OFFICE OF
POLICY, PLANNING AND EVALUATION

January 2, 1992

I am proud to introduce our new publication, <u>Cooling Our Communities: A Guidebook on Tree Planting and Light-Colored Surfacing</u>. This book is a practical guide that presents the current state of knowledge on potential environmental and economic benefits of strategic landscaping and altering surface colors in our communities. The guidebook, a joint effort of the Environmental Protection Agency and the Department of Energy's Lawrence Berkeley Laboratory, reviews the causes, magnitude, and impacts of increased urban warming, then focuses on actions by citizens and communities that can be undertaken to improve the quality of our homes and towns in cost-effective ways.

Summer temperatures in urban areas are now typically 2°F to 8°F higher than in their rural surroundings, due to a phenomenon known as the "heat island effect." Research shows that increases in electricity demand, smog levels, and human discomfort are probably linked to this phenomenon. Planting trees to provide shade and protection from winter winds, and lightening the color of building and pavement surfaces have the potential to significantly reduce energy use for cooling, and lower electrical bills. The guidebook shows that well-placed vegetation around residences and small commercial buildings can reduce energy consumption typically by 15 to 35 percent. Savings from lightening surface colors may be as high or greater, but are still being quantified. Widespread adoption of these strategies could help reduce urban temperatures and smog.

* * *

We designed the <u>Cooling Our Communities</u> guidebook with several general audiences in mind. Following are suggestions for ways each audience can apply the guidebook's findings and recommendations. The document also includes many technical appendices for the benefit of city planners, urban foresters, and electrical utilities needing more specific information about these principles.

Elected officials and other policymakers: The principles in this book have great potential to reduce expenditures for building energy, build citizen support for government tree planting programs, and improve the lives of our citizens. We hope you will actively support the types of activities and programs recommended here by sharing the guidebook with your staff and constituents, and consider launching volunteer or public/private partnership programs to implement these principles.

Foresters, landscapers, architects, and urban planners: Citizens are increasingly demanding these changes in their communities and are willing to volunteer time and resources to bring them about. You can support and encourage their efforts by using the guidebook to incorporate these approaches into your professional practice.

Utilities: Many power companies have already established tree planting programs to foster energy conservation. Major opportunities exist for utilities to cooperate with citizens, homeowners, and communities to expand the use of these recommended strategies.

Commercial interests: Demand is increasing for products and services that save people money and energy. We hope that retailers, manufacturers, and contractors of products and services involving vegetation, buildings and pavements will incorporate these energy saving ideas into their product and service lines, and advise consumers fully about the potential benefits of using them. Developers may increase the value of their properties by including these principles in their designs.

Citizen's and community groups: The successes and experiences of many of your colleagues across the entire United States are reflected in this book. Join them by taking action in your own communities to organize tree planting and light-colored surfacing projects.

Professional schools and programs: Community professionals can be the most effective supporters of improving environmental quality. Incorporating these design principles into your programs will help professionals in your disciplines understand and use these principles.

Editors, publication managers, and public affairs staff: To expedite informing your colleagues about the guidebook and its availability, we suggest you review or abstract the document in your in-house publications. We have included a sample abstract and order forms at the back of the book for you to copy and use as you wish.

       *   *   *

  Innumerable citizen groups and municipalities have clearly demonstrated the will to band together and plant trees in the United States. The guidebook supports these efforts, and identifies light-colored surfacing as a strategy that may have similar benefits. Now the challenge is to guide this volunteer spirit to achieve measureable environmental improvements in all of our communities. This publication is one of EPA's contributions to this on-going movement.

Richard D. Morgenstern
Acting Assistant Administrator

Cooling Our Communities

A Guidebook on Tree Planting and Light-Colored Surfacing

Editors:

Hashem Akbari, Lawrence Berkeley Laboratory
Susan Davis, Lawrence Berkeley Laboratory
Sofia Dorsano, The Bruce Company
Joe Huang, Lawrence Berkeley Laboratory
Steven Winnett, U.S. Environmental Protection Agency

U.S. Environmental Protection Agency
Office of Policy Analysis
Climate Change Division

January 1992

This document has been reviewed in accordance with the U.S. Environmental Protection Agency's and the Office of Management and Budget's peer and administrative review policies and approved for publication. Mention of trade names or commercial products does not constitute endorsement or recommendation for use.

Publisher's Note:

This is Lawrence Berkeley Laboratory Report LBL-31587.
This work was supported by the U.S. Department of Energy under contract No. DE-AC0376SF00098.

Those who wish to order the Guidebook should inquire at the address below:

Publications Requests:

GPO Document #055-000-00371-8
Superintendent of Documents
P.O. Box 371954
Pittsburgh, PA 15220-7954
ATTN: New Orders

For sale by the U.S. Government Printing Office
Superintendent of Documents, Mail Stop: SSOP, Washington, DC 20402-9328
ISBN 0-16-036034-X

Cooling Our Communities

A Guidebook on Tree Planting and Light-Colored Surfacing

Editors:
Hashem Akbari, Lawrence Berkeley Laboratory
Susan Davis, Lawrence Berkeley Laboratory
Sofia Dorsano, The Bruce Company
Joe Huang, Lawrence Berkeley Laboratory
Steven Winnett, U.S. Environmental Protection Agency

Project Directors:
Joe Huang, LBL
Steven Winnett, U.S. EPA
Kenneth Andrasko, U.S. EPA

Principal Investigator:
Hashem Akbari, LBL

SPONSORS:

— U.S. Environmental Protection Agency
— Heat-Island Project at Lawrence Berkeley Laboratory,
  University of California
— U.S. Department of Energy
— California Institute for Energy Efficiency
— Los Angeles Department of Water and Power
— Universitywide Energy Research Group, University of California
— Electric Power Research Institute
— American Council for an Energy Efficient Economy

U.S. Environmental Protection Agency
Office of Policy Analysis
Climate Change Division
401 M Street, SW (PM-221)
Washington, D.C. 20460
(202) 260-8825

Lawrence Berkeley Laboratory
Energy Analysis Program
Energy & Environment Division
1 Cyclotron Rd.
Berkeley, CA 94720
(510) 486-4000

Contents

Cooling Our Communities
A Guidebook on Tree Planting and Light-Colored Surfacing

Graphs

Illustrations

Maps

Photographs

Tables

Foreword

In the 1990 State of the Union address to the U.S. Congress, President Bush unveiled his America the Beautiful Tree Planting Program, one of the most ambitious anywhere in the world. Its goals are to plant one billion trees each year and improve forest management on targeted lands. This new EPA publication, *Cooling Our Communities,* focuses on one element of that program, community tree planting, and adds a new component, light-colored surfacing. It describes how citizens can help reduce air pollution, abate the greenhouse gas carbon dioxide, and potentially lower rising urban temperatures through two types of activities—planting trees around homes and other small buildings, and lightening the color of buildings and paved surfaces. Each can save energy, reaping environmental <u>and</u> economic benefits. This guidebook shows how the efforts of volunteers, spurred by growing environmental awareness, can be tapped to improve our communities.

My appreciation goes to the Department of Energy's Lawrence Berkeley Laboratory, which worked with EPA on this guidebook. It draws on the expertise of specialists in government, universities, and other organizations, and the experiences of many individuals. Many thanks to all who contributed to producing this report.

As President Bush announced the America the Beautiful program, he said, "Every tree is a compact between generations." I hope the findings and recommendations in this document provide the impetus for individuals and for members of private groups to plant trees for our common good, and for that of generations to come.

—William K. Reilly

January, 1992

Acknowledgements

This guidebook was completed as a special project by the Climate Change Division of the U.S. Environmental Protection Agency (EPA), and the Energy Analysis Program of Lawrence Berkeley Laboratory (LBL). The project's Principal Investigator is Hashem Akbari of LBL. The Project Directors are Steven Winnett and Kenneth Andrasko of EPA, and Joe Huang of LBL.

The guidebook represents the cumulative work of many people extending over two years. We would like to give special recognition to Arthur Rosenfeld at LBL and Kenneth Andrasko at EPA for the initial concept of producing a "heat island mitigation handbook," and then developing the original guidebook outline.

In addition to EPA and LBL, this project was also sponsored by the following organizations: the U.S. Department of Energy (DOE), the California Institute of Energy Efficiency (CIEE), Los Angeles Department of Water and Power (LADWP), the Universitywide Energy Research Group of the University of California (UERG), the Electric Power Research Institute (EPRI), and the American Council for an Energy Efficient Economy (ACEEE).

We wish to thank Peter Beedlow, Bruce Schillo, Gordon M. Heisler, Margot W. Garcia, Neil Sampson, Gary Moll, George Britton, James Demetrops, and Linda J. de la Croix for providing formal reviews of the guidebook. We also thank the numerous reviewers of the guidebook drafts, Gordon Binder, Dan Esty, Richard Morgenstern, Courtney Riordan, Edgar Thorton, Dennis Tirpak, Jane Leggett, Gregory McPherson, Timothy Oke, John Parker, Judy Ratcliffe, Allen McReynolds, and Marcia Bansley. In addition, the authors of the individual chapters also contributed in reviewing various drafts.

For their graphics, editorial, and other bookmaking contributions, we extend our appreciation to the staff of The Bruce Company presentations division, especially Allison Anderson, Paula Batchelor, Paul Jordan, Todd Neitring, Shelley Preston, Jeffrey Satterwhite, and Mildred Stewart.

The following people authored this report:

Akbari, Hashem. Energy & Environment Division, Lawrence Berkeley Laboratory, University of California, Berkeley. (Chapter 1; Chapter 3)

Arey, Janet. Statewide Air Pollution Research Center, University of California, Riverside. (Chapter 4)

Atkinson, Roger. Statewide Air Pollution Research Center, University of California, Riverside. (Chapter 4)

Carhart, Ralph. California Department of Transportation, Sacramento. (Chapter 8)

Davis, Susan E. San Francisco, California. (Chapter 1; Chapter 6)

Garbesi, Karina. Energy & Environment Division, Lawrence Berkeley Laboratory, University of California, Berkeley. (Chapter 4; Appendix C)

Huang, Joe. Energy & Environment Division, Lawrence Berkeley Laboratory, University of California, Berkeley. (Chapter 1; Chapter 2)

Lipkis, Andy. TreePeople, Inc., USA of Los Angeles, CA. (Chapter 5)

Lipkis, Katie. TreePeople, Inc., USA of Los Angeles, CA. (Chapter 5)

Liu, Phillip. University of California, Davis. (Chapter 1)

Martien, Philip. Bay Area Air Quality Management District, San Francisco, CA. (Chapter 3; Chapter 6)

McPherson, E. Gregory. USDA Forest Service. Chicago, IL. (Chapter 5)

Moll, Gary. American Forestry Association. Washington, D.C. (Appendix E)

Nordman, Bruce. Energy & Environment Division, Lawrence Berkeley Laboratory, University of California, Berkeley. (Chapter 4)

Panzer, Susan. Florida International University, Miami. (Appendix D)

Patterson, Fred. Energy & Environment Division, Lawrence Berkeley Laboratory, University of California, Berkeley. (Chapter 7)

Parker, John. Florida International University, Miami. (Appendix D)

Ratliffe, Judy. University of Arizona, Tucson. (Chapter 5)

Ritschard, Ron. Applied Sciences Division, Lawrence Berkeley Laboratory, University of California, Berkeley. (Chapter 2)

Rosenfeld, Arthur. Energy & Environment Division, Lawrence Berkeley Laboratory, University of California, Berkeley. (Chapter 3)

Sampson, Neil. American Forestry Association, Washington, D.C. (Chapter 2; Chapter 6)

Taha, Haider. Energy & Environment Division, Lawrence Berkeley Laboratory, University of California, Berkeley. (Chapter 2)

Executive Summary

Summer temperatures in urban areas are now typically 2°F to 8°F higher than in their rural surroundings, due to a phenomenon known as the "heat island effect." Recent research shows that increases in electricity demand, smog levels, and human discomfort are probably linked to this phenomenon.

Urban areas accumulate greater amounts of heat for several reasons. Many of these factors—including climate, topography, and weather patterns—cannot be changed. Two factors we *can* influence are the amount of *vegetation* and the color of *surfaces*. These two factors are responsible for the majority of additional heating attributable to human activities.

Strategically planting trees and lightening building and pavement surface colors have the potential to reduce energy use for cooling and lower electrical bills. This may also help lower summer temperatures in our communities, thereby reducing the production of tropospheric ozone and improving the quality of our environment. By reducing the generation of electrical power, these actions also decrease the emission of carbon dioxide (CO_2), the most important greenhouse gas, and may help lower the risk of global climate change.

Initial analysis suggests that billions of dollars may be spent each year just to compensate for the increased heat of an urban heat island. Planting trees and lightening

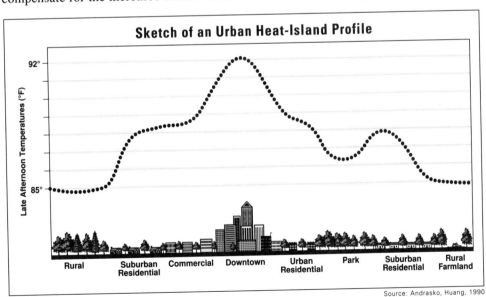

Sketch of an Urban Heat-Island Profile

Late Afternoon Temperatures (°F)

92°

85°

Rural   Suburban Residential   Commercial   Downtown   Urban Residential   Park   Suburban Residential   Rural Farmland

Source: Andrasko, Huang, 1990

Figure ES-1.
Sketch of a typical urban heat-island profile: This graph of the heat island profile in a hypothetical metropolitan area shows temperature changes (given in degrees Fahrenheit) correlated to the density of development and trees. (Also appears as Figure 1-4.)

Peak temperatures in Los Angeles, other cities of northern California, Texas, Washington, D.C., Shanghai, and Mexico City show that peak temperatures have risen throughout the century.

the color of our urban surfaces could lower our urban temperatures, reduce our cooling energy use, and lower smog levels. A study by the National Academy of Sciences indicates that these strategies may be able to save 50 billion kilowatt hours, or 25 percent, of the 200 billion kilowatt hours spent annually in the United States for air conditioning (NAS, 1991). Programs that encourage these energy-saving practices could also beautify urban areas, mask noise, reduce air pollution, enhance community relations, and provide valuable habitat for wildlife.

This guidebook is designed to introduce both lay and technical readers to the potential of tree planting and light-colored surfacing methods for reducing energy demand and lowering urban temperatures. It is the first collection of such material. Therefore, its findings and recommendations should be considered a foundation for future inquiry and work, and not a final analysis.

Why Are Urban Temperatures Rising?

The urbanization of the natural landscape—roads, bridges, dams, houses, and high-rises—has dramatically altered its waters, soils, and vegetation. In fact, the most stereotypically "urban" characteristics of cities are also those which can cause temperatures to rise. By replacing vegetation and soil with concrete and asphalt, we reduce the landscape's ability to lower daytime temperatures through evapotranspiration, and lose the obvious benefits of shade. And by using dark-colored materials on roads, buildings, and other surfaces, we create entire cities that absorb, rather than reflect, incoming solar energy.

The combination of reduced reflectivity—called "albedo"—and reduced vegetation has resulted in a temperature difference between urban and rural areas that is most clear in late afternoon and early evening, when roads, sidewalks, and walls begin to release the heat they have stored throughout the day. The difference is most extreme in densely developed areas. In fact, heat islands are broken up partially by parks and other vegetated areas, even within the downtown area (See Figure ES-1).

Meteorologists and other scientists have been aware of this phenomenon for over 100 years. But throughout the last century, increasing rates of urbanization and industrialization have exacerbated the heat island effect. Peak temperatures in Los Angeles, for instance, have risen by 5°F in the last fifty years. Peak temperatures in other cities of northern California and Texas, as well as Washington, D.C., Shanghai, and Mexico City, have also risen throughout the century. Figure ES-2 shows a historical comparison of rural and urban temperatures in California.

What Are The Effects Of Increased Urban Temperatures?

Increased Electricity Demand

Higher urban temperatures increase the demand for electricity.

A winter heat island in a cold climate can be a moderate asset because it lowers heating bills. In warm and hot climates, however, the higher temperatures result in increased energy demands for air conditioning. Initial research shows that for every 1°F increase in summer temperatures, peak cooling loads will increase 1.5 to 2 percent. Since urban temperatures during summer afternoons in the United States have increased by 2 to 4°F in the last four decades, we can assume that 3 to 8 percent of the current urban electricity demand is used to compensate for the heat island effect alone.

These percentages may seem nominal, but they cost a great deal. The 5°F increase in Los Angeles' peak temperatures since 1940, for instance, is estimated to have added electricity demands of 1.5 gigawatts (approximately one and a half new, large power plants)—with an estimated hourly cost of $150,000. Similarly, the cost of Washington, D.C.'s heat island has been estimated at $40,000 per hour. A rough estimate of the national electricity costs for the added urban heat is around $1 million per hour, or over $1 billion per year.

Increased Smog Production

Summer heat islands also increase smog production; the incidence of smog events may increase by 10 percent for each 5°F increase in temperature. In Los Angeles, for example, ozone levels are not likely to exceed the National Ambient Air Quality Standard (NAAQS)—currently 12 parts per hundred million (pphm)—when temperatures are below 74°F. Above that threshold, however, peak ozone levels exceed health standards more often (See Figure ES-3). Ozone levels frequently reach unacceptable levels at or above 94°F. Similar threshold phenomenon have been found in other areas as well.

Increased Emission of Carbon Dioxide And Other Pollutants

Increased air conditioning increases electricity generation at power plants. Plants that run on fossil fuels typically emit many pollutants, including sulfur dioxide, carbon monoxide, nitrous oxides, and suspended particulates. Perhaps more importantly, burning fossil fuels or wood produces large amounts of carbon dioxide, which many

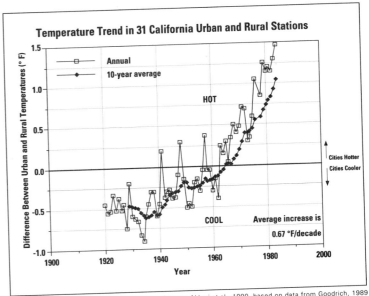

Source: Akbari et al., 1990, based on data from Goodrich, 1989

Figure ES-2.
Urban areas are getting warmer: Since 1940, the temperature difference between urban and rural stations has shown an increase of 0.67°F per decade. (Also appears as Figure 1-15.)

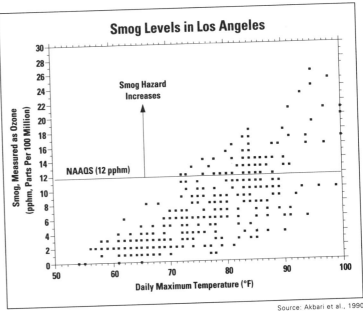

Source: Akbari et al., 1990

Figure ES-3.
Rising temperatures and smog: This graph shows ozone concentrations compared to daily peak temperatures in Los Angeles, California. As temperatures rise above 74°F, ozone concentrations can more frequently exceed the National Ambient Air Quality Standard (NAAQS) which is currently 12 parts per hundred million. (Also appears as Figure 1-23.)

Figure ES-4.
Sample residential landscape: A large tree is planted on the east side to shade the air conditioner, and on the west and south sides to cast maximum shadows on the house. Shrubs planted on all sides of the house help to reduce the temperatures of soil and walls. (Also appears as Figure 6-9.)

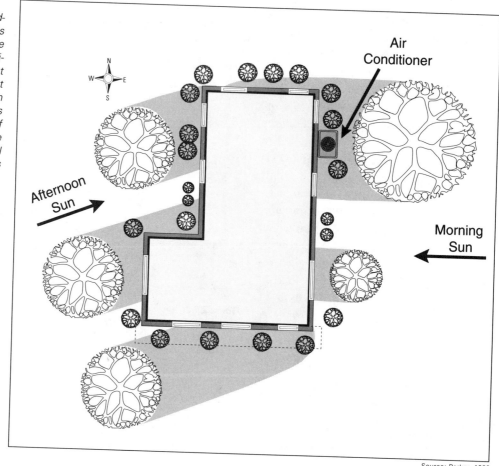

Source: Parker, 1982

scientists believe could contribute to changes in climate (IPCC, 1991). If so, urban heat islands could be contributing to this problem, since increased air conditioning leads to increased power generation and carbon dioxide emissions.

Tree Planting And Light-Colored Surfacing To Reduce Urban Temperatures

Trees affect climates and building-energy use in two ways. Direct benefits accrue from the shade that trees provide to buildings and surfaces. By blocking solar radiation, trees prevent structures and surfaces from heating up beyond the ambient air temperature. Indirectly, trees cool buildings by cooling the air surrounding them through evapotranspiration. In a process similar to sweating, trees use heat to evaporate water from a leaf before it can heat the air, thus cooling the air immediately around the leaf. The cumulative effect of many leaves and many trees can cool the air in a large area.

Direct Effects

Tree shade does a better job cooling a building and its interior than Venetian blinds, plastic coatings, or reflective patinas on glass. Field measurements have shown that through shading, trees and shrubs strategically planted next to buildings can reduce summer air-conditioning costs typically by 15 to 35 percent, and by as much as 50 percent or more in certain specific situations. Simply shading the air conditioner—by using shrubs or a vine-covered trellis—can save up to 10 percent in annual cooling-energy costs.

Placement of trees is very important. Proper placement can ensure that trees shade the areas most critical in lowering internal temperatures, and shade them at the most critical times of the day. For example, trees should be placed to shade the east, west and south sides of a building in order to block late morning, afternoon, and early evening sun (See Figure ES-4). In addition, trees which shade windows provide the most benefit. However, improperly positioned trees can increase the cost of energy.

During the winter, shade (especially from the south) can be a liability, as it blocks the warming rays of the sun, which can otherwise reduce heating energy requirements. Broadleaved or deciduous trees drop their foliage in the fall and allow most of the sunlight to come through the bare limbs. Proper pruning of larger trees allows the low-angled winter sun to come in under the lowest branches.

Evergreen or coniferous trees and shrubs can be positioned to reduce the influence of cold, winter winds on the heating requirements (See Figure ES-5). It is very important that these windbreaks not impede winter sunlight. Houses measured in South Dakota, for example, consumed 25 percent less fuel when located on the leeward sides of windbreaks than when exposed. Windbreaks on three sides—north, west, east— reduced fuel consumption by 40 percent. This guidebook discusses proper placement of trees and vegetation in detail. Figure ES-6 shows estimated direct savings in heating and cooling energy from a 30 percent increase in tree cover around older houses.

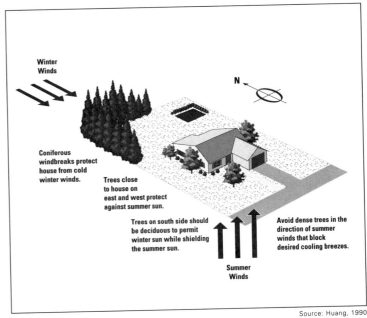

Source: Huang, 1990

Figure ES-5.
Strategic planting example: In temperate climates, trees must be chosen and planted to shield a house from both the hot summer sun and the cold winter winds. (Also appears as Figure 6-10.)

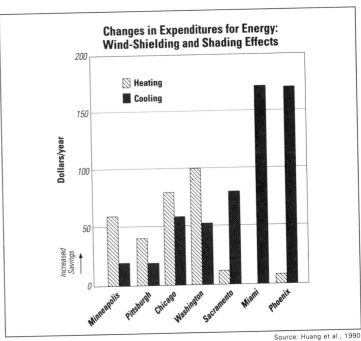

Source: Huang et al., 1990

Figure ES-6.
*Wind-shielding and shading effects: The net direct effects of a 30 percent increase in tree cover on the heating and cooling energy use of **older** houses, based on computer simulations. (Also appears as Figure 2-6.)*

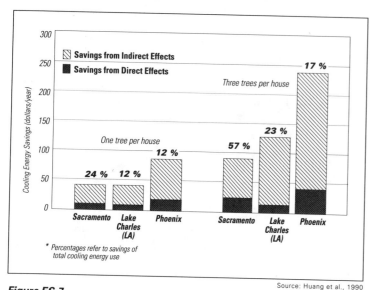

Figure ES-7.
Estimated cooling savings in a typical well-insulated new house from the combined direct and indirect effects of trees. Note that direct effects provide a relatively small percentage of the total energy savings for new housing stock. (Also appears as Figure 2-9.)

Source: Huang et al., 1990

Indirect Effects

The evapotranspirative properties of trees can produce even greater *indirect* effects on temperature and energy consumption. Figure ES-7 shows a comparison of the relative savings attributable to indirect and direct effects of trees. As the number of trees increase, the relative contribution of the indirect effect grows in comparison to the direct effects. Trees transpire up to 100 gallons of water in a day. In a hot dry climate, this cooling effect equals that of five air conditioners running for 20 hours. When the effects of evapotranspiration are combined with the effect of strategically placed shade, temperatures can drop by as much as 9°F in the immediate vicinity of the trees. Increasing vegetation cover by just 10 and 30 percent (about one and three properly placed trees per house, respectively) may reduce cooling energy by as much as 10 to 50 percent, depending on housing stock type, age, construction and other factors. (Typically, older and more poorly insulated buildings, and those in hotter, drier regions, will have larger energy savings.) These numbers apply only to shade trees carefully placed to maximize their shading effects.

City-wide programs to plant street trees and to fill our parks, corporate lawns, and plazas would enhance the shading and evapotranspirative benefits of urban trees. Such an increase in the urban canopy would improve our communities in other ways, too. For instance, trees filter air pollutants, mask noise, and prevent erosion. They provide habitat for wildlife and birds, and may inspire feelings of relaxation and happiness in humans. Massive tree-planting programs can revitalize our dying urban forests, while sponsoring community cooperation and civic pride.

Finally, urban trees can contribute to slowing or preventing potential changes in climate. Urban trees not only sequester carbon dioxide from the atmosphere, but they also help prevent carbon dioxide emissions in the first place by reducing the need for air conditioning. Researchers estimate that the energy conserving properties of community trees may increase their contribution to reducing carbon dioxide levels by a factor of five to ten compared to trees planted at a distance from buildings. If enough trees are planted, we may be able to reduce our cooling energy enough to avoid both the costly construction of new power plants as well as their economic and environmental costs.

Light-Colored Surfaces

Our built environments contain myriad surfaces, including building roofs and walls, streets, freeways, parking lots, driveways, school yards, and playgrounds. When these surfaces are dark, they absorb heat. When they are light, they reflect heat and stay cooler.

The measure of a surface's reflectivity is called albedo. Humans in tropical and sub-tropical communities (Greece and North Africa for example) have been white-washing their walls and streets to keep albedos high—or very reflective—and temperatures low for centuries. In this country and other countries, people may have forgotten the practical cooling effect that such light colors can have. Dark-colored houses and streets create hotter communities and increased use of air conditioning.

Many studies exist which show that increasing surface albedos lower surface temperatures (See Figure ES-8). To date, few field measurements exist that document reductions in energy use from changing dark-colored surfaces to light ones in houses and communities. Computer simulations of a typical house in Sacramento, California, indicate that its total air-conditioning bill could be reduced by up to 22 percent if the albedo of the roofs and walls are increased from 0.2 to 0.6 (See Figure ES-9). Such increases entail no drastic measures, and simply changing grey siding to off-white, and replacing dark-colored roof shingles with light-colored ones, would significantly increase the house's overall albedo.

Like trees and vegetation, reductions in temperatures and energy use from albedo modifications accrue to both individual buildings and entire neighborhoods. In fact, the indirect effects of albedo modification may be larger than the direct ones. Computer simulations of neighborhoods show that changing roof, wall, and street colors could significantly reduce air temperatures and cooling energy use. Researchers estimate that realistic albedo changes could reduce a city's air temperature by as much as 5°F in hot, sunny climates with many dark surfaces. This, in turn, would produce indirect energy savings as high as 40 per-

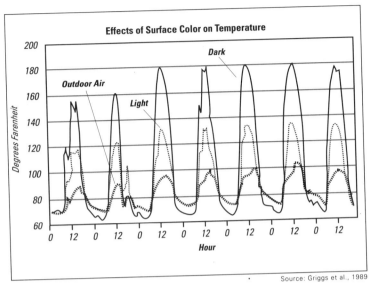

Source: Griggs et al., 1989

Figure ES-8.
Effects of Surface Color on Temperature: Actual measurements of roof temperatures showed that dark-colored surfaces become increasingly hotter throughout the day compared to light-colored surfaces. (Also appears as Figure 3-4.)

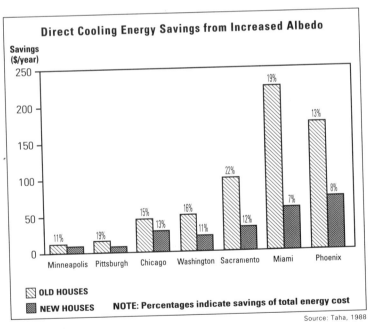

Source: Taha, 1988

Figure ES-9.
Cooling Energy Savings from Direct Effects of Increased Albedo: Significant energy savings from increasing the surface albedo in selected cities across the country as projected by computer models. Note higher dollar savings in sunbelt cities. (Also appears as Figure 3-6.)

Filling 100 million urban tree spaces and lightening surface colors on a large scale could reduce U.S. energy use by 2 percent and cut carbon emissions by 1 percent, annually.

cent. When the direct and indirect savings of albedo changes are combined, the total energy savings simulated by a computer approached 50 percent during average hours and 30 percent during peak cooling periods.

In addition to these significant savings in energy, albedo modifications are likely to be inexpensive. Because changes can be incorporated into normal maintenance cycles (i.e., repainting walls, replacing roof shingles, or repaving asphalt surfaces), they add little or no extra costs to building owners or city governments.

Trees And Light-Colored Surfaces

Clearly, both trees and light-colored surfaces can have a significant effect on the temperatures and energy consumption of our homes, offices, and communities. Taken together, however, the effect of these two measures is even more striking. Some scientists estimate that if 100 million urban tree spaces in this country were filled (that's three trees for one-half of the single-family homes in this country) and if light-colored surfacing programs were implemented, we could reduce our electricity use by as much as 50 billion kilowatt hours per year (2 percent of annual electricity use in the United States). In addition, the amount of CO_2 released into the atmosphere could be cut by as much as 35 million tons per year (about 10 million tons of carbon) roughly 1 percent of annual U.S. CO_2 emissions.

Do These Strategies Cause Problems?

Neither planting trees nor changing surface colors are faultless measures. Increasing trees may increase the amount of water needed for irrigation and the amount of solid waste generated in a community. Preliminary analysis suggests, however, that using trees to replace lawns can drastically reduce water needs in a community, and that using shrubs or groundcover to replace trees can reduce water usage even further. In arid climates, using native vegetation that is less dependent on high volumes of water also reduces water needs.

The problem of disposal (potentially large amounts of leaves, twigs, branches, and other debris from vegetation deposited in landfills) also does not loom as large on closer inspection. Leaves can be used for compost, while branches and fallen trunks can be used for firewood, large-scale composts, or boiler fuel. Clearly, any community embarking on a large-scale tree-planting program could also consider the merits of community-wide composting and yard debris programs. Depending on the region and other factors, the combined benefits of urban tree planting will often be greater than the costs incurred, especially when planting directly around houses (See Figure ES-10).

Questions regarding albedo primarily focus on glare and soiling. That is, a community containing many light-colored surfaces may be uncomfortable to the eye. This does not seem to be a problem; cities in the Tropics and Middle East have had predominantly white surfaces for centuries. By contrast, some critics have claimed that white surfaces will soil too quickly to be effective. Studies show, however, that even soiled, light-colored surfaces can have a higher albedo than dark-colored ones.

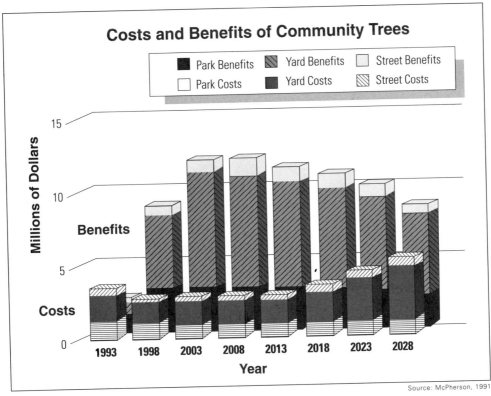

Costs and Benefits of Community Trees

Legend:
- Park Benefits
- Park Costs
- Yard Benefits
- Yard Costs
- Street Benefits
- Street Costs

Y-axis: Millions of Dollars — 0, 5, 10, 15

Benefits

Costs

X-axis (Year): 1993, 1998, 2003, 2008, 2013, 2018, 2023, 2028

Source: McPherson, 1991

Figure ES-10.
Projected annual costs and benefits of the Trees for Tucson/Global ReLeaf reforestation program: This graph shows the relative benefits of the location of planting. Benefits are plotted in the back row, and costs in the front row. Note the high benefits associated with planting trees around houses (yard.) (Also appears as Figure 2-13.)

Developing Programs To Plant Trees And Change Surface Colors

One way to begin programs for tree planting and light-colored surfacing strategies is through public education. That is, providing information on the albedo of building materials, the shade potential of trees, and energy-savings of direct and indirect measures will inspire consumers to implement some measures. Developing ordinances will also spur energy-conserving measures.

Many communities in this country already have tree-planting programs and ordinances in effect. The simple addition of landscaping and albedo modification suggestions could enhance the overall benefits of existing programs.

Because no urban community in the United States or abroad has yet initiated a formal program of albedo modification, we have no experience with successful implementation practices, potential drawbacks, and conflicts with other urban issues. We would like to stress, however, that our preliminary analysis indicates that the energy and environmental benefits of albedo modifications are high, while the costs and potential risks can be strikingly low.

Conclusions And Recommendations

Research on the effects of urban heat islands is coming at a time of great public concern about local and global environmental conditions. Air pollution, water pollution, and the possibility of global climate change all mandate that we decrease our energy use. In addition, America's urban forests are in a state of decline. Half of the potential

Figure ES-11.
This figure illustrates strategic tree-planting and light-colored surfacing activities that could yield energy-conserving results for homeowners.

spaces for trees along streets are unfilled, and only one quarter of urban trees that die each year are replaced.

At the same time, our city sizes are growing at unprecedented rates. By the year 2000, fifty percent of the world's population will live in cities, where only 14 percent lived 100 years ago. Correlating population size to heat-island intensity is still inexact. It is clear, though, that heat islands intensify as urban areas grow. Already, urban temperatures in this country can be 8°F hotter than those in surrounding areas, and urban temperatures in tropical and sub-tropical countries are as much as 15°F higher than their surroundings.

Specifically, the following tasks could be undertaken to reduce urban temperatures and the attendant levels of energy use and smog production:

1) Undertake or expand community-wide programs for shade tree planting and add albedo modification. These programs can consist of volunteer programs in conjunction with community tree planting and development groups, and public education.

2) Promote energy conserving activities by providing information on albedo of building products, suggestions for landscaping designs, and the energy savings possible—through retailers of building materials and trees, through forestry extension agents, city foresters, contractors, and through utilities and municipalities.

3) Provide incentives for developers to build well-arbored, light-colored, energy efficient buildings and communities.

4) Encourage Public Utility Commissions to provide utilities with incentives to support tree planting and surface color enhancements.

5) Utilities can support these activities as a way to reduce demand for peak power and perhaps reduce the need to build new power facilities.

6) Corporations can encourage energy conservation by sponsoring tree planting and light-colored surfacing programs among their employees and in the communities in which they and their employees reside.

7) Professional groups can create professional education materials so that their memberships are conversant with new techniques for community planning, tree planting, and other modifications to traditional practices.

8) Municipalities can pass tree ordinances, specify the use of light-colored paving materials in road building and renovations, provide financial incentives, or zone for light-colored building materials in commercial areas, strengthen the ability of roads and parks departments to plant new trees and maintain existing ones, and foster community efforts in these areas.

9) Professional schools and other educational programs could incorporate these principles in the training of builders, engineers, architects, city and urban planners and designers, arborculturists, foresters, and landscape architects.

Today, inspired by President Bush's "America the Beautiful" tree-planting program, and by efforts like the American Forestry Association's Global ReLeaf Network, and those of many successful city tree-planting organizations, citizens across the Unites States are planting trees in their communities. By combining those programs with these landscaping and albedo modification suggestions, we can create communities that are cooler, more aesthetically pleasing, and more energy efficient.

Introduction

The Urban Landscape

Construction Of The Urban Habitat

Over the past two million years, humans have drastically modified their environment. With fire, they cleared large areas of forest and grass lands. With plant and animal cultivation, they created entirely new landscapes—by genetically "engineering" native plants, transporting species to new areas, and re-directing water for irrigation. When humans started building urban centers, they began the most radical transformation possible—the replacement of vegetated landscapes with constructed cityscapes.

During the past century, this environmental transformation accelerated at an unprecedented pace. Industrialized society—with its emphasis on manufacturing, transportation, and urbanization—has affected many areas on the planet. Indeed, the impacts of industrialization on the landscapes and atmosphere are so significant that some people say no place on earth is free of human influence.

Much of this influence is not readily evident. Pollutant gases and contaminated soils are not always discernible. The ozone hole is not visible in the southern sky. The ocean hides the products of our disposable society in deep basins.

The most visible places of human influence are the cities. Rolling hills and pastureland have been leveled and paved over with asphalt roads and concrete sidewalks. Productive fields have been replaced with parking lots. Buildings are constructed where trees once naturally grew and thrived. Smog and noise often fill the air.

In creating these urban areas, humans inadvertently have also created their own microclimates with heightened air temperatures, unique windflow patterns, noise, and pollution. The material in this book, *Cooling Our Communities: A Guidebook on Tree Planting and Light-Colored Surfacing,* is specifically concerned with increased temperatures of the urban environment, the problems caused by this increase, and the potential methods for modulating the temperatures of our homes and communities while reducing electricity demand and costs.

The "intensity" of the heat island—that is, just how much hotter a city is than its countryside—may seem slight. The effect of the heat islands is usually a temperature rise of 2 to 8 degrees Fahrenheit (°F). Multiplied across the country, however, these higher urban temperatures may be costing us billions of dollars each year in energy expenditures, smog damage, and increased water consumption. Analysis of data from electric utilities indicates that for each degree Fahrenheit increase in temperature, peak power demand rises by one to two percent. Besides costing rate payers more than one million dollars an hour during hot periods, increased power generation raises levels of atmospheric carbon dioxide—a major contributor to the greenhouse effect. Research also indicates that these increased temperatures exacerbate levels of smog in cities.

It is clear that urban heat islands have major effects on energy costs and the quality of urban life. It is also clear that effective ways of mitigating heat islands exist, and that, fortunately, these methods are fairly simple and inexpensive to implement.

Opportunities For Cool Communities

Urban areas accumulate greater amounts of heat for several reasons. Many of these factors—including climate, topography, and weather patterns—cannot be changed. Two heat island factors we *can* influence are the amount of *vegetation* and the color of *surfaces*. These two factors are responsible for the majority of additional heating attributable to human activities.

Vegetation cools cities by directly shading individual buildings, and by evapotranspiration. Evapotranspiration is the process by which a plant releases water vapor into the air. Entire neighborhoods and cities can be cooled by evapotranspiration. Unfortunately, in the last several decades, more and more trees were removed from urban environments. As vegetation disappeared, temperatures began to rise. Today, only one tree is planted in our cities for every four removed.

The color of a city's surfaces determines the amount of solar energy absorbed or reflected. Dark building materials—roofing tiles, shingles, tar, asphalt, and gravel—absorb more sunlight than light-colored surfaces. In this country, most buildings and roads are dark. Each time we build them, we continue to drive up the temperature of our cities.

Two of the most cost-effective methods of reducing heat islands are strategic landscaping and light-colored surfacing. Strategic landscaping refers to planting trees and shrubs around buildings and throughout cities to provide maximum shade and wind benefits. Light-colored surfacing means changing dark-colored surfaces to ones which more effectively reflect—rather than absorb—solar energy.

The combined effects of planting more trees and incorporating more light-colored surfaces can be astonishing. Preliminary research indicates that late afternoon air temperatures on a hot summer day can be reduced by 5 to 10°F, resulting in cooling energy savings of up to 50 percent, depending on location. Implementing these measures may be cheaper than implementing other efficiency programs.

In addition to mitigating environmental concerns, planting trees and changing surface colors provide many other physical, functional, and psychological benefits to urban dwellers. Trees help reduce noise and particulate matter in the air, and provide habitat for wildlife. Both trees and light-colored surfaces enhance the aesthetics of urban spaces, thereby contributing to the psychological well-being of their inhabitants.

The Guidebook

This volume is an initial attempt to address this problem. It compiles existing information on the causes, effects, and most viable mitigation strategies of urban heat islands. As such, it necessarily has some strengths and some weaknesses.

The primary strength of this volume is that it collects the most current research on heat islands in the country. A number of researchers, in particular the Heat Island Project of the Energy Analysis Program at Lawrence Berkeley Laboratory, have been studying the problem of heat islands for several years. This book documents and reflects their efforts. In addition, this is the first book to suggest the ways in which homeowners and policymakers can take steps to reduce heat islands.

The concepts of strategic landscaping and light-colored surfaces are not difficult to understand, but implementing community-wide programs requires considerable planning and constant maintenance.

The first chapter of the guidebook introduces the causes of heat islands and their effects on urban areas. The second and third discuss planting trees and changing surface colors to reduce those heat island effects. The remaining chapters discuss implementation of programs for heat island mitigation, and describe several programs already in operation.

The authors developed the guidebook for the benefit of lay readers. Citizens, policymakers, and urban planners are provided with a general view of the scientific research that is underway to understand and mitigate the effects of urban heat islands. In the back of the book, the authors have included technical appendices to assist analysts seeking more detailed information.

Definitions

There are several technical terms that appear throughout the guidebook and are defined here for the reader's convenience.

Albedo. The ability of a surface to reflect incoming electromagnetic radiation measured from 0 to 1. A surface with an albedo of 1 reflects all incoming radiation, while one with an albedo of 0 absorbs all of it.

Building cooling load. The hourly amount of heat that must be removed from a building to maintain indoor comfort is known as the building's "cooling load." This measurement, generally used by architects and engineers, is given in British Thermal Units (Btus).

Caliper. The standard measure for the diameter of a tree measured six inches above the ground (for trees larger than one half inch and smaller than four inches in diameter).

Cooling electricity use. The amount of electricity used to meet the building cooling load is referred to as its "cooling electricity use."

Gigawatt. A gigawatt is a unit of energy equal to a billion watts or a million kilowatts.

Kilowatt (kW). A kilowatt is a unit of electric power equal to 1000 watts, which is the work represented by an electric current of one ampere under the pressure of one volt.

Kilowatt-hour (kWh). A kilowatt-hour is a unit of energy equal to that expended by one kilowatt of electricity in one hour.

Megawatt (mW). A megawatt is a unit of energy equal to 1000 kilowatts.

Microclimate. The localized climate conditions within an urban area or neighborhood.

National Ambient Air Quality Standard (NAAQS). The NAAQS is a measurement of ozone concentration, currently equivalent to 12 parts-per-hundred-million. Smog levels that exceed this measurement are considered problematic.

Peak building cooling load (or peak load). The maximum hourly amount of heat that must be removed from a building to maintain required indoor comfort conditions is known as "peak building cooling-load." In this book, this term often appears in a shortened form as the "peak load."

Peak cooling electricity use. The maximum amount of electricity needed to meet the cooling load of a building is referred to as its "peak cooling electricity use."

Peak electricity demand. The maximum electricity used to meet the cooling load of a building or buildings in a given area is known as "peak electricity demand." Peak electricity demand is measured in kilowatts.

Quad. One quadrillion Btus (British Thermal Units), approximately equivalent to the yearly production of 17 large nuclear power plants (1000 megawatts each).

Utility load. The total electricity demand for a utility district is referred to as the "utility load" of that district.

1

Hashem Akbari
Susan Davis
Joe Huang
Philip Liu
Haider Taha

The Urban Heat Island: Causes and Impacts

What Is An Urban Heat Island?

One of the most telling characteristics of a city is its temperature. Visit any city on a hot summer day and you will feel waves of blistering heat emanating from roads and dark buildings. Travel from the city to the countryside after sunset, and you will notice that the settled areas are still hot and muggy, while the rural areas are rapidly cooling.

Even within a city, different neighborhoods have different temperatures, depending on the surroundings. Parks are the coolest, for example. Neighborhoods with many trees are cooler than those with few. Downtown areas full of concrete and tall buildings are the hottest of all. These differences may seem obvious, but they also illuminate an often-ignored fact: human activities affect the climate within which we live. More specifically, in creating urban landscapes, humans have made them significantly hotter—usually between 2 and 8°F hotter—than their surrounding rural areas.

The "Urban Heat Island" is a moderate asset during the winter, raising city temperatures and lowering heating bills. During the summer, however, heat islands intensify "heat waves," increasing electricity use for air conditioning, adding to human discomfort, and exacerbating urban smog.

Figure 1-1.
Comfort in the shade and moist air: Temperatures can noticeably vary even within a city, depending on the amount of surrounding vegetation and surface colors.

Data from electric utilities indicate that for each degree increase in temperature, power use rises by 1-2 percent because of the increased need for air conditioning. Nationwide, this increased demand could cost ratepayers more than a million dollars per hour or possibly over one billion dollars per year.

Meteorologists who first noticed this phenomenon more than a century ago, labelled it the "urban heat island." These heat islands influence most of the major cities around the world. In the United States, for instance, the temperature of New York City can be 10°F hotter than its outlying areas. Inner-city St. Louis is 2 to 8°F hotter than its surroundings. Perhaps the most striking effect of heat islands is found in tropical cities that receive a great deal of sunshine. Records indicate that the heat island effect in New Delhi, India, can be 10°F, while in Mexico City, Mexico, it can raise urban temperatures by an additional 18°F.

Figure 1-2.
Rural building (and air conditioner) shaded by trees: Shading urban homes with strategically placed vegetation can help to regain both the quality of environment and cooling advantages of the rural landscape.

What Causes Urban Heat Islands?

While the nature and effects of urban heat islands are still being studied, the causes are well established. Denuded landscapes, impermeable surfaces, massive buildings, heat-generating cars and machines, and pollutants all help to make urban areas hotter.

The replacement of vegetation or soil by concrete or asphalt reduces an urban landscape's ability to lower daytime temperatures through evaporation and plant transpiration. In a rural or irrigated landscape, a large amount of daytime solar energy is actually spent on evaporating water, not on raising air temperatures. Trees and other vegetation perform this function through the process of "evapotranspiration." In this process, the plant draws moisture from the ground, utilizes what it needs for growth and moderating its own temperature, transpires the excess, and cools the surrounding air.

When a natural vegetative cover is replaced by asphalt or concrete, it loses its ability to moderate temperatures. Instead, the solar energy normally delegated to the evaporation process is left to raise surface temperatures.

Urban areas get hotter than rural settings not only because their ability to cool evaporatively is reduced, but also because they reflect less incoming solar energy. This reflective capacity is called "albedo."[1] Asphalt, in particular, has low albedo; it absorbs almost all the solar energy falling on it. This, combined with asphalt's inability to evaporate water, means that streets and parking lots paved with this material often reach blistering temperatures on sunny summer afternoons.

Buildings also contribute to the urban heat island in a number of ways. Like pavement and sidewalks, buildings do not have the capacity to moderate heat through evaporation. Instead, they absorb and store the day's heat, and then radiate it back to the urban atmosphere at night. You can feel this heat if you stand close to a brick building early on a summer evening.

In downtown areas, the densely clustered, tall office buildings create "urban canyons" that take hours to cool off every night. In addition, buildings and other architectural structures obstruct the natural flow of breezes, making wind speeds noticeably lower in the cities. This obstruction prevents winds from carrying heat build-up away from the city and from assisting in the reduction of the heat island.

Urban pollution also affects the heat island, depending on the time of day and season of the year. During daylight hours, pollution lowers heat build-up slightly, because it blocks incoming solar energy. At night, however, pollution prevents heat from escaping by covering the city like a blanket, and thereby increasing the heat island effect. Finally, heat and pollution from cars, machines, and other mechanical systems contribute to winter heat islands. During the summer, however, solar energy is so intense that it overwhelms the heat output from these human activities. Consequently, the severity of the summer heat island is determined largely by the interplay of the urban landscape and solar radiation.

Urban areas get hotter than rural settings not only because their ability to cool evaporatively is reduced, but also because they reflect less incoming solar energy. This reflective capacity is called "albedo."

---

[1] Albedo differs from "reflectivity" in that it is measured across all wavelengths, rather than just the visible spectrum. Since more than half of the solar radiation is invisible to the eye, albedo is a more precise term when discussing the ability of surfaces to reflect solar radiation.

Figure 1-3.
Urban canyons block breezes: Urban canyons are typically found in the downtown area of large cities. There, tall and densely clustered buildings obstruct the flow of natural breezes that could carry heat build-up away from the city at night.

What Is The Temperature Pattern In A Typical Urban Heat Island?

With the exception of slight variations due to geographical or climatological features, the overall pattern of heat islands is remarkably consistent from city to city. Starting from the countryside, temperatures rise distinctly at the edge of the city. Temperatures continue to rise slowly closer to downtown, with pockets of cooler air hovering over parks or other wooded areas. The highest temperatures, or "peaks," in the urban heat island are almost always in the downtown areas. The center of the city usually contains the highest density of buildings, and there seems to be a direct correlation between the amount of buildings per unit area and variations in temperatures. Figure 1-4 illustrates the heat island effect for a hypothetical metropolitan area. Figures 1-5 and 1-6 show recorded heat island effects in two cities.

Variations in the urban heat island over time are also consistent from city to city. The thermal processes causing summer heat islands occur when the sun is shining. The difference in temperatures begins to grow in mid-morning. The heat island, however, is most pronounced two to three hours after sunset, when paved areas and buildings slowly release their stored heat into the urban atmosphere. Figure 1-7 shows how the recorded heat island contours in St. Louis changed over the course of a day.

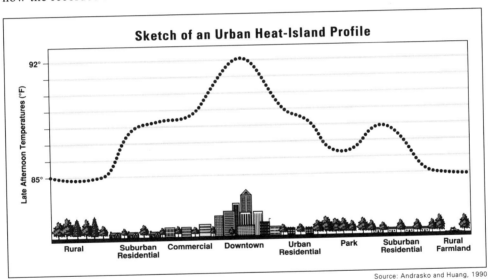

Sketch of an Urban Heat-Island Profile

Source: Andrasko and Huang, 1990

Figure 1-4.

Sketch of a typical urban heat-island profile: This profile of a heat island in a hypothetical metropolitan area shows temperature changes (in degrees Fahrenheit) correlated to the density of development and trees.

How Much Hotter Is An Urban Heat Island ?

Although most cities today suffer from heat island effects, their intensities—that is, just how much hotter the cities are than their surrounding areas—depend on a number of factors. Climate, topography, and physical layout certainly influence a city's average temperature. Short-term weather conditions also have a strong effect. Breezes in a city, for instance, prevent the formation of heat islands by mixing cooler air from surrounding areas with warmer urban air. On windless, cloudless days, stagnant urban air hovers over cities and holds heat that is released from city surfaces.

In the last century, increasing urbanization and industrialization have exacerbated the heat island. As cities have grown, increasing numbers of buildings have crowded out trees and other vegetation. It is estimated that, at present, only one tree is planted

Figure 1-5.
Winter heat island in London: This map shows temperature variations in downtown and surrounding London, England. Even in winter the contrast of high temperatures in the inner city and lower temperatures in surrounding rural areas is observable. Here, the difference is 12°F.

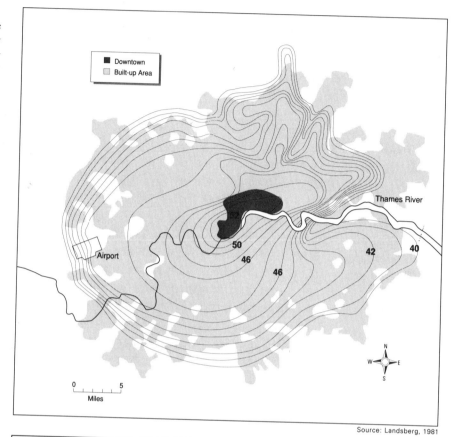

Source: Landsberg, 1981

Figure 1-6.
Neighborhood temperatures in Montreal: This map shows temperature variations (degrees Fahrenheit) in LaFontaine Park and surrounding areas of Montreal, Canada. Notice that the temperatures are lower over the park, due to the cooling effects of trees.

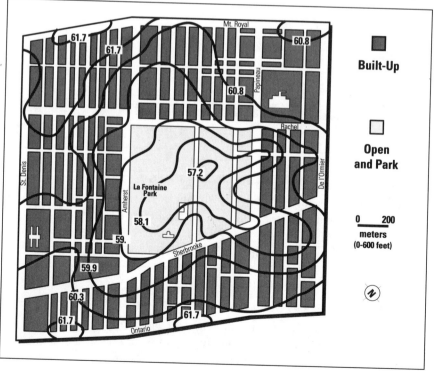

Source: Oke, 1977

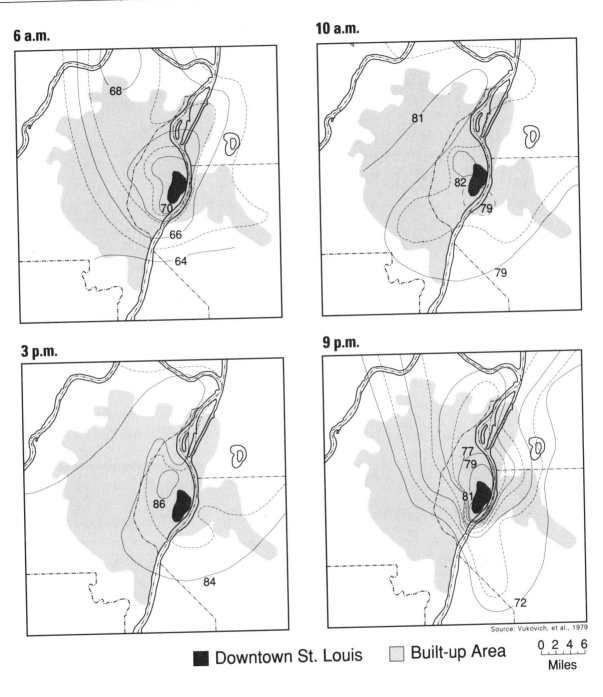

6 a.m.

10 a.m.

3 p.m.

9 p.m.

Source: Vukovich, et al., 1979

■ Downtown St. Louis ▢ Built-up Area

0 2 4 6
Miles

Figure 1-7.
Heat island profile in downtown St. Louis, Missouri: Although heat islands differ in their intensity and their size, most exhibit a similar pattern throughout the day. Notice that at 10:00 a.m., the temperature difference between downtown areas and surrounding areas is apparent, but it is only about 3°F. This is because although the sun has been shining for several hours, the dark surfaces have not yet absorbed enough heat to make the temperatures rise. At 3:00 p.m., the temperature difference is still slight—in this instance, only 2°F. By 9:00 p.m., however, after the sun has set, there is a marked 7°F difference between downtown and the area surrounding the city, because the pavements and other dark areas are releasing the heat stored there throughout the day. That difference continues throughout the evening and into the early morning hours. Indeed, the 6:00 a.m. frame shows a significant, lingering heat island of 6°F for this city.

Population can be seen as one indicator of a heat island's intensity. This can be particularly troublesome for cities in the tropical areas of the world, where populations are expected to skyrocket in the

for every four removed in American cities. For example, New York City has lost 175,000 trees, or 20 percent of its urban forest, in the past ten years. This loss of vegetation and its replacement by buildings or pavement causes the urban heat island to intensify.

Population also can be seen as one indicator of a heat island's intensity. Several studies of different cities in North America and Europe have shown that cities with larger populations tend to have more intense heat islands (See Figure 1-8).

This does not bode well for the future. Already, the number of urban

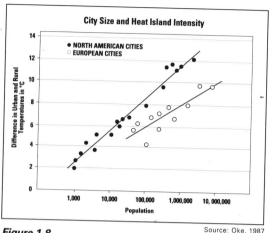

Figure 1-8.

Source: Oke, 1987

Maximum difference in urban and rural temperatures: Researchers have found correlations between city size and city temperature.

dwellers has risen from 600 million in 1900 to 2 billion in 1986. If this growth continues, more than one-half of the world's population will live in cities by the end of this century, where 100 years ago, only 14 percent lived in cities. In the United States, 90 percent of the population is expected to be living in, or around, urban areas by the year 2000 (Brown, 1987).

The situation will be even more dramatic in developing countries. Already, twenty-one of the thirty-four cities with more than 5 million inhabitants are in developing countries. Current projections estimate that eleven of those cities will have populations of between 20 and 30 million by the year 2000. In other words, our cities may be hot now, but they are going to get even hotter (Brown, 1987).

What Do Historical Records Show About Urban Temperature Trends?

Complete historical records of urban temperatures are not available at this time for a number of reasons. First, not all cities have maintained temperature records. Second, available records are usually only a century old, and contain so many changes in weather station location and instrumentation that comparisons are extremely difficult. Third, most temperature data taken in the last forty years have come from airport, rather than urban, weather stations. These data may underestimate urban temperature trends, because airports are usually located in the outskirts of cities, where temperatures are generally cooler. Fourth, data on summer temperatures have not always been compiled for all cities.

Despite these data limitations, climatologists and researchers can still see that cities across the planet are getting progressively hotter than their surrounding areas. Since the turn of the century, average annual temperatures in many cities have increased by as much as 5°F. The next section discusses first historical trends in absolute urban temperatures in several cities in California, selected cities elsewhere in the United States, and several cities abroad. It then focuses more closely on the relative differences between urban and rural temperatures, or the urban heat island. In the absence of summer data, we used average annual and maximum annual temperatures.

Absolute Urban Temperatures

The historical data for several Californian cities with mild to warm climates show an obvious warming trend. Figure 1-9 shows that the maximum yearly temperatures in Los Angeles dropped 0.5°F per decade from the late 19th century until 1930. Summer temperatures began rising, and have continued to rise at a steady rate of 1.3°F per decade. Today, maximum temperatures in downtown Los Angeles are about 5°F higher than in 1940. Average yearly temperatures in Los Angeles since the 1940s have risen by about 0.8°F per decade.

The cooling trend in the first third of the century probably was a result of irrigation and agricultural development on what had been sparsely vegetated ground. The profusion of fields and orchards had the inadvertent, but beneficial, effect of cooling the city. After the 1930s, however, as the urban population began to expand, agricultural areas were replaced by buildings and dark roads. As these surfaces heated and cooling effects of vegetation were lost, city temperatures began to rise.

Other cities in California are also warming. San Francisco's average August temperatures are increasing at a rate of 0.2°F per decade, as shown in Figure 1-10. This rate is lower than that in Los Angeles, but still significant, especially if we remember that San Francisco is well ventilated and open to the ocean. Other cities in California, including Oakland, Sacramento, and San Diego, are also warming at significant rates. Figures for these cities are located in Appendix A at the back of this guidebook.

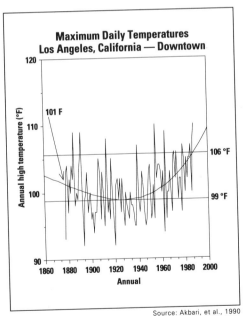

Source: Akbari, et al., 1990

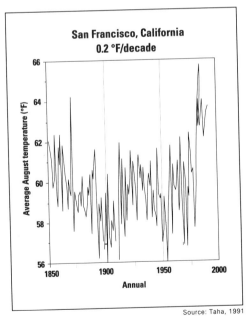

Source: Taha, 1991

Figure 1-9.
Los Angeles (CA) temperature record: Meteorological records show that yearly maximum temperatures have been rising 1.3°F per decade since 1940. Today, peak downtown temperatures are about 5°F higher than they were 50 years ago.

Figure 1-10.
San Francisco (CA) temperature record: Even though this city is located on a peninsula, average August temperatures for San Francisco show a 0.2°F rise in temperature per decade.

Warming trends are also evident in other parts of the country. Figure 1-11 shows annual mean temperatures for Washington, D.C. from 1871 to 1987. Since 1900, the annual mean temperatures have risen by a steady 0.5°F per decade, resulting in a total increase of about 4°F over 80 years. The actual increase is probably higher than indicated in this figure, since the weather station was moved from downtown to cooler airport locations in 1942 (indicated by the vertical line in Figure 1-11). Similarly, Ft. Lauderdale's (FL) summers have been warming at about 0.2°F per decade, as shown in Figure 1-12.

Data from foreign countries indicate similar, if less drastic, temperature increases. Figure 1-13 shows that the annual mean temperatures in Shanghai (China) have increased by 1.2°F over the last 100 years. Figure 1-14 shows that the annual mean temperatures in Tokyo, Japan, have increased by 3°F between 1915 and 1965. Table 1-1 summarizes the observed temperature trends for cities mentioned in this section and in Appendix A.

Differences Between Urban And Rural Temperatures

Because of the scarcity of data directly comparing urban and rural temperatures, it is often difficult to ascertain how much of the urban warming trend resulted from changes in regional weather, and how much is the result of the urban heat island effect. But the available data indicate that urban temperatures are rising faster than temperatures of surrounding rural areas.

In California, comparisons of 31 urban and rural weather stations show that urban sites were all relatively cooler before 1940, as illustrated in Figure 1-15, because cities were the centers of irrigation. After 1940, however, urban temperatures became

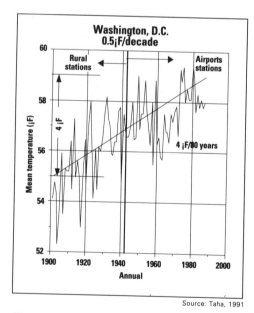

Source: Taha, 1991

Figure 1-11.
Washington, D.C. temperatures: Since 1900, annual mean temperatures in Washington, D.C. have risen by a steady 0.5°F per decade.

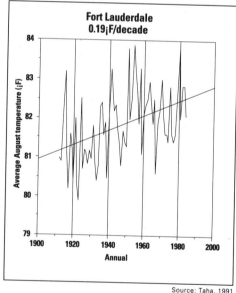

Source: Taha, 1991

Figure 1-12.
Fort Lauderdale (FL) temperatures: Average August temperatures for Fort Lauderdale show a 0.2°F rise in temperature per decade. The increase is lower in this city because it is oceanside.

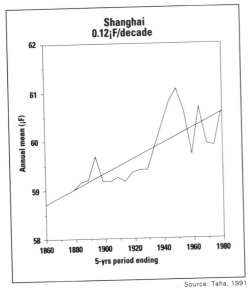

Source: Taha, 1991

Figure 1-13.
Shanghai (China) temperatures: Annual mean temperatures in Shanghai have increased by 1.2°F since 1860. See also Figure 1-16 which shows a record of the "temperature difference" between urban and rural areas of Shanghai during 1960 and 1980.

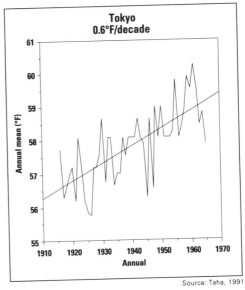

Source: Taha, 1991

Figure 1-14.
Tokyo (Japan) temperatures: In Tokyo, the annual mean temperatures increased by 6°F between 1915 and 1965.

Table 1-1. *Measured temperature trends in selected cities*

City	**Trend** (° F/decade)	Type of Recording
Los Angeles	1.3	highs
Los Angeles	0.8	means
San Francisco	0.2	means
Oakland	0.4	means
San Jose	0.3	means
San Diego	0.8	means
Sacramento	0.4	means
Washington	0.5	means
Baltimore	0.4	means
Ft. Lauderdale	0.2	means
Shanghai	0.12	means
Shanghai	0.2	minima
Tokyo	0.6	means

Sources: For identification of individual sources see description under Further Reading.

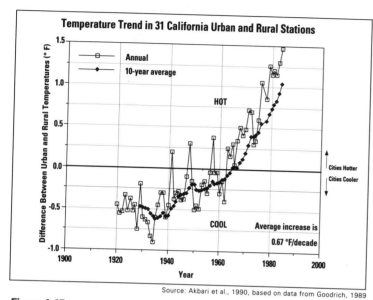

Figure 1-15.
California heat islands: Since 1940, the temperature difference between urban and rural stations has shown an increase of 0.67°F per decade.

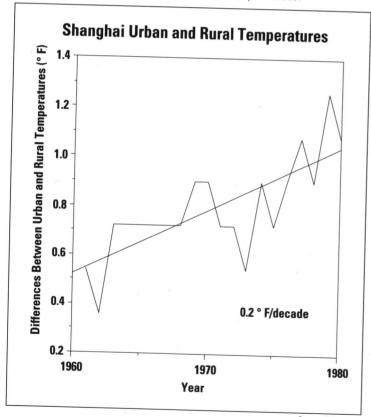

Figure 1-16.
Shanghai heat island: Since 1960, the temperature difference between urban and rural Shanghai has increased by 0.2°F per decade.

as high, if not higher, than those in the suburbs. After 1965, this trend became quite obvious; temperatures rose at about 0.7°F per decade.

Similarly, the difference between annual mean urban and rural temperatures in Shanghai grew from 0.4°F in 1962 to 1°F in 1980 (See Figure 1-16). Under ideal conditions (clear and calm nights, for example), a heat island of 10°F has been measured in that city.

Tropical cities provide excellent examples of increasing heat island intensity. Indeed, it is not unusual for average temperatures in tropical and subtropical cities to be as much as 10 to 18°F higher than surrounding areas. Heat islands of 16°F have been measured in Mexico City (Mexico), and of 11°F in Bombay and Poona (India).

Urban Heat Islands And Energy Use

Heat islands can have either beneficial or detrimental impacts on energy use, depending on geography, climate, and other factors. In a cold climate, an urban heat island is a moderate asset because it raises wintertime temperatures and lowers heating bills. In warm to hot climates, however, it exacerbates cooling energy use in the summer. For U.S. cities with populations larger than 100,000, peak utility loads will increase 1.5 to 2 percent for every 1°F increase in temperature. Since urban temperatures during summer afternoons in the United States have increased by 2 to 4°F in the last four decades, it can be assumed that 3 to 8 percent of the current urban electricity demand is used to compensate for the heat island effect alone.

The negative effects of urban heat islands should be a concern for all cities with significant cooling seasons. Figure 1-17 shows the United States separated into four general climate zones: Cold, Temperate, Hot-Arid, and Hot-Humid. Cities in the first zone typically have cold long winters and mild short summers. The effect of urban heat islands in these locations is generally positive, with some improvement of winter conditions and small increases in energy use during the short summer. Current thinking suggests that lightening surfaces and planting trees, however, will probably have little effect on winter heat islands. Hence, mitigation strategies for summer heat islands would still be a benefit in these areas.

Cities in the second zone have moderately cold winters, and mild to hot summers varying in length from three to four months. The effect of urban heat islands in these locations are generally detrimental, since their winter benefits do not compensate for their significant degradation of summertime conditions and increased air-conditioning demand. Cities in the last two zones have short mild winters and long hot summers. There, the urban heat island definitely intensifies temperatures and increases demand for air conditioning.

Correlations between temperature and energy use can be established by comparing utility-wide electricity loads to temperatures at the same time of day. Selecting the same hour each day is necessary to minimize non-climate related effects on electricity demand, such as those from utility-imposed schedules. Most utility districts experience peak electricity demands around 4:00 p.m. in the summer. (When hourly temperature data are not available, we correlate daily temperature averages with peak loads. This difference in method seems to have little effect on the results.)

Comparisons of temperatures to utility loads for the Los Angeles area have consistently shown that the two are interrelated. There are two electric utilities serving

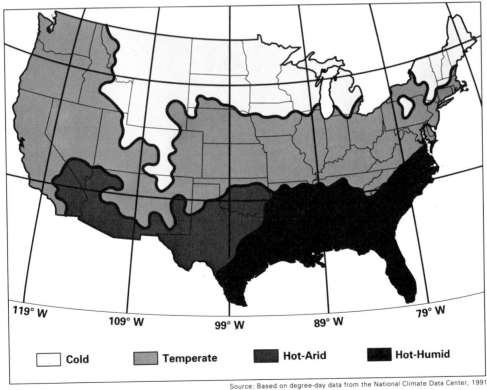

Figure 1-17.
Climate regions based on heating and cooling requirements.

| | Cold | | Temperate | | Hot-Arid | | Hot-Humid |

119° W   109° W   99° W   89° W   79° W

Source: Based on degree-day data from the National Climate Data Center, 1991

the metropolitan area, the Los Angeles Department of Water and Power (LADWP) and Southern California Edison (SCE). The 1986 data for LADWP showed that the peak demand increased by 72-75 megawatts (MW) or 2 percent for each 1°F increase in temperature (See Figure 1-18). Similarly, the data for the larger SCE district showed peak demand increases of 225 MW, or about 1.6 percent, for each 1°F increase in temperature (See Figure 1-19).

If we combine the data for the two districts, the net rate of increase in Los Angeles is 300 MW/°F. Therefore, the 5°F increase in Los Angeles' peak temperatures since 1940 translates into an added electricity demand of 1.5 gigawatts due to the heat island effect. Since peak electricity is worth approximately 10 cents per kilowatt-hour (kWh), this added burden costs the Los Angeles basin $150,000 per hour.

In Washington, the increase in electricity demand is reported to be 100 MW or 2 percent for each 1°F increase in temperature. This means that the 4°F increase over the past 80 years has contributed 400 MW to the utility load, at a cost of $40,000 per hour. Since there are approximately 1300 hours of air conditioning in Washington, the increase in yearly energy costs approaches $50 million. Table 1-2 and Figure 1-20 present data from various utility districts showing similar relationships between demand and temperature.

These rates of increase may not seem very high. But their impact on the national energy bill is impressive. The total electricity consumption for residential and commercial air conditioning in the United States is estimated at about 260 billion kilowatt hours per year, worth over $20 billion. Our initial calculations indicate that the electricity costs for summer heat islands alone could be as much as $1 million per hour, or over $1 billion per year. Hence, the nation-wide response of peak-cooling electricity load to temperature in the United States could range from 0.5 to 3 percent for each 1°F rise in temperature. Figures 1-21 and 1-22 show the results from a computer study of the potential energy impacts of rising temperatures in the southern part of the United

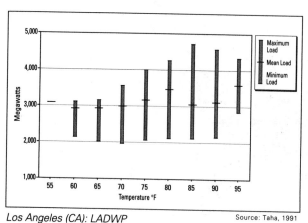

Los Angeles (CA): LADWP

Source: Taha, 1991

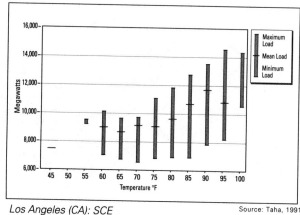

Los Angeles (CA): SCE

Source: Taha, 1991

Figure 1-18 and Figure 1-19.
Electricity Load: These plots show 4:00 p.m. electricity loads—maximum, mean and minimum loads—for two utility districts correlated with air temperatures: Los Angeles Department of Water and Power (Figure 1-18) and Southern California Edison (Figure 1-19). Note that as air temperatures rise, electricity loads also increase, due to increased demand for air conditioning.

Table 1-2. *Correlation between temperatures and electricity demand for selected utility districts based on measured data for 1986.*

Utility District	Increase (MW/°F)	Increase (% /°F)
Los Angeles (LADWP)	75	2.0
Los Angeles (SCE)	225	1.6
Washington, D.C.	100	2.0
Salt River Project (Phoenix)	56	2.0
Dallas-Ft. Worth (TX)	250	1.7
Tucson (AZ)	12	1.0
Colorado Springs (CO)	4	1.0

Source: Taha, 1991

Figure 1-20 . *Electricity records for four cities: These plots also show the correlation of air temperatures with electricity load in the cities of Dallas (upper left), Colorado Springs (upper right), Phoenix (lower left), and Tucson (lower right). Again, notice that as temperatures rise, so does the increase in electricity demand from increased air-conditioning use.*

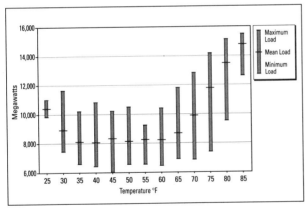

Dallas (TX)

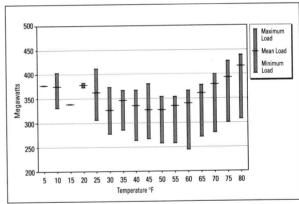

Colorado Springs (CO)

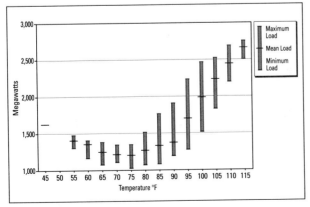

Phoenix (AZ)

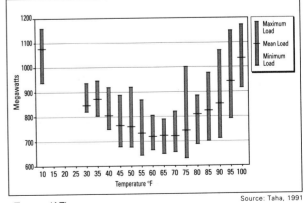

Tucson (AZ)

Source: Taha, 1991

Cooling Our Communities
A Guidebook on Tree Planting and Light-Colored Surfacing

Figure 1-21.
Estimated temperature increases in the United States: Estimated increases in average and peak temperatures in various regions in the United States due to global climate change, under the assumptions of one study.

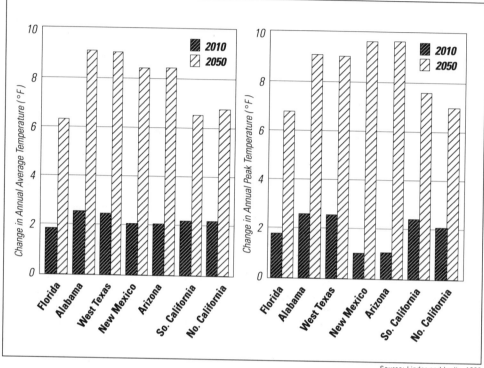

Source: Linder and Inglis, 1989

Figure 1-22.
Estimated electricity increases in the United States: Estimated increase in peak and annual electricity use in various regions of the United States with increases in regional temperatures.

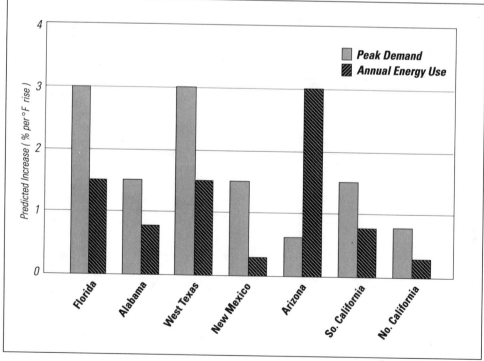

Source: Linder and Inglis, 1989

States. Figure 1-21 shows the estimated changes in average temperatures due to global climate change, although results are speculative until climate change models provide better regional resolution. Figure 1-22 shows the estimated impacts of these temperature changes on electricity use in the same regions.

The increasing demand for electricity will continue if our cities continue to warm, either from heat islands or global warming. Such warming can affect a utility in two ways. First, it can increase the amount of new generating capacity that a utility has to build and maintain to meet increased cooling demand. Second, logistical problems arising from the reallocation of resources, in terms of scheduling, importing, and exporting, could cost utilities across the country millions of dollars.

Urban Heat Islands and Smog Levels

In addition to increasing cooling energy use, heat islands and long-term urban warming affect the concentration and distribution of urban pollution, because heat accelerates the chemical reactions in the atmosphere that lead to high ozone concentrations.

Polluted days may increase by 10 percent for each 5°F increase. In Los Angeles, for example, ozone levels are not likely to exceed the current National Ambient Air Quality Standard (NAAQS)[1] when temperatures are below 74°F. Above that threshold, however, peak ozone levels increase. At 94°F and above they reach unacceptable levels (Figure 1-23). A similar threshold phenomenon was found in 13 cities in Texas (Figure 1-24). There, high urban temperatures

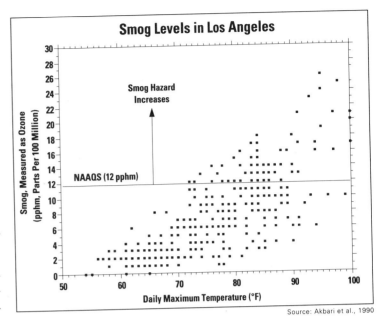

Source: Akbari et al., 1990

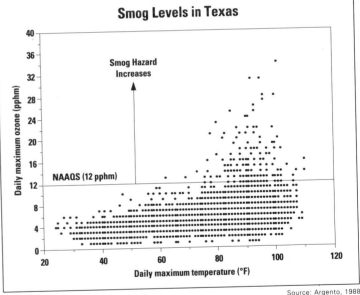

Source: Argento, 1988

Figures 1-23 and 1-24.
Ozone concentrations compared to daily peak temperatures in downtown Los Angeles in 1985 (Figure 1-23); and ozone concentrations compared too daily peak temperatures in 13 cities in Texas (Figure 1-24). Note that as temperatures rise, ozone concentrations reach dangerous levels (levels above the current National Ambient Air Quality Standard—NAASQ—of 12 parts per hundred million.)

---

[1]The current National Ambient Air Quality Standard (NAAQS) is an ozone concentration of 12 parts per hundred million (pphm). Ozone concentrations that exceed this measurement are considered problematic.

associated with the heat island effect also increase the probabilities of exceeding the NAAQS.

The relationship between air temperature and air pollution levels, however, is not simple. Other characteristics of city air, including dew point (the temperature at which air becomes saturated and begins producing dew), air pressure, cloud cover, and wind speed, also affect pollution levels. Emissions and concentrations of acidic gases and particles also are greater in urban areas. And the deposition of acidity in urban areas may be increased locally by enhanced rain volume due to heat-island-generated differences in air circulation.

To add to the complexity of these interactions, urban geometry also plays an important role in the transport and removal of pollutants. On the one hand, the roughness of urban buildings and landscapes increases air turbulence, thereby enhancing the dispersion of pollutants. On the other hand, if pollutants land in sheltered areas—like street canyons—they may reside longer than they would in a breezy rural environment.

Heat island effects on urban winds also influence the concentration and dispersal of pollutants. When incoming winds are fairly slow, winds within cities actually increase, due to heat-island-generated differences in temperatures. Conversely, when incoming winds move more quickly (a condition when heat islands cannot develop as fully), winds within the city slow down, due to the roughness of the buildings and urban structures.

Heat islands also affect urban pollution in less direct, but equally important, ways. Increased air-conditioning results in an increase in power generation, which produces larger amounts of pollutants. Average daily emissions from a representative (500 megawatt electric) coal-fired power plant consist typically of about 28 tons of sulfur dioxide (SO_2), two tons of carbon monoxide (CO), 28 tons of nitrous oxides (NO_2), and 1.4 tons of suspended particulates. These latter two are the major constituents of urban smog.

Urban Heat Islands And The Greenhouse Effect

The data just described show that temperatures in cities, especially large ones, have been increasing for at least the last four decades. There is no evidence that this warming trend will stop, or even slow. Indeed, based on results that scientists have obtained from computerized climate models, this trend may even accelerate because of the greenhouse effect.

The greenhouse effect occurs when the atmospheric concentration of greenhouse gases (carbon dioxide, methane, and nitrous oxides, among others) forms a blanket over the earth's surface. This blanket reduces heat loss through re-radiation from the planet's surface, which leads to increased global temperatures.

A natural greenhouse effect has existed for millions of years. Without it, the earth would be 50 to 60°F colder than it is. Human activities, however, particularly the burning of fossil fuels, are now changing the concentration of greenhouse gases radically. (This may cause the earth to warm at a rate that could far exceed any other

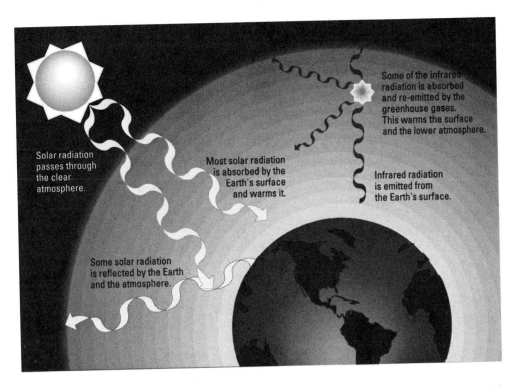

Solar radiation passes through the clear atmosphere.

Most solar radiation is absorbed by the Earth's surface and warms it.

Some of the infrared radiation is absorbed and re-emitted by the greenhouse gases. This warms the surface and the lower atmosphere.

Infrared radiation is emitted from the Earth's surface.

Some solar radiation is reflected by the Earth and the atmosphere.

Figure 1-25.
The Greenhouse Effect: Greenhouse gases in the entire atmosphere warm the earth just as glass traps warm air in a real greenhouse.

experienced on earth.) Researchers and analysts are working to understand the potential impacts of global climate change in an effort to learn possible methods for adapting to and slowing changes, such as reducing the emissions of greenhouse gases.

Scientists from organizations all over the world are forecasting that if current trends continue, we could see an increase in the mean global temperature of 2 to 5°C (3.6 to 9°F) by the end of the next century (IPCC, 1991). This could alter ocean and atmospheric currents, shift precipitation patterns, raise sea levels, and lower the levels of inland waterways. There could be reductions in the range of existing forests, the loss of significant portions of the U.S. coastal wetlands, and regional adjustments in agriculture due to a northward shift in productive regions. Finally, the higher temperatures could require increases in the production of electric power to meet additional air-conditioning needs. This generation could cause increases in the concentrations of ozone in the troposphere, that part of the atmosphere within 8 to 10 kilometers of Earth's surface (Morgenstern, 1991). In short, changes in climate have the potential to alter social, economic, agricultural, political, and ecological systems.

Important greenhouse gases include carbon dioxide (CO_2), methane (CH_4), chlorofluorocarbons (CFCs), nitrous oxide (N_2O), and tropospheric ozone. Among these gases CO_2 is considered the primary factor affecting global warming. This gas is a by-product of both fossil fuel combustion and deforestation. On a global scale, world energy use represents the largest anthropogenic source of CO_2; it exceeds the amount released from deforestation by two to five times. Taken together, the burning of fossil fuels combined with deforestation has quadrupled global rates of anthropogenic CO_2 emissions over the past 150 years. Atmospheric concentrations of CO_2, for example, have risen from about 315 parts per million to about 350 parts per million

Figure 1-26.
Electricity use and carbon dioxide (CO_2) emissions: Turning on the air conditioner at home increases CO_2 emissions at the power plant where they are released into the atmosphere.

this century, up sharply from estimates of approximately 290 parts per million in the 1800s (Lashof and Tirpak, 1991). The U.S. Department of Energy estimates that the CO_2 emissions in the United States could increase by 380 million tons of carbon by the year 2010, and by 900 million tons of carbon by the year 2030, 66 percent above current emission levels (IPCC, 1990). If emissions remained constant at 1985 levels, the atmospheric concentration of CO_2 might reach 440-500 parts per million by 2100 (Lashof and Tirpak, 1991).

Heat islands also may contribute to global warming. Scientists do not know what the direct impact of urban temperature increases may be on global temperatures. As the temperature of urban areas rises, they demand increased energy for cooling, which requires additional power generation. Each kilowatt hour of electricity generated, in turn, releases about one half pound carbon—in the form of carbon dioxide—into the atmosphere. (The average city of 100,000 people uses approximately one billion kilowatt hours per year.) An unchecked cycle of increasing temperatures leading to increased electricity demand followed by increased power generation, atmospheric emissions, and higher temperatures, might begin. This means that if energy demand can be reduced by alleviating heat islands, the amount of CO_2 released into the atmosphere also can be reduced.

Whatever global climate change does occur would amplify an increase in urban temperatures, if current trends continue. Preliminary work by a number of researchers indicates that if the current trends of heat islands continue, cities would be 10°F hotter in 50 years. As mentioned earlier, Figure 1-21 shows the results obtained by one research group of estimated increases in temperatures for various regions of the United States. This heating would result in greater discomfort, higher ozone levels, more electricity use, and more carbon dioxide emissions. An effective program of heat-island mitigation could help curb this dramatic urban warming.

If urban temperatures are not lowered in the near future, both energy and smog generation will continue to increase, as will the costs associated with that generation. This increase may occur whether global warming happens or not, and it could result in some social and economic consequences.

The America the Beautiful
Urban and Community Forestry Assistance Program

In 1990, Congress passed President Bush's America the Beautiful Act as part of the 1990 Farm Bill. The President's goal for the program is to plant one billion trees per year. The Community Forestry element of the America the Beautiful program calls for a nationwide, multi-year effort to plant and maintain trees in all 40,000 cities, towns, and communities throughout the country. The goal of the program is to plant 30 million trees, the largest community tree planting and maintenance program in history. It seeks to reverse the current trend of deforestation in the Nation's cities and towns, where on average only one tree is planted for every four that die or are removed.

The Act gives leadership to the U.S. Forest Service in the Department of Agriculture and creates a non-profit foundation called the National Tree Trust. The Forest Service, working with state forestry agencies and other partners, is providing technical advice and support to communities and volunteer groups in their tree planting and tree care endeavors. The National Tree Trust Foundation is bringing the public, private, and civic sectors together, soliciting funds to assist communities, and encouraging volunteer community tree-planting programs. Funds raised by the Foundation can be used to assist communities in preparing sites, and selecting, planting, and maintaining trees.

To get involved with the America the Beautiful Urban and Community Forestry Assistance Program, or for more information, contact your state forester, or write to the National Tree Trust, 1455 Pennsylvania Avenue NW, Suite 250, Washington, D.C., 20005.

—Source: USDA Forest Service, 1991

Further Reading

Several books by climatologists describe urban climate and the heat island effect, including *The Urban Climate* by H. Landsberg (1981), and *Boundary Layer Climates* by Oke (1978). The technical papers by Oke (1975, 1987), and Duckworth and Sandberg (1954) describe measurements of heat island intensities. The paper by Myrup (1969) describes a simple computer analysis of the urban heat island. The proceedings from the Urban Climatology Workshop in Mexico City (Oke, 1986) has numerous articles by Oke, Landsberg, and others on urban heat islands in tropical cities.

The proceedings from the Heat Island Workshop by LBL (Garbesi, ed. 1989) contain numerous articles on various aspects of the urban heat-island issue, including computer analyses of urban climates, estimated costs of heat islands, and the energy saving potentials of and implementation methods for mitigation strategies. In addition, there are several LBL reports by Akbari and others on the energy costs and potential mitigation strategies of urban heat islands.

The papers by Hartig, Hull and Harvey, Schroeder, Ulrich, and Verderber describe the psychological effects of trees on humans.

Urban temperatures and heat island discussions in this chapter were based on data from Goodridge (1987, 1989) and Karl et al. (1987, 1988, 1990). The historical temperature data from California urban and rural weather stations were obtained from Goodridge (1987, 1989) and further discussed in a paper by Akbari et al. (1989). The weather data for Washington, D.C. were obtained from the Potomac Electric Power Company whereas the temperature data for Baltimore and Ft. Lauderdale were obtained from Karl et al. (1990). The urban temperature data for Shanghai and Tokyo are based on studies by Chow (in Oke 1986, pp. 87-109) and Fukui (1970). The heat island data for Mexico City, Bombay, and Poona are taken from Oguntoyinbo (in Oke 1986, pp. 110-135) and Jauregui (1973). The computer-based estimates of future changes in annual and peak temperatures for various parts of the United States are taken from a report by Linder and Inglis (1989).

Utility load data for the two Los Angeles area utilities were obtained from the Los Angeles Department of Water and Power and the Southern California Edison Company. The utility load data for Salt River Project, Dallas-Ft. Worth, Tucson, and Colorado Springs were obtained from their respective utilities. The estimated temperature sensitivity of peak demand and energy use for various parts of the country are again taken from the Linder and Inglis report (1989).

Comparisons of smog levels to temperature in Los Angeles are based on data from the California Air Resources Board. Comparisons of ozone levels to temperature in Texas cities are based on data from Argento (1988). Estimated amounts of power plant emissions are taken from a Department of Energy report (1988). General data on the relationship between heat islands and urban pollution can also be found in Feng (1990), Summers (1966), and NAPAP reports (1990). Information on heat islands and wind speeds can be found in Balling and Cerveny (1987), Bornstein et al. (1977), and Lee (1979). Finally, analyses of urban air quality modeling are available in Bennett and Saab (1982), Freeman et al. (1986), and Ivanyi et al. (1982).

2

Joe Huang
Ronald Ritschard
Neil Sampson
Haider Taha

The Benefits of Urban Trees

Vegetation is one of the simplest and most effective ways to cool our communities and save energy. Trees, shrubs, and vines can protect individual buildings from the sun's heat in the summer, and from frigid winds in the winter. On hot, sunny days, evapotranspiration from trees and shrubs also can reduce temperatures and energy use for whole neighborhoods, even entire cities. Indeed, this collective cooling can have a greater influence on energy use than shading and wind shielding.

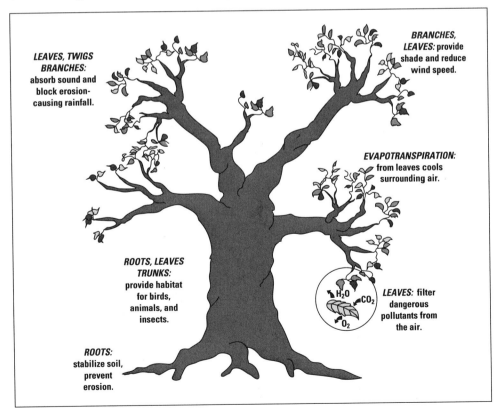

LEAVES, TWIGS BRANCHES: absorb sound and block erosion-causing rainfall.

BRANCHES, LEAVES: provide shade and reduce wind speed.

EVAPOTRANSPIRATION: from leaves cools surrounding air.

ROOTS, LEAVES TRUNKS: provide habitat for birds, animals, and insects.

H_2O CO_2 O_2

LEAVES: filter dangerous pollutants from the air.

ROOTS: stabilize soil, prevent erosion.

Figure 2-1.
The numerous ecological qualities of trees: Indeed, almost every part of a tree provides a beneficial function. The leaves alone can provide cooling from evapotranspiration, shelter from wind, sound absorption, and sequestering of carbon dioxide.

Vegetation has other benefits as well. It is cheap, fairly simple, and aesthetically pleasing (nobody raves about the appearance of insulation or air conditioners). It can increase property value, block noise, and stabilize soil. These benefits increase as trees get older and bigger.

The effectiveness of vegetation, of course, depends on its density, shape, dimensions, and placement. But in general, any tree, even one bereft of leaves, can have a noticeable impact on energy use.

Direct Effects Of Vegetation

Trees affect urban climates and building energy use in two ways. Shading and lowering wind speeds modifies the interaction between a building and its surroundings. These are called "direct" effects. "Indirect" effects, like evapotranspiration, are those that change the surrounding urban environmental conditions. In general, direct effects—like shade—accrue to one building while the benefits of indirect effects accrue to a whole neighborhood or city.

During the winter, shading is not desirable in temperate and cold climates, because it will increase heating needs. Blocking the wind, however, is a benefit in the winter. During the summer, the opposite is true: shading helps reduce energy needs, while wind screening can reduce cooling breezes. With strategic planting, we can maximize the positive effects in both seasons, while minimizing the negative ones.

Shading

Trees in full leaf can be very effective in blocking the sun's radiation. While the full extent of a canopy's shade depends on the species, vegetation of the right shape and density can block up to 95 percent of the incoming radiation. Even leafless trees (such as deciduous trees in winter) can intercept up to 50 percent of the sun's energy.

Tree shade reduces cooling energy use inside a building in three ways. First, shading windows helps prevent direct solar radiation from entering the structure. Second, shading walls, windows, and roofs keeps them from getting hot, thereby reducing the amount of heat reaching the interior. Third, shade similarly keeps the soil around a building cool, which can then act as a "heat sink" for the house.

The shade of trees actually does a better job cooling a building and its interior than Venetian blinds, plastic coatings, or heavy, reflective coatings on glass. Figure 2-2 illustrates the dynamic relationship between deciduous shade trees and incoming solar radiation.

> Several studies have shown that trees can increase property values by 3 percent to 20 percent. The American Forestry Association in 1985 estimated that the future value of an urban tree is $57,000 for a 50 year-old mature specimen. This estimate includes an average annual value of $73 for air conditioning, $75 for soil benefits and erosion control, $50 for air pollution control, and $75 for wildlife habitats. The total value over the tree's lifetime would be the total annual value of $273 (1985 dollars), compounded at 5 percent interest for 50 years.
>
> — Neil Sampson

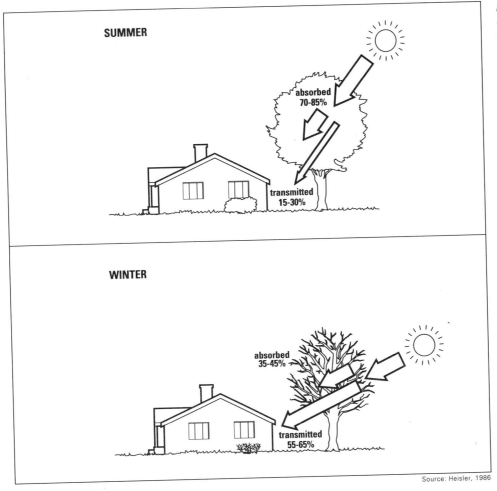

SUMMER

absorbed 70-85%

transmitted 15-30%

WINTER

absorbed 35-45%

transmitted 55-65%

Source: Heisler, 1986

Shade And Energy Use

Field measurements have found that the shade of trees and shrubs planted immediately adjacent to buildings can directly reduce cooling needs. Dr. John Parker, a researcher at Florida International University, estimated that trees and shrubs planted next to a South Florida residential building can reduce summer air-conditioning costs by 40 percent (Parker, 1983). Reductions in summer power demand of 3 kilowatts (59 percent) during mornings and 5 kilowatts (58 percent) in afternoons were also measured. Parker noted that the most effective position for trees is close to windows and glazed areas. He also indicated that directly shading the air conditioner can increase its efficiency by up to 10 percent during the warmest periods. Measurements taken in Central Pennsylvania suggest that shading a small mobile home can reduce air conditioning by up to 75 percent (Heisler, 1986). See Chapter 6 for more exact steps on landscaping for energy conservation.

Tree shading is beneficial during the summer, but not in the winter, when the warming rays of the sun are desirable. The penalties from tree shading in winter, however, are not as significant as the benefits are during the summer. The sun is less intense in winter, and deciduous trees shed their leaves which allows most of the sunshine to reach the house.

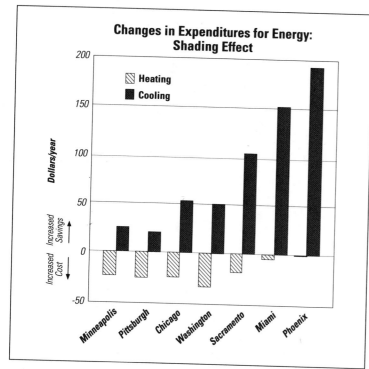

Figure 2-3.

Source: Huang et al., 1990

The effects of shading from a 30 percent increase in tree cover on the heating and cooling energy use of older houses, based on computer simulation.

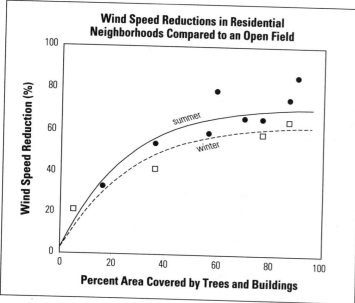

Figure 2-4.

Source: Heisler, 1989

Tree cover and wind speed reduction: Measured studies show that an added 10 percent tree cover can reduce urban wind speeds by 10-20 percent. Even in winter, wind-speed reductions are as much as 50-90 percent of the summer reductions.

Figure 2-3 shows the results of computer simulations of the impact of additional tree shading on the heating and cooling energy use of typical houses in seven cities. Although tree shading increased winter heating bills, these increases are more than offset by the much larger savings in cooling energy use.

Even the heating penalties shown in Figure 2-3 must be interpreted with care, since they relate only to the effects of tree shading. In reality, trees also reduce wind speeds, which is a benefit during the winter, as described in the following section. Consequently, the net impact of added trees on building energy use is beneficial, even in the winter.

Wind Reduction

Trees also reduce wind speeds. Indeed, the area within a single crown or stand of trees can be very calm, even when the wind is strong outside the stand. Houses in neighborhoods also help keep wind speeds down. Increasing the number of trees, however, can help get wind speeds down even further. This is a benefit in the winter, but a detriment in the summer when cooling breezes are welcomed.

How much foliage does it take to reduce wind speeds? Dr. Gordon Heisler, of the U.S. Forest Service, has found that even scattered trees can significantly decrease the wind speed in residential neighborhoods. Figure 2-4 shows the results from Heisler's study of wind speeds in various neighborhoods. Depending on the density of housing, an added 10 percent tree cover in a residential area can reduce wind speeds by 10 percent to 20 percent, while an added 30 percent tree cover can reduce it by 15 percent to 35 percent. The study also showed that even in wintertime, when most trees are leafless, wind speeds can be reduced by as much as 50-90 percent of their summer values.

In the winter, such wind reductions help keep a building warmer. In the summer, blocking the wind sometimes has the undesirable effect of blocking cooling breezes, too. It is possible, however, to plant trees around buildings to channel winds and create cooling ventilation. (Chapter 6, presents additional information on strategic planting to channel wind.)

Wind and Energy Use

Wind-speed reductions resulting from tree planting can either decrease or increase both cooling and heating energy use, depending on local weather conditions. In Figure 2-5, for example, we can see that wind-speed reductions simulated in computer models lowered both heating and cooling energy use in Chicago, IL, Miami, FL, and Washington, D.C. In Phoenix, AZ, Pittsburgh, PA, Sacramento, CA, and Minneapolis, MN, however, the heating energy use was reduced but the cooling energy consumption was increased.

Field measurements have also indicated that reduced wind speeds can be beneficial to heating-energy users. Houses monitored in South Dakota, for example, consumed 25 percent less fuel when located on leeward sides of windbreaks than when exposed. With wind breaks on three sides of houses, fuel consumption was reduced by an average of 40 percent. Between January and February, exposed houses used 442 kilowatt-hours per month to keep the temperature at 60°F, but only 270 kilowatt-hours per month when sheltered by vegetation.

Net Energy Impacts of Trees

Since the direct effects of planting trees around a house include both shading and wind shielding, it is important to evaluate the net impact of these two effects on a building's heating and cooling energy bill. In Figure 2-6, we have simulated both

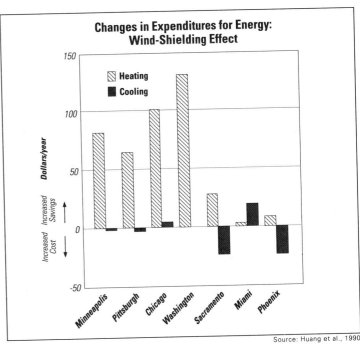

Source: Huang et al., 1990

Figure 2-5.
The effects of wind shielding from a 30 percent increase in tree cover on the heating and cooling energy use of older houses, based on computer simulation.

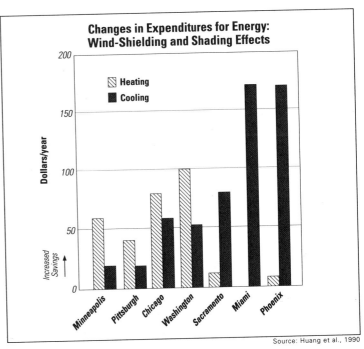

Source: Huang et al., 1990

Figure 2-6.
The net direct effects of windshielding and shading from a 30 percent increase in tree cover on the heating and cooling energy use of older houses, based on computer simulation.

the wind-shielding and shading effects from planting three trees around a typical house built before 1973. The estimated energy savings shown in the figure combine those estimated for the individual effects shown earlier in Figures 2-3 and 2-5. When the wind-shielding and shading effects are considered together, trees are shown to reduce both the heating and cooling energy use in both hot and cold locations. During the winter, trees reduce heating costs through their wind-shielding effects, while during the summer, trees reduce cooling costs through their shading effects. In fact, the computer study shows annual energy cost savings from three additional trees to be $75 to $175 per household in all seven cities.

Indirect Effects of Vegetation

Evapotranspiration, the process by which plants release moisture in the form of water vapor, requires energy from solar radiation or warm air. When solar energy is expended for evapotranspiration instead of directly heating the air, the increase in temperatures during the day will be reduced.

This process can have a significant effect on air temperatures. Trees can transpire up to 100 gallons of water a day. In a hot, dry location, this produces a cooling effect similar to that of five average air conditioners running for 20 hours. In a hot, humid location, however, evapotranspiration is not an effective cooling process.

Evapotranspiration and shading effects together can reduce air temperatures by as much as 9°F, LBL researchers have found. Even cropped surfaces can be 5°F cooler than their denuded surroundings. Temperature measurements by LBL in suburban Davis and Sacramento, CA, indicate that the air temperature in neighborhoods with mature tree canopies are 3 to 6°F lower in the daytime than newer areas with no trees.

Even more pronounced cooling effects have been measured in large urban parks, where evapotranspiration is increased by wind. In such parks—referred to as oases—temperatures can be up to 7°F lower than surrounding neighborhoods. The cooling influence of these oases extends far beyond the immediate foliated area. In experiments in Davis, for example, LBL researchers found that temperatures of the air leaving an orchard remained low for a distance five times the height of the trees.

The indirect effects trees have on reducing air temperatures through evapotranspiration are much more difficult to predict using computers than are the direct effects of shading and wind-shielding. Preliminary results produced by researchers, however,

The American Forestry Association's Global ReLeaf Utility Program is successfully convincing utility companies to plant trees for energy conservation. The Utility Program invites companies to sponsor Global ReLeaf as part of a customer education/community and public relations program. Individual customers learn how to plant trees to save energy and money. Communities are encouraged to develop tree-planting projects—and to support them. The program also gives utility employees background on the savings potentials of trees and strategic landscaping methods, and coaches utility companies on corporate outreach and the development of citizen-based environmental activities.

corroborate the previously mentioned field measurements. These simulations predicted that increasing the tree cover by 25 percent in Sacramento and Phoenix would decrease air temperatures at 2 p.m. in July by 6 to 10°F (Figures 2-7 and 2-8).

Evapotranspiration and Energy Use

Researchers at LBL have also used computer simulations to study the combined direct and indirect effects of vegetation on the energy use of typical one-story buildings in Sacramento, Lake Charles (LA), Phoenix, and Los Angeles. In these simulations, the effects of trees on building energy use were categorized either as direct effects due to shading and wind shielding or indirect effects due to evapotranspiration. The effects of 10 percent and 25 percent increased vegetation cover (corresponding to one and three trees per house) were simulated first separately, to test the contribution of each effect, and then in combination, to yield comprehensive, more realistic results. Figure 2-9 summarizes these results. Because of the difficulty in simulating the indirect effects of evapotranspiration, the results should be regarded as more hypothetical than those shown in Figures 2-3, 2-5, and 2-6.

In Los Angeles, the reductions are small because the base cooling energy use is relatively low (only 65 cooling hours per year), and it is assumed that natural ventilation is used whenever possible. Therefore, the results for Los Angeles have been omitted from Figure 2-9. A 10 percent increase in tree cover in the other three cities (corresponding to one tree per house), however, produced savings of 24 percent in Sacramento and 12 percent in Phoenix and Lake Charles, corresponding to dollar savings of $40 to $90. The corresponding

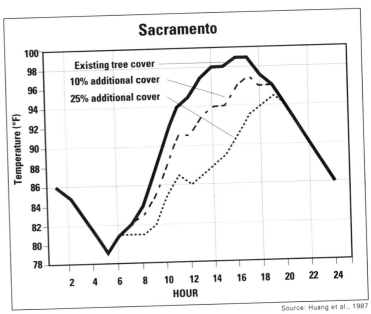

Source: Huang et al., 1987

Figures 2-7.
Temperature reductions in Sacramento due to added tree cover on a typical summer day in July, based on computer simulations.

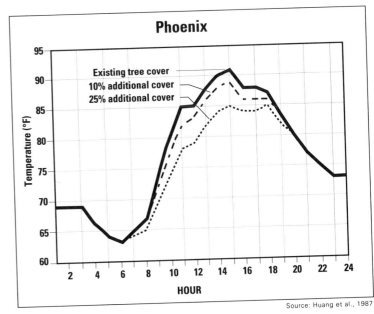

Source: Huang et al., 1987

Figure 2-8.
Temperature reductions in Phoenix due to added tree cover on a typical summer day in July based on computer simulations: Increasing tree cover can significantly decrease city-wide temperatures.

Figure 2-9.
Estimated Cooling Energy savings in a typical, well-insulated, new house from the combined direct and indirect effects of trees. Note that direct effects provide a relatively small percentage of the total energy savings for new housing stock.

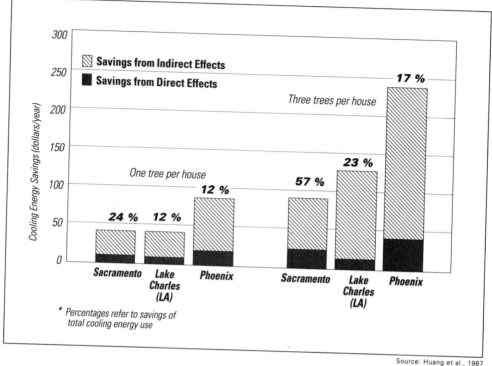

Source: Huang et al., 1987

If we were to plant 100 million trees, and implement light-surfacing programs, we could reduce our electricity use by 50 billion kilowatt hours per year (2 percent of annual electricity use in the United States), and reduce the amount of CO_2 dumped into the atmosphere by as much as 35 million tons per year.

savings in peak electricity use vary from 9 percent in Phoenix to 20 percent in Sacramento and Los Angeles.

A 25 percent increase in tree cover (corresponding to three trees per house) was estimated to have an even more dramatic impact on summer cooling bills, with reductions in cooling energy use of 57 percent in Sacramento, 17 percent in Phoenix, and 23 percent in Lake Charles. The monetary value of these energy savings are from $100 to $250 a year, per household.

According to this study, the direct effects of shading account for only 10 to 35 percent of the total cooling energy savings. The remaining savings result from temperatures lowered by evapotranspiration. The ratio of these two savings is also affected by how well a house is insulated and caulked. Older houses (which have a lower thermal integrity) will show greater savings from shading than newer, tighter houses.

These simulated and measured findings indicate that trees can be of potential benefit to the urban dweller if care is taken in positioning them. Trees can save both heating and cooling energy use particularly if properly considered during the building design stages.

Trees And The Greenhouse Effect

By reducing cooling energy use, trees do more than save residents money. They also can help mitigate, even reduce, the greenhouse effect, which many scientists think could cause widespread disruptions and dislocations in the next 100 years.

As discussed in Chapter 1, scientists now believe that if all 100 million urban tree spaces were filled, and if rooftops and parking lots were painted light colors, we could reduce our electricity use by 50 billion kilowatt hours each year, thereby reducing the amount of CO_2 dumped into the atmosphere by as much as 35 million tons per year (NAS, 1991). Scientists call this benefit "avoided carbon." In addition, trees absorb carbon dioxide for photosynthesis and store some of the carbon. This process, called "sequestering," helps mitigate the amount of carbon dioxide emitted by power plants when they generate power for air conditioning. Figure 2-10 illustrates the cycle of potential carbon sequestering by trees.

Rural Versus Urban Trees

One obvious question that comes up when we talk about planting trees—whether to reduce energy costs or the amount of carbon dioxide in the atmosphere—is "why not plant trees in rural areas?" After all, there are more spaces for trees in the countryside than in urban areas, and rural conditions support tree longevity far more than do urban conditions.

It's actually not an either/or question. Both urban and rural planting programs have benefits. For heat island mitigation and global warming reduction, however, urban trees are far more efficient.

A tree planted in the countryside sequesters CO_2 from the atmosphere. A tree planted in the city also sequesters CO_2, yet its cooling effects have an additional benefit: by shading and reducing air temperatures around buildings, it reduces the need for air conditioning, thereby reducing the amount of CO_2 dumped into the atmosphere

Figure 2-10.
Trees can help reduce the greenhouse effect in two ways. First, trees directly absorb CO_2—the primary greenhouse gas—from the atmosphere during photosynthesis. Second, shade from trees can reduce air-conditioning energy use, which reduces the amount of CO_2 emitted by power plants.

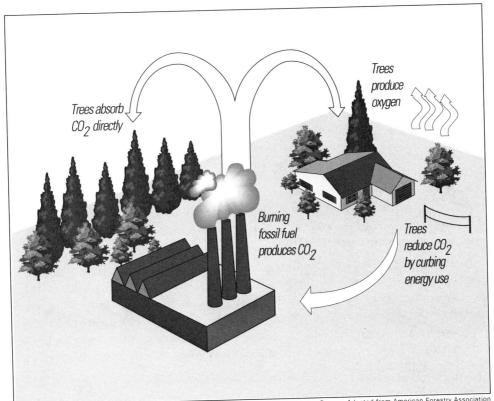

Trees absorb CO_2 directly

Trees produce oxygen

Burning fossil fuel produces CO_2

Trees reduce CO_2 by curbing energy use

Source: Adapted from American Forestry Association

On a carbon savings basis alone, urban trees provide greater benefits than rural trees, because they reduce carbon emissions by reducing cooling energy consumption. Researchers estimate that an urban tree can save five to ten times more overall carbon than a rural tree.

at the power plant. Indeed, the annual amount of carbon saved per tree from cooling energy savings (88 pounds saved per tree per year) is five to ten times greater than the amount of carbon sequestered on a per tree basis.[1]

Researchers have developed indicators such as the "Cost of Conserved Energy" (CCE) to compare the potential savings in energy conservation with the cost of the investment. To establish these costs (which are expressed in dollars per kilowatt hour), researchers divide the annualized cost of a conservation measure by the annual energy savings.

Researchers use a similar formula to calculate the Costs of Conserved Carbon (CCC). To make this calculation, researchers divide the cost of conserved energy by the amount of carbon burned in a power plant to generate one kilowatt hour of electricity. The result is expressed as dollars per ton of carbon.

In fact, if enough trees are planted, we can reduce our cooling energy use enough to avoid the costly and unsightly construction of new power plants and the burden of their economic, social, and environmental costs. See Appendix B for a more detailed discussion of calculating these costs and efficiency measures.

Using Trees To Reduce Urban Air Pollution

The air in many of America's larger communities fails to meet air quality standards much of the time, although many communities have made significant improvements in recent years. In Los Angeles, the air was classed as "unhealthful" about one-third of the time in 1979; this was down only 100 to 110 days a year by 1983. In New York City, unhealthful air was recorded over 150 days in 1979 and dropped only to 80 in 1983. Clearly, in spite of intensive efforts and pollution control, the quality of the urban community as human habitat remains threatened by air pollution.

This is a complex problem that demands considerable attention. But there is a role here for trees, as well, in addition to reducing energy use and CO_2 emissions, trees act as free-standing air purifiers.

Tree leaves and needles precipitate significant amounts of particulates from the air. One researcher estimates that a street lined with healthy trees can reduce air-borne dust particles by as much as 7,000 particles per liter of air (Bernatsky, 1978). In addition, some nitrogen oxides (NO and NO_2) and airborne ammonia (NH_3) can be taken up by foliage, with the nitrogen going to plant use. Trees can also utilize some sulfur dioxide (SO_2) and ozone (O_3), but many species suffer severe damage from exposure to high concentrations.

Most of the pollution reduction ability of trees is, however, finally related to the soil, since pollutants are either washed to the ground from leaf surfaces or fall directly as the result of having collided with tree structures or entering wind eddies caused by the vegetation. The ability of soils to neutralize pollutants and prevent subsequent water contamination varies considerably. Species and sub-species of trees also vary in their sensitivity to different pollutants. Some handle high pollution levels

---

[1] The estimated average carbon savings of 88 lbs. carbon are the product of the energy savings per tree (220 kilowatt hours) and the number of pounds of carbon saved per kilowatt hours (.44 pounds).

reasonably well; others serve as sensitive indicators of the degree of environmental deterioration.

Thus, it is possible to utilize trees and other vegetation as part of a pollution reduction scheme, but only within limits. Such a strategy cannot replace efforts to reduce pollution at its source. Where trees and forests have been stunted or killed by pollution, the basic environmental life machine has been reduced in capacity, and all life on earth is affected by this change.

Trees And Urban Noise

Trees also filter another type of pollution: urban noise. This is a pervasive and troublesome feature of the urban environment. Trees can be a significant factor in reducing unwanted sound levels. The leaves, twigs, and branches absorb sound, particularly high frequency sounds that are the most bothersome to humans. Indeed, a belt of trees 98 feet wide and 49 feet tall has been shown to reduce highway noise by 6 to 10 decibels—a sound-energy reduction of almost 50 percent.

In addition to reducing unwanted noise, trees produce alternative sounds that can "mask" other noises and make them less noticeable. With the wind rustling through leaves and with birds singing, the drone of a nearby freeway is less noticeable and less bothersome.

Psychological Benefits Of Trees

While it is difficult to quantify what philosophers, naturalists, and theologians have been telling us for centuries about the soothing aspects of natural landscapes, enough research has been done to prove that a qualitative effect does exist. That is,

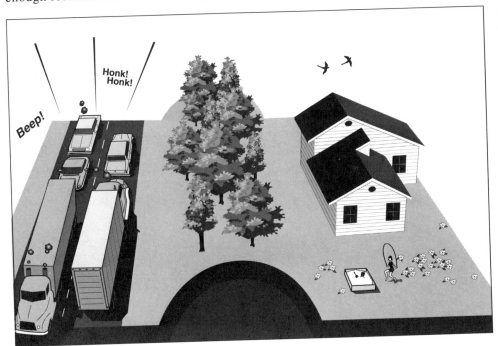

Figure 2-11.
Benefits of berm: A row of trees can be particularly effective in screening undesirable urban noise.

trees significantly reduce that familiar feeling of being severely stressed, while they increase feelings of peace and well-being.

A number of researchers have examined the effects of trees on emotional states. Roger Ulrich, the Associate Dean for Research at Texas A&M University, for instance, studied subjects' reactions to color slides of rural scenes and urban scenes. He found that subjects were more interested in, and felt more positively about, the rural scenes than urban ones. Ulrich also recorded the subjects' brain alpha waves (which have been correlated with feelings of relaxation) during the slide presentation. Alpha amplitudes were higher when subjects saw rural scenes than when they saw urban ones.

A number of studies also have linked recreation in nature areas to psychological well-being. One study found that visitors to Chicago's Morton Arboreteum associated feelings of peacefulness, quiet, and tranquility with their stay. Similarly, research has found that the mostly low-income, inner-city dwellers visiting Detroit's Belle Isle Park experienced significant stress reduction. Finally, one study had encouraged subjects to spend 40 minutes walking in an urban area with trees, 40 minutes walking in a denuded urban area, or 40 minutes relaxing with magazines and music. Those subjects who walked under the trees reported more positive feelings than did those doing other activities.

In a more recent study, Ulrich first showed 120 subjects a stressful movie and then showed them one of six different videotapes of urban and natural settings. As the subjects watched the tapes, researchers took readings on their heart rates, muscle

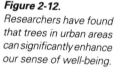

Figure 2-12.
Researchers have found that trees in urban areas can significantly enhance our sense of well-being.

tension, skin conductance, and pulses. Both psychological self-ratings and the physiological measurements showed that subjects recuperated from the stressful movie more rapidly, and more thoroughly, with exposure to natural settings.

Physiological benefits related to trees can be equally striking. One study of hospital patients recovering from surgery found that individuals had shorter post-operative stays, fewer negative evaluative comments in nurses' notes, fewer post-surgical complications, and fewer painkillers needed when they saw trees from their window, rather than a brick wall. Similarly, prisoners with cell window views of nature had fewer stress syndromes (including head-aches and digestive upsets) than those looking at buildings or other prisoners.

Wildlife And Recreation

It is a well-documented fact that humans seek forested areas for recreation. What is less well understood is that, for many of America's urban residents, the most important recreational forest (either by choice or necessity) is the forest that is around them every day.

Forest and park managers are faced with the fact that not all people want or need the same kind of experiences. A study by researcher J.F. Dwyer found that people in downtown Chicago preferred more intensively developed and managed parks as a location for visiting and other social interaction, while suburbanites wanted more natural, undeveloped areas to "get away from people."

One of the major attractions of either kind of forest is wildlife. Trees may provide colors, shapes, sounds, and other sensory pleasures, but wild animals provide the animation that particularly delights most forest visitors. From the ubiquitous gray squirrel and pigeon of the central city to the shy deer or rabbit of the greenway, people enjoy watching the wildlife that characterizes trees, forests, and their surrounding environs.

Water Quality And Hydrology

Trees intercept falling raindrops and moderate their passage to the ground. Runoff, erosion, and flooding during intensive rainfall can be significant problems in an environment largely dominated by concrete, asphalt, and rooftops, and lacking the moderating canopy of trees. Water flows concentrated by impervious surfaces hit unprotected soils or stream channels with terrific force, causing accelerated soil erosion and significant water pollution along with very high flood flows. Trees that shelter impervious areas can cut the rate at which water hits the surface, and tree roots can provide protection that slows water flows and reduces soil erosion. Gary Moll, urban forester at the American Forestry Association, estimates that a city with 30 percent tree cover has a leaf and branch surface area that adds up to four times as much intercepting surface as provided by the city's buildings and concrete. As a result, cities with maximum tree cover can experience significant reduction of peak flood flows. This translates into less construction cost and land dedicated to floodways and storm sewers, less instances of overflow and resulting damage to life and property.

It also results in less pollution flushed into rivers, lakes and estuaries—pollution which can eradicate important economic fisheries, destroy recreational opportunities, and even poison the drinking water supplies of millions of people. These problems can almost always be traced to the use and management of the land in the watershed. If that land is urbanized, the existence and condition of its trees will have a significant impact on the condition of the watershed.

Forested areas in urban regions may also become significant in waste-water treatment. Partially treated urban wastewater has been sprayed on forest lands with good effect in several cities. This not only provides a least-cost way of providing tertiary water treatment, but also has beneficial effects on forest productivity, aquifer recharge, and stream flow. In State College, Pennsylvania, for example, a number of researchers have reported that 16 years of spraying partially treated sewage on a forest watershed did not contaminate groundwater, but did return 90 percent of the water to the aquifer. Different forest ecosystems, different soils, and varying aquifer characteristics need be factored into such a program, and intensive monitoring is needed to assure that performance is meeting health standards. But this method of waste-water treatment is almost certain to appeal to more and more communities as water supplies get scarcer and conventional waste treatment facilities become more expensive to operate.

Conclusion

Trees save energy by shading, wind-shielding, and evapotranspiration. But they shouldn't merely be seen as green air conditioners. Trees also help mitigate the greenhouse effect, filter pollutants, mask noise, prevent erosion, and calm their human observers. These are all benefits that air conditioners simply cannot provide. In addition, trees and shrubs enhance our environment, provide recreation for our children, and through group planning and planting, can sponsor a feeling of community within neighborhoods.

Indeed, people all over the country have begun planting trees, not just for energy conservation, but for all these other reasons as well. In cities ranging from Atlanta to San Francisco, and Chicago to Los Angeles, people are planting trees both near their homes and in their neighborhoods. Planting for energy conservation can easily become a part—or the foundation—of such efforts.

Few cities have implemented urban forestry programs for the sake of energy conservation. Those cities which have done so, however, have had high rates of success. In Nanjing, China, for instance, after 34 million trees were planted in the late 1940s, average summer temperatures dropped 5°F. Similarly, fingers of green open space convey cool night air into downtown Stuttgart, in West Germany, and help reduce daytime temperatures.

The Trees for Tucson/Global Releaf reforestation program proposes planting 500,000 desert-adapted trees before 1996. An economic-ecological model calculated the costs and benefits associated with the program. The computer simulation accounted for planting locations, planting rates, growth rates, and mortality rates when projecting average annual benefits and costs. Costs modeled included planting, pruning, tree removal, and irrigation water. Benefits accounted for include cooling energy savings, and avoided dust and stormwater runoff costs. The simulations do not include the effects of trees on property values (generally considered to be positive), aesthetics, wildlife habitat, human stress, nor on factors that are not local.

Projected net benefits are $236.5 million for the 40-year planning horizon. The benefit-cost ratio and internal rate of return of all trees are 2.6 and 7.1, respectively. Trees planted in parks are projected to provide the highest benefit-cost ratio (2.7) and trees along residential streets the lowest (2.2). Tree removal costs are the most important management expense and energy savings for air conditioning provide the greatest benefits (attributed mostly to house or "yard" trees). Average annual cooling energy benefits per tree are projected to be 227 kWh ($16.34) for evapotranspirational cooling and 61 kWh ($4.39) for direct shade. Ninety-seven percent (464 lb.) of the total carbon conserved annually per mature tree is attributed to reduced power plant emissions.

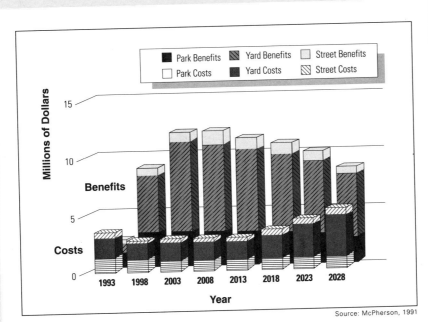

Source: McPherson, 1991

Figure 2-13.
Projected annual costs and benefits of the Trees for Tucson/Global Releaf reforestation program.

Figure 2-14.
Consider the seasonal path of the sun when planning landscaping improvements. Strategic placement of deciduous trees on the southwest and west sides of a building can help maximize the cooling effects of shade in summer and can allow sunlight to reach the building in winter.

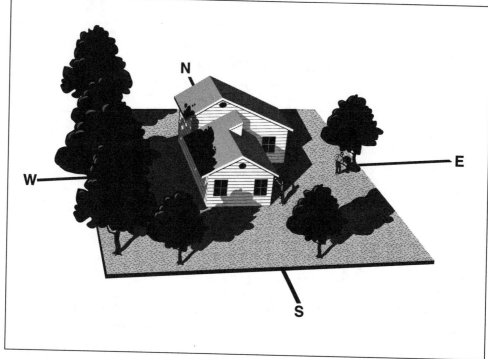

Source: Missouri Natural Resources Department (Koon, 1989)

Further Reading

There have been numerous studies on the wind-shielding and shading effects of trees by Heisler (1981, 1984, and 1986) and DeWalle (1983 and 1988). The microclimate effects of different amounts of tree cover have been measured by McGinn (1982), Taha et al. (1988), Rainer et al. (1989) and Heisler (1989).

McPherson measured the effect of different landscaping treatments on building energy use using scale models (1989). Computer studies of the energy savings from the direct effects of trees were done by Huang et al. (1989) and McPherson et al. (1988). Another study by Huang et al. (1987) modeled the indirect effects of tree evapotranspiration on temperatures and building energy use.

Two very informative books published on the subject of tree planting in urban communities are: *Shading Our Cities* (Island Press, 1989) by Moll and Ebenreck, a thorough discussion of urban forestry for both general and professional readers, with guidelines for program development; and *The Simple Act of Planting A Tree* (Jeremy P. Tarcher, Inc., 1990) by Lipkis and Lipkis, directed especially to citizens, also with detailed guidelines for community programs.

3

Hashem Akbari
Phil Martien
Arthur Rosenfeld

Using Light-Colored Surfaces to Cool Our Communities

The practice of using light-colored surfaces to keep buildings and outdoor urban areas cool is not new. In many tropical countries, particularly those with large amounts of sunshine, the traditional architecture has many examples of light-colored walls, roofs, and streets. In this country, architects and urban planners have overlooked this energy-conscious design principle relying instead, on mechanical air conditioning to maintain comfort during the summer months. Unfortunately, the dark-colored surfaces commonly used here increase air-conditioning costs for individual houses—because their walls and roofs get hot, and for all buildings in the city—because temperatures of the entire area rise. Yet computer models of urban climates have shown that the use of light-colored surfaces in cities can reduce air conditioning costs for everyone, most often without additional cost.

Computer models of urban climates have shown that the use of light-colored surfaces in cities can reduce air-conditioning costs for everyone, often without additional cost.

Figure 3-1.
Traditional light surfaces: In sunny countries, such as Greece, walls, roofs, and streets have been painted in light colors for centuries.

Greek National Tourist Agency, 1990

Studies done at Oak Ridge National Laboratory in Tennessee have found that dark-colored roofs routinely exceed 160°F, on summer days, while surfaces with flat white paint reach 135°F and those with glossy white paint seldom exceed 120°F.

Because no urban community in the United States or abroad has yet initiated a formal program of albedo modification, we have no experience with successful implementation practices, potential drawbacks, and conflicts with other urban issues. This chapter, then, is more theoretical, and less specific than those on tree planting, which benefit from a wealth of programs and written materials. We would like to stress, however, that our preliminary analysis indicates that the energy and environmental benefits of albedo modifications are high, while the costs and potential risks can be strikingly low.

What Is Albedo?

Urban landscapes consist of myriad surfaces, including building roofs and walls, streets, freeways, parking lots, paved walkways, driveways, school yards, and playgrounds. Each of these surfaces either absorbs or reflects a significant portion of the sunlight falling on it. Scientists use the term albedo to define the ability of a surface to reflect incoming solar radiation. The opposite of albedo is "absorptivity," or the ability of a surface to absorb incoming radiation.

Albedo is measured on a scale from 0 to 1. A surface with a relatively high albedo of 0.75 reflects most of the incoming solar energy, while one with a low albedo of 0.25 or 0.10 will absorb most of it.

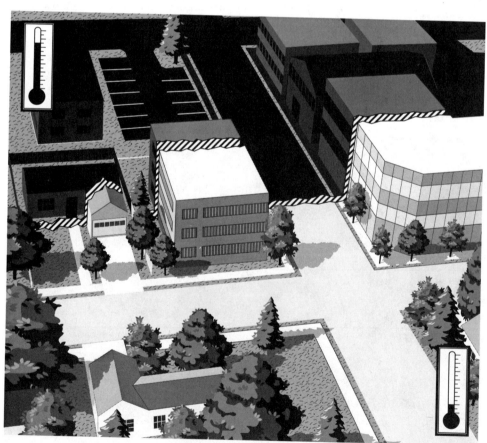

Figure 3-2.
Surface contrast: Simply changing the surface colors of our urban communities could significantly decrease their temperatures.

Source: Huang, 1991

In general, light-colored surfaces have high albedo, and dark-colored surfaces have low albedo. However, there are cases where a light-colored surface will absorb so much near-infrared radiation that it will have a low albedo. Similarly, other surfaces which appear quite dark to the eye, such as green grass, are good reflectors of infrared radiation and have albedos from 0.25 to 0.30. Texture and geometry also affect a surface's albedo. A complex, bumpy surface tends to absorb more radiation than does a flat surface made of the same material. Figure 3-3 shows the albedo for a number of typical urban surfaces.

Solar energy that is not reflected is absorbed by the surface (unless it allows the radiation to penetrate, as water or glass do). That means that albedo directly determines the effect solar radiation has on surface temperature. A light-colored surface with high albedo will absorb less sunlight and remain cooler than a dark-colored surface of lower albedo and similar thermal properties. Buildings with dark- or low-albedo surfaces will tend to have higher air-conditioning loads, because the heat from the hot walls and roofs eventually seeps inside. Studies done at Oak Ridge National Laboratory in Tennessee have found that dark-colored roofs routinely exceed 160°F on summer days, while surfaces with flat white paint reach 135°F, and surfaces with glazed white paint seldom exceed 120°F. Similarly, on a 90°F day, the surface temperature of asphalt can reach 140°F (See Figure 3-4). This can increase air temperatures by 5°F and more. Figure 3-5 shows that during the summer, light-colored surfaces are, on average, 15°F cooler than dark-colored ones.

Modifying the albedo of a building will lower the heat build-up from sunlight on the walls and roofs, and reduce the amount of electricity needed for air conditioning. Computer simulations of a typical house in Sacramento, California indicate that its

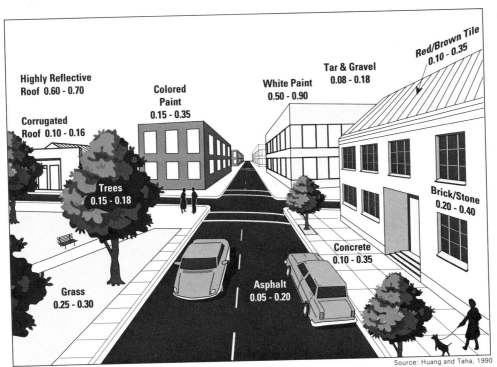

Figure 3-3.
Surface albedo values: The more solar radiation a surface absorbs, the hotter it gets. The more radiation it reflects, the cooler it stays. Today's urban communities contain surfaces with many different albedo values. Surfaces with high albedo values reflect more solar radiation and are generally cooler.

Highly Reflective Roof 0.60 - 0.70

Corrugated Roof 0.10 - 0.16

Colored Paint 0.15 - 0.35

White Paint 0.50 - 0.90

Tar & Gravel 0.08 - 0.18

Red/Brown Tile 0.10 - 0.35

Trees 0.15 - 0.18

Brick/Stone 0.20 - 0.40

Concrete 0.10 - 0.35

Grass 0.25 - 0.30

Asphalt 0.05 - 0.20

Source: Huang and Taha, 1990

Figure 3-4.
Daily surface temperature: Dark-colored roofs get much hotter throughout the day than do light-colored roofs.

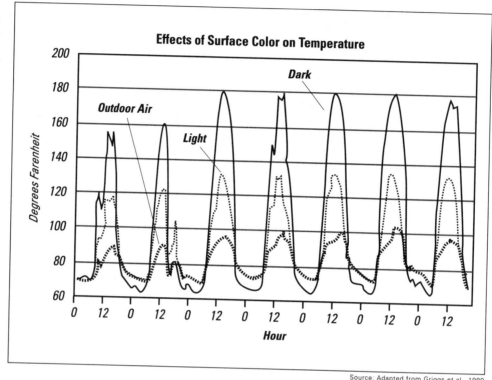

Source: Adapted from Griggs et al., 1989

total air-conditioning bill can be reduced by up to 20 percent if the albedo of the roofs and walls are increased from a typical 0.30 to a light-colored 0.90.

We call this kind of energy saving from albedo modifications "direct savings," since they relate solely to the individual house. If similar albedo modifications are implemented on a large number of urban surfaces, the collective albedo of a neighborhood or city will be changed and the air temperatures lowered as a result. This will then reduce the amount of cooling energy needed for all houses in that city or neighborhood. These are "indirect savings."

In general, changing the albedo of a building produces direct savings only for houses, single story industrial buildings, or small commercial buildings. Changing the albedo of large buildings will not produce significant direct savings because they have small surface-to-volume ratios and tend to generate a lot of internal heat. However, even large buildings will realize significant indirect savings from city-wide albedo modifications. That is, while large buildings do not gain direct savings from increasing albedo, they do gain indirect savings from the generally lowered temperatures produced by wide-scale reductions in albedo.

Will Changing Surface Colors Save Energy?

Many studies exist which show that increasing surface albedos lowers surface temperatures. To date, there is little measured data on the *direct energy savings* from changes in building albedo. Measurements of the indirect energy savings from large-scale changes in urban albedo are, for obvious reasons, even more difficult and have not been attempted. However, both the direct and indirect effects can be estimated using computer

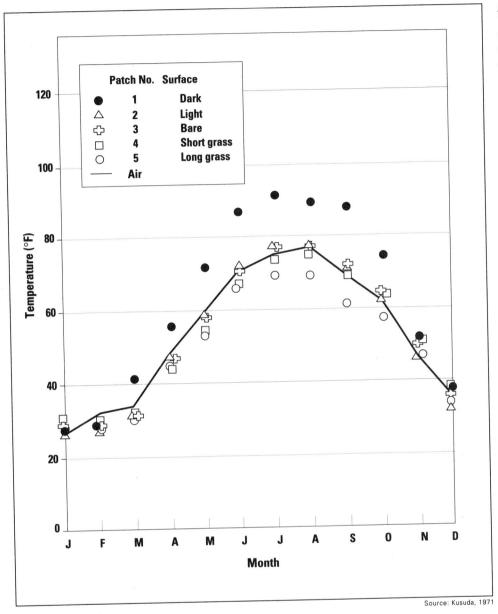

Figure 3-5.
Year-round ground sur-face temperatures: Dark-colored surfaces are also hotter throughout the year than light-colored sur-faces or even ground veg-etation.

Source: Kusuda, 1971

programs that model building energy use and urban climate conditions. These show that increasing the albedo of urban surfaces can significantly reduce both energy consumption for individual buildings and the outdoor temperatures of cities.

For example, researchers at Lawrence Berkeley Laboratory have used a detailed computer program to simulate the energy use of a typical one-story ranch house in Sacramento, California, with an average albedo of 0.25, roughly equivalent to grey walls and a dark-shingled roof. When they increased the wall albedo by 0.13 (painting the walls off-white for instance), the amount of energy needed for cooling dropped by 2.7 percent. When they increased the building's albedo by 0.60, by perhaps using a light-colored shingle roof, its cooling energy use dropped by almost 19 percent.

In a poorly insulated house, such as those built before 1970, increased albedo could reduce cooling-energy use by 5 percent for each 0.01 increment in albedo. For better insulated houses like those built today, increased albedo can reduce cooling-energy use by 3 percent for each 0.01 increment in albedo.

In other computer simulations, researchers found that the energy savings from increased albedo are much larger for poorly insulated houses, as insulation helps to block the heat from the outside surfaces. They simulated both poorly and well-insulated houses, with an initial albedo of 0.30, and then increased it by 0.40. In the poorly insulated house, cooling-energy use dropped by 11 to 22 percent. In the well-insulated house, cooling-energy use dropped by 8 to 13 percent. Although the total savings are two times larger for the poorly insulated house, they are significant even in the well-insulated house (See Figure 3-6).

Albedo also has indirect effects. These seem to be larger than the direct ones. An urban climate model has been used to simulate how changing a city's collective albedo affects air temperature. The results showed that the indirect cooling energy savings for typical houses could be 3 percent to 5 percent for each 0.01 increase in overall city albedo. In a poorly insulated house, such as those built before 1970, increased urban albedo can reduce the cooling-energy use by 5 percent for each 0.01 increment in albedo. For better-insulated houses like those built today, increased albedo can reduce cooling-energy use by 3 percent for each 0.01 increment in albedo.

Researchers have also found that the albedo of a typical U.S. city can be increased realistically by up to 0.15. Based on computer simulations, this albedo increase will reduce a city's air temperature by 5°F, which, in turn, would produce indirect energy savings of around 40 percent. When the direct and indirect savings of albedo changes are combined, the simulated total energy savings approach 50 percent during average hours and 30 percent during peak cooling periods.

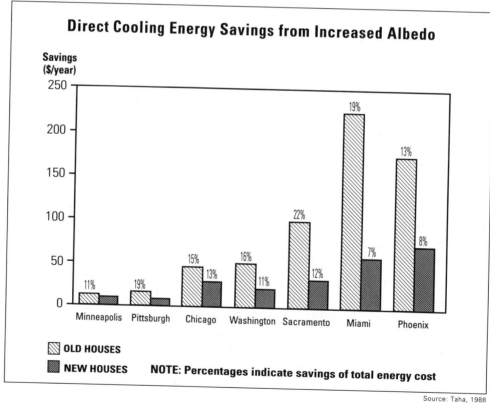

Figure 3-6.
Cooling energy savings from the direct effects of increased albedo: Computer models project significant energy savings from albedo increases in cities all across the country. Note higher dollar savings in sunbelt cities.

Source: Taha, 1988

On a national level, researchers estimate that increased albedo can save annually, in residential and commercial building, 22 billion kilowatt hours (0.25 quads), with annual monetary savings over $2 billion. This estimate assumes that only half of the surfaces in a typical city are available for albedo modifications.

How Much Will Albedo Modifications Cost?

Albedo programs can be implemented at little cost, because they can be incorporated into routine maintenance schedules and budgets. While no model programs have been implemented so far, extrapolations from individual buildings show that increasing albedo can be an extremely cost-effective strategy for reducing summer electricity usage on a city-wide scale.

As mentioned before, changing albedo in the course of routine maintenance is very cost effective, since in many cases it may cost nothing extra at all. Researchers estimate that the Cost of Conserved Energy (See Appendix B) for repainting and resurfacing is between 0 and 6 cents per kilowatt-hour. This compares quite favorably with the cost of peak power residential electricity, which is about 10 cents per kilowatt-hour.

Potential Problems With Albedo

Perhaps the greatest problem with albedo modification at this time is that no community or institution has initiated a program yet. Computer models can make worthwhile estimates of the energy and environmental benefits of albedo modification, but they cannot hypothesize about the potential problems of such programs. And, because of the paucity of materials, a number of researchers have challenged the viability of albedo modification, based on questions of soiling, glare, and citizen cooperation.

Will Light Urban Surfaces Cause Too Much Glare?

Some researchers worry that lightening the color of a city's streets and buildings will cause uncomfortable glare for city dwellers. There are no reports, however, of residents complaining about too much brightness in Mediterranean and Middle East cities, many of which have predominantly white surfaces. It may also be possible to develop materials that create less glare than those currently available.

Similarly, some researchers have questioned whether traffic markings on lightened streets would be as visible as those on dark roads. Researchers at LBL, however, believe that new marking designs (perhaps a dark median strip with traditionally white markings) can be developed to ensure public safety.

Will Light Urban Surfaces Soil Too Quickly?

On the other end of the spectrum, some question exists as to the durability of white surfaces, especially under the wear and tear of weathering and soiling. In some parts of the country, for instance, light-colored roofs may discolor from leaves, tree secretions, and air-borne dust and dirt. In that case, even a high-albedo roof would become a low-albedo roof in a matter of time, thereby mitigating both the energy and aesthetic benefits of the original conversion. Studies done at Oak Ridge National

Figure 3-7.
Residents of cities in tropical and mediterranean areas have whitewashed their buildings for centuries, sometimes repainting outside walls annually to ensure comfort. Today, we can look to that example to learn how to cool our cities and save energy, with a method that is both aesthetically pleasing and easy to implement.

Laboratory, however, have shown that even soiled, highly reflective roofs have a higher albedo than dark roofs.

Weathering from the oil drippings and tire scuff marks of vehicles could pose more serious problems for light-colored streets. Again, while no studies have been done on this potential issue, common sense observations of currently existing concrete roads show that the soiling does not significantly alter the surface color. If we move to lighter surfaced asphalt, we may want to lighten the color of auto tires as well.

Will Light Surfaces Increase Heating Bills In The Winter?

If light-colored surfaces reflect solar radiation, we may lose in the winter by paying increased heating bills, even as we gain in the summer when cooling bills drop. Except for computer simulations, no researchers have investigated, in a carefully designed experiment, whether or not changing surface colors will result in a net benefit or net cost on an annual basis. This is an issue primarily for areas subject to cold winters, however. Areas where air conditioning is used most of the year will benefit from light-colored surfaces because the cost of that space cooling will be kept down throughout the year.

Will Citizens Resist Changing Surface Colors?

One final question that arises in the course of discussions on albedo modification is "How will we convince citizens that this is an appropriate measure?" Questions of implementation—including citizen action and ordinances are discussed in Chapter 7 of this guidebook.

How Can We Implement Urban Albedo Modification Programs?

Just as some states have building energy standards that specify minimum requirements for window shading, awnings and shades, it is also possible to stipulate minimum albedo values for building surfaces such as roofs or walls, or to give energy credits or tax rebates for using materials with high albedos.

Different approaches are needed to promote high-albedo materials, depending on whether it is private or public property. For private property (such as homes or commercial property), the best approach is probably a combination of public information, energy credits, or ordinances. Specifically, we recommend that community officials, school districts, and materials manufacturers:

1. Promote greater awareness of the potential for energy conservation in the selection of building materials and surface colors.

2. Provide information to the public on the albedo (reflectivity) of different building products.

3. Increase awareness among financiers, developers, and homeowners of the lower operating costs, energy savings, and greater return on investment possible from lightening surface colors.

We also recommend that professional schools and other educational programs incorporate these principles in the training of builders, engineers, architects, city planners, and urban and landscape designers.

For public property, such as roads or sidewalks, the approach should be to convince the responsible city departments and school districts of the costs and benefits (financial and environmental) in the use of alternate materials with higher albedo.

Finally, considerably more technical research needs to be done in order to:

1. Gain a better understanding of the feedback mechanism of large-scale albedo modification.

2. Document existing urban albedos in various cities by combining data on land-use patterns with those on the albedo of various urban surfaces.

3. Study the long-term albedos of building materials under typical urban conditions to account for wear and urban grime.

4. Evaluate the trade-offs between reductions in cooling energy use and possible increases in heating energy costs with the use of light-colored surfaces.

See Chapter 7 for suggestions on developing ordinances and other legislation.

 Further Reading

As we discussed in the text, no formal albedo modification programs have been implemented to date. Therefore, there is a dearth of measured data on the energy savings from albedo changes, particularly as related to indirect effects of neighborhood-wide albedo programs.

There have been, however, a number of technical studies documenting the relationship between surface temperatures to the surface color and texture by Kusuda (1971), Givoni (1981), and Griggs (1989). Computer studies of the impact of albedo changes on building energy use were done by Taha et al. (1988). Studies of the overall albedo of the urban landscape were done by Myrup (1972) and Aida (1982), while Reagan (1979) measured the albedo of typical building materials. Practical information on building and road materials can be found in trade journals, including Concrete Construction, American City and Country, and publications of the Asphalt Institute, in Maryland. In addition, much of the information on material availability and viability can be obtained by directly contacting manufacturers in this country and abroad.

4

Jane Arey
Roger Atkinson
Karina Garbesi
Bruce Nordman

Implementation Issues: Water Use, Landfills, and Smog

Widespread tree planting has a number of beneficial effects, including shading, conserving energy, reducing pollutants in the atmosphere, enhancing visual appeal, and sequestering carbon dioxide. Such a program can also raise questions—and potential problems—for the communities involved.

With proper landscape design, residents can save both water and energy.

Several questions that may arise in the early planning stages of heat-island reduction include whether tree planting programs conflict with water conservation programs, whether trees pollute, and whether they create municipal solid-waste problems. Much research remains to be done on these issues. The following discussions, however, will give policymakers some guidelines for their own analyses.

Will Urban Tree Planting Waste Valuable Water?

As discussed in previous chapters, trees can help reduce energy used for cooling in buildings, both by shading and evapotranspiration. In recent years, increased public awareness of these benefits, coupled with concerns about the environment, have led to numerous proposals to plant trees. The American Forestry Association, for example, has proposed planting 100 million trees in U.S. cities in its Global ReLeaf Campaign. Similarly, in October of 1988, the Mayor of Los Angeles announced a proposal to plant two to five million trees in the city.

Trees, however, need water to survive, and ground water can be a scarce resource in arid communities such as in the West or Southwest.[1] Planners and residents in these communities may be concerned that tree programs will increase water use, and that the costs and burdens of this increase will override energy benefit. Similarly, it may appear that tree planting programs tailored to arid climates will reduce water usage—which is good—but simultaneously will reduce cooling from evapotranspiration and thereby reduce its beneficial effect.

---

[1] While no clear distinction has been made in this chapter between groundwater and city water generally speaking, however, it concerns only groundwater.

Tree planting need not always result in increased water use. Appropriate landscaping strategies can actually reduce water use, even as the amounts of shade or vegetation cover

Is there a trade-off between energy savings and water use in arid urban areas? Urban environments are too complex to expect precise calculation of landscape water usage and its effects on urban climates. It is possible, however, to estimate the relative water usages of different landscape scenarios. It is also possible to identify planting strategies that maximize cooling energy benefits while minimizing water consumption. Research shows that residents can save water and energy with proper landscape design.

Landscaping In Arid Climates

Early settlers in the American Southwest tried to mold their new environment in the image of the lush green landscapes of Europe and the Eastern seaboard. Planted in the dry and desert regions of the West, however, these imported landscapes of deciduous trees and green lawns created a large demand for water. With population increasing and the specter of water shortage looming ever closer, a new trend is emerging. This trend emphasizes replacing imported "artificial" landscapes with native ones that use less water and are more in keeping with local climates and water availability.

Many cities now have ordinances that encourage water-conserving landscapes. Some water districts even offer cash incentives to homeowners who replace high-water-use landscapes with low-water-use ones, or with gravel. In Arizona, local governments use landscape ordinances to comply with a state law to eliminate groundwater overdraft. The city of Mesa offers a $231 rebate if 50 percent of the total landscaped area is covered with inorganic mulch, such as decomposed granite. Similarly, California's Urban Water Management Act of 1983 pressures water retailers to conserve water. The Act emphasizes landscape water conservation, because landscapes consume 30 to 50 percent of residential water. In fact, the state is counting on landscape water conservation to help meet future water demands in the state.

Many landscape water conservation programs are already under way. Of 166 water retailers responding to a questionnaire by the California Department of Water Resources in 1986, at a local level, 39 percent had existing landscape-water conservation programs and 23 percent had proposed programs. The North Marin Water District, for example, in northern California, offers $50 for each 100 square feet of lawn removed and replaced with water-conserving plant materials.

The existence of such policies suggests a strong institutional resistance to tree planting programs that threaten to increase landscape water use. It is important to point out, however, that tree planting need not always increase water usage. Indeed, appropriate landscaping can actually reduce water use, even as the amounts of shade, or in some cases, total vegetation cover, increases.

Estimating Urban Water Needs

A number of factors must be considered when estimating the effect that tree planting programs will have on urban water use. First, which elements of the landscape will be displaced by the trees? If trees are planted in parking lots, for instance, their influence will be much different than if they replace lawn areas. Second, will the trees replace or supplement existing vegetation. That is, the water use of an area in which trees replace lawn will be different than that in which trees are added to lawn.

In a recent study by researchers at Lawrence Berkeley Laboratory, urban vegetation was divided into three broad classes: turf (or lawn); trees and palms; shrubs and groundcovers (referred to simply as "turf," "trees," and "shrubs"). Based on available data on the water use of other plants, each class received a "typical water use" rating. Changes in urban landscape water use were estimated by simulating changes in the amount of area covered by each vegetation class. The calculations, assumptions, and methodology of the simulation are discussed in detail in Appendix C.

Researchers have found that turf generally uses more water than trees, and trees use more water than shrubs or groundcovers.

Trees, Shrubs, And Grass: Which Uses More Water?

LBL researchers found, and landscapers agree, that, in general, lawns use more water than trees, and trees more water than shrubs and groundcovers (See Figure 4-1).[1]

The lower water usage of trees means that if trees replace grass, landscape water requirements typically will decrease. If shrubs and groundcovers replace trees, still more water savings can occur (See Figure 4-2). In this case, however, energy savings will decrease, because these vegetations provide less shading for cooling.

Water Usages For Different Landscape Scenarios

The ways in which changes in landscapes affect water use were estimated beginning with a base case scenario, in which grass occupied 13 percent of the total urban area, trees took up 10 percent, and shrubs took up 4 percent. (This made a total vegetated area of 27 percent, as was the case in Los Angeles in 1986.) Scenarios were developed by modifying the landscape three ways. First, the total vegetated area remained constant, but lawn area was replaced with varying amounts of trees and shrubs. Second, the total vegetated area was increased, while varying the areas of lawn, trees, and shrubs. Finally, lawn area was reduced by replacing it with drought-adapted trees and shrubs, thereby simulating low-water-use practices, also called "Xeriscape." The following examples illustrate these scenarios.

Replace lawn area with typical trees and shrubs. In this scenario, the total vegetated area remains the same. But the area covered by trees is doubled (to 20 percent of the total urban area), the area covered by shrubs stays the same, and the lawn area is reduced from 13 to 3 percent. In this case, water use actually decreased by 18 percent. That means that in the hypothetical city of the study, water use could decrease by 18 percent, while doubling tree cover to replace existing lawn area.

Increase total vegetated area, while varying the relative cover of lawn, trees, and shrubs. In this scenario, the total vegetation cover increases from 27 to 33 percent by doubling the tree and shrub cover, and reducing the lawn area from 13 to 5 percent.

Watering trees at the same level as grasses can harm them in some cases. A joint report by the Municipal Water District of Orange County and the Department of Landscape Architecture at Cal Poly University revealed that the average lifespans of 44 tree species in Southern California were shortened by 58 percent when planted in lawns. For one drought-adapted species of Eucalyptus (red iron bark), the estimated tree lifespan in a lawn was reduced by 90 percent.

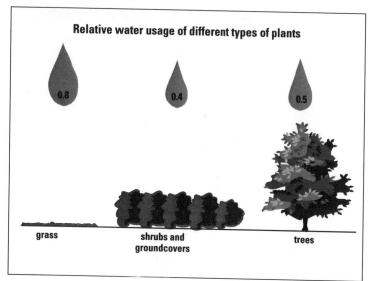

Figure 4-1.

Estimated typical water usage of varying plant types in relative amounts: The amount of water needed by plants varies with location and climate. Generally, lawns use more water than trees, and trees use more water than both shrubs and groundcovers.

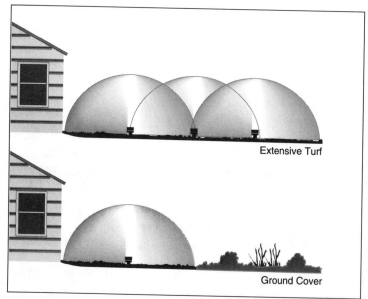

Figure 4-2.

Source: McPherson and Sacamano, 1989

Water consumption and turf: Extensive turf area consumes more water than turf area combined with groundcover.

This would be the case, for example, in a planting program in which shade trees are planted near houses, and some lawn areas are replaced with trees and shrubs. In this case, landscape water use stayed the same. When typical trees and shrubs are used to expand the amount of total vegetation, landscape water use increased.

Xeriscape (minimize lawn area and use low-water-use trees and shrubs). In this scenario, low-water-use trees, shrubs, and groundcovers replace the total vegetated area, which is expanded from 27 to 47 percent, by tripling tree cover, more than doubling shrub cover, and reducing lawn area from 13 to 7 percent. Even with this increase, water use was held constant. But when total vegetation area increased to 33 percent of the total urban area (by doubling tree and shrub areas, and reducing lawn area to 5 percent), water use was reduced by 30 percent.

In identical distributions, low-water-use plants save 20 to 43 percent of the water used by typical plants. This is in keeping with the results of landscaping studies on Xeriscape design (low-water-use landscaping) which show savings of as high as 50 to 60 percent over traditional designs.

Multi-layered canopy (lawn shaded by shrubs and trees). The most interesting case of a multi-layered canopy is that of lawn shaded by trees. In such a case, we cannot simply combine the contributions of tree and lawn, as if they were on different plots of land, because the shading of the lawn will modify its water requirements. We found that on a hot, sunny day, tree shade can reduce lawn water requirements by as much as 95 percent. In other words, even the combined water use of tree and lawn can be lower than that of an unshaded lawn.

Importantly, the numerical results of both the study's vegetation distribution model and its calculation of the water needs for a multi-layered landscape are rough estimates, based on the assumed starting conditions of the models. In order to obtain numerically meaningful estimates for a given location, appropriate initial conditions must be used. For example, if an area starts with a lot of turf and high-water-use trees, tree planting programs which replace lawn area and other high-water-use species with low-water-use species are likely to reduce landscape water use significantly. Areas which already have low-water-use species will not show large water savings.

Even the combined water use of tree and lawn can be lower than that of an unshaded lawn.

Trees, Energy, And Water: Implications For Urban Temperatures

Any trees planted near occupied structures of modest height should mitigate cooling energy needs in hot communities by shading. But it is the *total* landscaping strategy which will determine if evapotranspiration increases or decreases, and, therefore, if the net evapotranspiration will lessen or increase the existing savings from shading. That is, if water use by vegetation is increased, cooling is enhanced. If water use decreases, the energy savings from evapotranspiration will also decrease.

The extent to which changes in evapotranspiration affect changes in near-ground air temperature (and hence cooling-energy needs) depends on a number of factors, including the density and geometry of the urban canopy (including buildings), wind conditions, and temperature. The data are not yet available to back up such detailed modeling of the urban climate system. It is impossible, therefore, to exactly calculate the energy/water trade-offs. However, field experiments by E. Gregory McPherson and his colleagues at the University of Arizona demonstrate that both water and energy can be saved by planting low-water-use trees and shrubs around residences. This indicates that the losses from reduced evapotranspiration do not seriously threaten the benefits of trees and shrubs in dry cities.

Planning Ahead

It is clear from the analysis above that trees can be added to most urban landscapes without increasing water use—if trees, or some combination of trees, shrubs, and groundcover, replace lawn area. If total vegetated area remains constant, landscape water requirements can decrease rapidly as trees replace lawns. As a result, tree planting programs to conserve cooling energy are not only consistent with current landscape water conservation programs, but ought to be an integral part of planning. That is, we can save water, while we save energy, with proper landscape design.

On a hot, sunny day, tree shade can reduce lawn water requirements by as much as 95 percent if the lawn is entirely shaded.

Plant A Diversity Of Species

One word of caution: If we find—as is likely—that we need to choose low-water-use species for our tree planting programs in arid cities, we should not repeat the historical mistakes of agriculture and forestry. Too often, planners in these sectors sought out and planted the single most effective species available. Unfortunately, monocropping has proven highly susceptible to pest outbreaks—which could destroy the positive economics of the planting program. Instead, we should maximize the many other positive environmental benefits by planting a diversity of species.

Optimize Benefits

In addition, any planting program should optimize benefits for wildlife, as well as for people. Planting native species in arid areas not only assures the selection of drought-adapted and low-water-use species, but provides food and shelter for local wildlife. This approach can be aesthetically pleasing, as well as environmentally and socially sound. Perhaps the best example of this approach is the extensive use of native desert species in Santa Fe, New Mexico. This beautiful city appears to be a gentle extension of the surrounding natural environment. It provides a sense of place for the residents, and thereby engenders an appreciation of the native landscape.

Maintain A Regional Context

When assessing the benefits and costs of tree planting programs, it is important to maintain a regional context. The initial distribution of vegetation in the region must be accounted for, as well as the local cost and availability of both energy and water. In some areas, like California, potential water savings in agriculture might dwarf savings obtainable from urban landscaping. In such cases, water conserving practices in agriculture might free up considerable amounts of water for urban landscapes and wild areas.

Tips on Low-Water-Use Landscaping

Issues of water re-allocation are beyond the scope of the guidebook. But they need to be considered in the long run. Here are two categories of recommendations for low-water-use landscaping:

Immediate Actions

1) Plant low-water-use trees first next to one- and two- story buildings (trees could also be used to shade larger structures by including planting terraces on buildings with a pyramidal structure).

2) Replace lawn with trees where possible.

3) Plant low-water-use shrubs and groundcovers where vegetation is desired.

4) Use native plants where possible to provide food and habitat for native wildlife.

5) Include natural shading in building energy codes.

Future Actions

1) Create greenways connecting parks using native vegetation, thereby providing migration corridors for wildlife and hiking opportunities for residents.

2) Consider sectoral reapportionment of water from agriculture to urban areas.

Will Urban Trees Burden Landfills?

In 1988, EPA estimated that yard debris constitutes 20 percent of the country's municipal solid waste—about 30 million tons. In recognition of this fact, tree planners must consider the solid waste implications of planting programs.

Whether or not increasing the number of trees will increase the amount of debris to be placed in landfills depends, in part, on climate, species, and the street and lot layout. Resident behavior and the existing solid waste and storm drain systems, however, also have significant effects on the amount of debris produced and how it is handled.

Fallen leaves are the primary waste of trees. The fate of those leaves depends on where they land. If leaves fall in a yard or public lot, they can be left on the ground to decompose, or they can be gathered and composted on-site, in which case they become a useful soil amendment. If the leaves fall on the street, they may be gathered by streetsweepers or washed down the storm drain system.

In many communities, leaves also are collected as yard debris. Composting these leaves produces a useful product, but requires funds for both collection and processing. If they end up in a landfill, they contribute to an already burdened system, but they probably do not create harmful leachates.

Other tree wastes include fallen or pruned branches, and dead or diseased trees. Most residents probably will not compost branches, or leave them on the ground. More likely, they will be landfilled, burned, or collected as yard debris. Similarly, removed trees probably will end up in the fireplace, a landfill, or the municipal compost, if there is one.

A city-wide tree planting program also may have less direct, but equally important effects on a city's solid waste system. Increased shade, for instance, may alter plant growth beneath the trees, and create more or less vegetative debris. This is a particularly important consideration with urban planting programs, because so many trees will have turf beneath and around them.

Similarly, objects typically exposed to sunlight, including lawn furniture, awnings, gutters, paint, and shingles, may last longer in the shade, and be thrown out less often. Finally, some critics worry that street trees will break sidewalks and sewer pipes, and thereby create more material for landfill. Choosing appropriate species, and planting carefully, however, should mitigate that problem.

Choosing the appropriate tree species for streets, and planting them carefully, can prevent breaks in sidewalks and sewer pipes, and avoid creating more material for landfill.

Trends In Solid Waste

A number of states have banned the deposit of yard debris in landfills. The alternative is to chip or shred yard debris to facilitate both composting and the use of wood chips for boiler fuel.

Similarly, by the time young trees that are planted now have significant foliage and branches, or by the time they become diseased or die, solid waste systems across the country probably will have changed. Exactly how the systems will change—and how that will affect content—is only speculative at this point. Hopefully, more residents will be composting on-site, more cities will have yard debris collection programs, and more areas will ban the landfilling of that debris. If this happens, more yard debris will become compost or broiler fuel, and the percentage ending up in already overburdened landfills will lessen considerably.

In other words, urban tree planting may very well increase solid waste costs in cities, but it won't necessarily increase solid waste amounts in our landfills.

Will Urban Trees Worsen Urban Smog?

In the last few years, media attention has focused sporadically on the idea that trees pollute. This is not a mistaken notion. Studies of individual plants and air quality measurements show that some kinds of vegetation do emit organic compounds into the atmosphere. Other studies have shown that biogenic emissions undergo the same general reactions in the atmosphere as do organic compounds emitted from human activities (including motor vehicles, solvents, fuel storage and use, landfills and hazardous waste facilities and refineries).

Like anthropogenic, or human-caused emissions, then, these biogenic emissions can contribute to low-level ozone, better known as photochemical smog.

Compounds Emitted From Vegetation

The chemical compounds emitted by vegetation contain carbon, hydrogen, and, in some cases, oxygen, and can be classified as follows:

Isoprene

Isoprene (C_5H_8) is emitted from such deciduous trees as oak, aspen, sycamore, and willow, primarily during daylight. Emission rates increase as both light intensity and temperatures increase. Indeed, one recently published study indicates that the isoprene emitted from aspen at high temperatures (returned to the atmosphere) may represent up to 8 percent of the carbon dioxide sequestered from the atmosphere by the tree's photosynthesis process.

Monoterpenes

These organic compounds ($C_{10}H_{16}$) are emitted from coniferous trees and a wide variety of other vegetation, including a large number of agricultural crops. Over 14 individual monoterpenes have been identified as vegetative emissions. Like isoprene, monoterpene emission rates increase with temperature. The two compounds emitted from a Monterrey pine tree, for instance, increase by a factor of 10 when temperatures rise from 24°F to 79°F. Not affected by light intensity, monoterpenes are emitted 24 hours a day.

Other Biogenic Organic Emissions

In addition to isoprene and the monoterpenes, many other organic compounds have been identified as vegetation emissions. These include aldehydes and alcohols containing 1 to 6 carbon atoms; alkanes and alkenes; compounds related to monoterpenes, including ether, alcohol and carbonyl derivatives of the monoterpenes; and sesquiterpenes. The atmospheric chemistry of these diverse compounds is not well understood at the present time.

Biogenic Emissions In Air Quality Degradation

Scientists now know that ozone and other photochemical oxidants are produced when oxides of nitrogen interact with reactive, non-methane, organic compounds under the influence of sunlight. Organic compounds emitted from both anthropogenic and biogenic sources are involved in these photochemical reactions.

Studies suggest, in fact, that the atmospheric lifetimes of biogenic emissions are at least one order of magnitude shorter than those of anthropogenic emissions, and that biogenic emissions may be three to five times more reactive than anthropogenic organics in the formation of ozone. The high reactivities counterbalance the low concentrations, making biogenic emissions important contributors to the formation of ozone and other oxidants in urban and rural areas.

Furthermore, research in Atlanta, GA, has shown that including biogenic emissions in computer models of urban air pollution can have major implications for control strategies designed to reduce ozone. Indeed, this same study concluded that controlling nitrogen oxides may be the most favorable, or perhaps only possible, strategy for achieving low ozone levels, since reducing the present vegetation is clearly undesirable for many reasons.

Clearly, the possibility that increased tree plantings could result in increased emissions of highly reactive biogenic organic compounds must be taken into account. Of great importance is the finding that the emission rates of biogenic compounds vary widely from species to species. There is a clear potential to minimize adverse effects of urban trees by screening candidate tree species for their emissions and choosing, if possible, only those exhibiting low emissions of organic compounds for planting.

Current Uncertainties

Unfortunately, at this time, the biogenic organic compounds emitted from ornamental trees, and their emission rates, are very poorly known. Indeed, to date, the emission rate data for biogenic compounds from all types of vegetation are sparse, and have generally only been obtained from a very limited number of observations.

A long-term experimental program to determine the organic compounds emitted from the candidate tree species, and their emission rates, over at least one, and preferably several, growing seasons, should be conducted in each community. This can be done either through a local university, or, if possible, through a local air quality control board.

Conclusion

Each issue raised in this chapter needs to be researched further, on both a theoretical and a practical level. Preliminary analysis indicates, however, that the most obvious problems—water use, waste, and air pollution—can be easily mitigated.

Indeed, as we examine temperature reduction strategies for our urban areas with increasing scrutiny, it becomes increasingly clear that one of their primary attractions is their simplicity.

 ## Further Reading

There are a number of excellent studies of urban vegetation cover, including the studies by Brown and Winer (1986) of vegetation in Los Angeles, Miller and Winer (1984) on the same subject, and Rowntree (1984) on eastern cities.

For information on landscape water use, California's Office of Conservation (1986) has published a number of reports on urban water management and the state's water future in general. The works by Swearengin (1987) and Nelson (1987) on Xeriscape, and Meyer and Strohman (1989) on irrigation also are helpful.

For explications of the interactions between plants and climates, see both Oke (1978) and Jones (1983). The case studies by McPherson et al. (1989) are perhaps the only quantitative analyses available on the trade-off between energy and water conservation and are excellent. See also: *Southwestern Landscaping That Saves Energy and Water* (The University of Arizona, Extension Publication 8929, 1989) by McPherson and Sacamano.

Information on native species and other low-water-use species are available from a number of sources. Books on native plants are usually locally available, as well as others on drought-tolerant and low-water-use non-native, but tolerant, species. Excellent examples include Perry (no date available), Coate (1986), and Duffield and Jones (1981).

There is also software available to help landscapers choose aesthetically appropriate native and low-water-use species. For example, Acacia Software of Santa Barbara has produced a plant database with regional modules for California and the southwestern United States. The landscaper can specify any number of plant criteria, including water and sun requirements, plant or tree height, canopy shape, blossom color, maintenance needs, and climate of origin to obtain a list of plants which are site-appropriate. The program even has a category of plants that are good substitutes for lawn. See the references section of this book for further sources on choosing plants and trees.

5

E. Gregory McPherson
Judith D. Ratliffe
Neil Sampson

Lessons Learned from Successful Tree Programs

Today, planting trees to modify the urban environment has become a popular civic cause. Spurred by the American Forestry Association's (AFA) Global ReLeaf program, which exhorts citizens to "Plant a tree, cool the globe," and motivated by local concerns such as potential urban deforestation, citizens across the country are putting trees in the ground at rates some municipalities have not seen in years.

With all this activity, it is important to evaluate the best planting programs for ideas to improve existing programs and create successful new ones. This chapter presents "tales from the trenches" as told by the planters themselves. They are the ones with the real experience and the ones who provide the best information and support. This chapter summarizes a survey of 13 programs in communities of all sizes and from all parts of the country. This survey focused on street programs—because trees planted in the public right-of-way are truly community trees—and programs deemed successful by the AFA and by other urban forestry experts. In addition, see Appendix F for ideas on types of trees and planting locations.

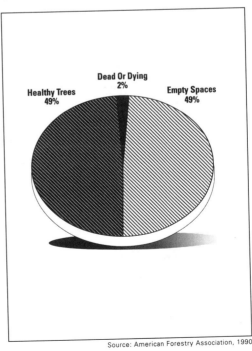

Source: American Forestry Association, 1990

Figure 5-1.
Summary report: Today's urban forests contain just as many empty tree spaces as healthy trees (AFA National Street Tree Survey).

The survey also emphasizes programs that have been in existence for some time. Longevity is a prime indicator of a program's success in gaining sufficient funding and in sustaining—even heightening—community support and involvement. In all but two cases, the programs we found have been in existence for at least five years. Many have been functioning for much longer.

To obtain the necessary information, an extensive questionnaire was sent to contact people at each program. Those questionnaires formed the basis of telephone interviews conducted in October, 1989. The questions were open-ended in nature and aimed at drawing out the kind of in-depth experiential information that short answer surveys seldom yield.

Readers will find that these 13 programs vary considerably in philosophy, structure, operating procedures, use of volunteers, and other important aspects. One primary difference is that some are city government programs and others are private. Such a mix provides a variety of perspectives on tree planting. The mix also offers insights as to how public and private programs can work and learn together. In the end, the shared goals, challenges, and approaches are more important than the differences between the programs. In addition, some of these other programs in the United States have been highlighted in boxes to further illustrate particular successes or innovations in program development and activities.

Surveying The Condition Of The City

The latest survey of city trees and their condition was completed in 1989 through the National Urban Forest Council, with support from the U.S. Forest Service, the American Forestry Association, Michigan State University, and a host of state and city agencies and volunteers. In the first phase, 413 cities were surveyed with a statistically selected sample set that ranged from five plots in small communities to 30 in the larger cities.

The data provide information on the amount, size, and condition of the street trees growing on the "tree lawn" that commonly exists between curb and sidewalk. Those street trees account for about 10 percent of the total tree population in most cities. The survey data, expanded to national estimates, suggests that there are about 60 million street trees in the United States today, with an estimated value of some $30 billion (Kielbaso and Cotrone, 1990).

Of concern, however, is the fact that the data indicate that over half of the available street tree spaces are empty. Tree planting needs, for street trees alone, are estimated in the range of 60 to 75 million trees. Developing effective and viable

Large-scale urban tree planting campaigns can be started immediately, but the practical implications of planning, planting, and care go far beyond the stroke of policymakers' pens. Simply put, legislation—and even funding—for tree planting programs will not necessarily result in thriving urban forests.

— Andy and Katie Lipkis, TreePeople (Los Angeles)

street tree programs could help fill in these gaps. Unfortunately, we don't seem to be gaining on this challenge in most cities, where fewer trees are often planted than die or get removed. In the very large cities, this ratio is even worse—as many as four trees die or are removed for each new one planted in some cities (Moll, 1987).

About Organizational Structure
Paid Staff

Almost every privately funded street-tree planting organization we examined had a core of paid professional staff. The justification for this is simple. Most volunteers have other obligations and once a program becomes successful, they can not keep up with the work. Even the most energetic and clearly focused volunteers lose steam when they are asked to run an organization for too many months or years. A paid staff, on the other hand, can develop the high levels of professionalism needed to avoid squandering a program's potential.

When should the first paid staff-person be hired? Hire as soon as possible. This establishes the organization as serious and professional from the start, which is important if you need to usher permits, waivers, and other paperwork through multi-layered bureaucracies. A paid staff—however small—also conserves the energy of important board members, who often run the group themselves in the beginning.

Staff size can range from one person to a fleet of knowledgeable professionals. Trees Atlanta, for instance, a private program operating since 1984, has a paid executive director, Marcia Bansley, who acts as a general contractor on each planting project, and a paid part-time volunteer coordinator. Working with volunteer professional landscape architects and landscape contractors, Bansley investigates the planting feasibility of selected sites, obtains necessary cooperation from property owners, and arranges for the city to issue necessary permits, mark utility lines, and make sidewalk cuts. With the advice of volunteer horticulturists, she also purchases the trees from an approved species list, puts the project out to bid, and supervises the actual planting. On the other end of the spectrum, TreePeople, a private program in Los Angeles, currently boasts a staff of 23 full-time and 10 part-time employees. In 1986, the organization had only 10 full-time staff members.

When it comes time to expand staffing, the key is to have a complete and detailed idea about what extra staff will allow the program to do. Then the issue is raising the money to hire them. Because every program will have its own priorities and organizational structure, growth direction for programs will differ. Many programs do quite well for some time with a single paid staff person, usually an executive director. However, as a program becomes more successful, a single executive director may become overwhelmed. Because staffing involves money, top-notch business expertise on the board is vital in weighing the pros and cons of expanded staffing, and in arriving at a sound business decision.

Sometimes expansion of staff in a particular direction is linked with seizing a special opportunity. For example, a number of the private programs contacted are going to add an educational component, or intensify an existing one, by making use of the educational package developed by Global ReLeaf. In Houston, this chance dovetailed nicely with

Hire paid staff as soon as possible to relieve the burden on volunteers and board members and to handle the range of activities associated with a successful, professional organization.

Board and professional staff members work most effectively when their areas are clearly defined.

the desire of several board members to plant trees along the perimeters of school campuses. This involved obtaining a grant to bring a complete program together, and hiring someone to administer it. Dona Chambers, the program's executive director, knew that educational programs can be great for public relations, but she also knew she had less and less time to devote to that task. A second hire will be someone who can pull together the educational program, work on public relations, and "earn their own keep," Chambers said, by raising money to fund the new program.

Advisors And Boards Of Directors

A board of directors comprised of high-profile leaders is also invaluable to a private planting organization, for it gives the program credibility. Ideally, board members work, too. But sympathetic community leaders with little time to volunteer may be used effectively as advisory committee members. They put star power on the letterhead, but have no time-consuming duties. They also have valuable contacts and more access to those contacts than a fledgling grassroots group. After such a committee is formed, a working board is also formed.

The boards of directors of successful groups tend to be, in the words of Peter Gradjansky, planting program manager for San Francisco's Friends of the Urban Forest, "supportive and not overly directive." That is, board and professional staff members work most effectively when their areas of endeavor are clearly defined. For instance, when board members do foundational work—such as setting policy, making financial decisions, fundraising, and selecting sites—and staff builds upon it, organizations run smoothly. But when directors get over-involved in day-to-day operations, say, by calling staff members directly to give specific orders on pet projects, trouble arises quickly. It is far more effective to use a paid executive director, who does not sit on the board but attends board meetings and communicates between the two groups.

Committees are most effective when board members are asked to serve on sub-committees performing specific tasks. Houston's Trees for Houston program, for instance, a private program incorporated in 1982, has a 30-member board of directors which is organized into standing committees responsible for membership, ordinances, maintenance, long-range planning, fundraising, and other activities. A separate advisory board lends its members' names to official publications.

Volunteers

Volunteers are all important. Every private program and most of the governmental programs we surveyed work with volunteers to some extent or another. The difference, however, is that private organizations tend to *depend* on volunteers, whereas governmental programs work with volunteers mostly on special projects aimed at educating the public about urban forestry.

Within private organizations, volunteers work at a wide variety of jobs, including planting, fundraising, office work, and vehicle maintenance. Probably no organization we contacted had a happier relationship with volunteers than TreePeople in Los Angeles, where hundreds of volunteers do everything from running the office, to digging holes, to organizing plantings.

Again, volunteers cannot replace paid staff. Cor Trowbridge, director of the TreePeople's Citizen Forester program, says, "As an organization grows, it becomes more important that certain things be taken care of. Answering the phone has become one of the most important jobs here. It just can't be volunteer anymore."

A Few Words to the Wise

To avoid turf battles, proceed with initiatives diplomatically. Don't harangue other departments about what they're doing wrong. Begin small. Arrange to make species recommendations for an upcoming planting project. Be ready to back up suggestions with examples of how proper species selection will save the city money through lowered maintenance and replacement costs. After a few successes, make it obvious that both entities will benefit from the relationship. Then move on to larger issues, such as the development of an approved species list.

Such informal links are truly a challenge in Chicago, with its maze of interconnected but legally separate taxing bodies (including the city, the parks district, the water reclamation district, the board of education, and others), each of which has jurisdiction over planting on lands it administers. When Edith Makra was directing Chicago's NeighborWoods program, she labored to pull together the splintered responsibility for tree services in her city. Whenever she planned a planting within a jurisdiction, she was careful to include Chicago's Bureau of Forestry (legally mandated to plant and care for only parkway trees) in the process. The bureau had all the city's urban forestry expertise, but other city entities had no tradition of taking advantage of it and they too often planted poor species in bad locations, thus squandering their portion of limited municipal planting funds. In effect, Makra introduced the different players to one another. Makra's networking activities convinced Mayor Richard Daley to encourage her to run the new GreenStreets program, where she is charged with fostering inter-agency cooperation.

GreenStreets works to make tree planting, preservation, and maintenance a high priority within each jurisdiction, by increasing the Bureau of Forestry's budget, by securing federal and state grants to plant and preserve trees, by working with the state legislature to pass legislation favorable to urban forestry, and by motivating business to have a stake in reforesting the downtown. In addition, Makra oversees the development of a city forest master plan.

Private programs also need to learn to coordinate with public agencies and departments. For instance, in San Francisco, Friends of the Urban Forest orchestrates the city permitting process, makes arrangements for site inspection and sidewalk cuts with the city, and contracts to have holes augured the day before planting. In addition, each property owner who receives a tree must sign an agreement with the city to care for the tree and accept liabilities connected with it.

— Andy and Katie Lipkis, TreePeople

Nothing can replace the dedication of volunteers, especially in the early stages of tree program development. Frequent public recognition of achievements, along with entertaining and educational activities, and contact through the mail all help to maintain a high level of enthusiasm.

Others agree. Nothing can replace the dedication of early volunteers who do everything necessary for a fledgling organization. Once a program is up and running, though, volunteers are best used on special projects, especially plantings. When these events are approached as celebrations, they can be fun, rewarding, and productive. San Francisco's Friends of the Urban Forest, for example, provides planters with coffee and doughnuts in the morning, and a potluck meal at the end of the day.

To keep volunteer enthusiasm high, our contacts suggest frequent public recognition of individual and group achievements, regular scheduling of both fun and educational activities, and maintaining contact through newsletters and other mailings. To mobilize for important special events, use an organized method of contact—a computerized mailing list perhaps, or an established telephone tree.

Trowbridge notes that professional volunteers, including architects, landscape architects, urban planners, and lawyers, are contributing to TreePeople's success in increasingly sophisticated ways. He also emphasizes, however, that these busy people have limited time. Their skills are best suited to special projects with focused goals and limited duration.

Links To Other Government Programs
Public Programs

Formal links to other departments involved in tree work are invaluable to government urban forest programs. Too often, urban forestry departments are isolated from parks and recreation, public works, or planning departments. The resulting communication problems can wreak havoc on the urban forestry department. Horror stories abound about trees that are poorly selected or poorly placed because other departments did not confer with the urban forestry experts.

Urban foresters are ultimately charged with maintaining their cities' public trees. Almost all the foresters we surveyed said they wanted to be more involved in overall planning and planting processes. Paul Dykema, former urban forester for the City Forestry Section in Albuquerque, New Mexico, said that it is important for foresters to get their "fingers into as many pots as possible."

A formally integrated forestry system, however, is not in the foreseeable future of most cities. Lacking that, our contacts said, informal communications can be most effective. For instance, in Albuquerque, where the city's tree planting began in the 1950s, tree planting is carried out by the park construction divisions, the public works department, and private property owners, as mandated by the city's street tree ordinance. All of these activities are guided by the design and development division of the parks and recreation department. The urban forester is charged with maintaining trees planted by the city. In most cases, street trees planted by citizens are maintained by the citizens themselves.

One tip: Don't expect volunteers to dig holes. Contract out this backbreaking labor. It's fine if the holes have to be filled in overnight for liability reasons. The next morning volunteers will just be removing loosened dirt.

Ongoing Care

Planning, training, selecting species, and mobilizing labor and resources to provide ongoing care and management requires considerable forethought and commitment. Proposed programs must go beyond paying for planting trees. They also must address the education and training required to prepare a community for planting, and the resulting forests' long-term care, management, and survival needs.

The right kind of tree planting program has several key components:

Educate the public to stimulate independent action on private property and community action on public property. Reaching, informing, and involving the public is best achieved by working closely with the news media.

Involve local communities in investigating and defining local needs, problems, and opportunities. Solicit ideas on how trees could help.

Train the community in the technical aspects of species selection, planting and maintenance and in the social skills of networking and fundraising.

Plant the first few trees. Is the community ready for the challenge ahead? How can you lay further groundwork?

Commitment is the key to a healthy urban forest.

Community members need to be dedicated to the ongoing care of those first trees, and all that follow. The city must demonstrate that it values the work by doing its share to support the effort.

—Andy and Katie Lipkis, TreePeople

Arrangements between these departments and divisions are coordinated informally. Despite the absence of mandated procedures for achieving a coordinated effort, and despite the lack of an approved planting master plan, employees involved in tree planting feel that great strides are being made towards viewing tree planting and maintenance as a team effort, and towards understanding the need to view the city as a whole when making design, planting, and tree care decisions.

Urban planting in Fort Collins, CO, also depends on informal links for integrated management and consistency. The Forestry Division functions without a community forest master plan, but has a close working relationship with the planning department.

New trees get planted several ways. Builders are required to plant street trees as part of the construction permitting process. For each home built, builders also must contribute to the Park Land Fund, which creates new residential parks throughout the city. All street development projects undertaken by the Department of Public Works include street tree plantings paid for as part of the bonding process. The Forestry Division replaces all large trees that must be removed with one or more small trees. And to the extent possible, that division identifies unplanted sections in established areas, and provides street trees and park trees. This system, the city forester feels, generally results in good species selection and placement.

Funding
Public Programs

Santa Maria Park Superintendent and Urban Forester Bailey Hudson best described the problem of funding both private and public urban forestry programs when he noted that as long as they are considered only an "amenity service," funding is not assured. Cities have many other problems which seem more pressing.

Tim Buchanan, city forester of Fort Collins, Colorado, agreed. "People are used to the thinking that says, 'We have to take care of our roads,'" he said. "The average citizen still has a lot to learn about the concept of an urban forest. We have to get better at demonstrating that we have money needs, and do more documentation and analysis than other competing departments."

Everybody we surveyed agreed that public education about the benefits of urban forests is crucial to increasing funding. An informed public will not tolerate an inadequate city forestry program, while informed funders will give willingly to a popular cause, both for the publicity and the sense of goodwill.

One tried and true method for increasing trees in the face of low government budgets is to require tree planting with new construction, roadway improvements, and other projects. This method gets trees in the ground, but it makes no provisions for maintenance. Later, as pressures from other departments mount, it becomes easy for City Council to cut back on crucial maintenance programs. Such moves, of course, can have drastic effects on tree health and public safety.

Urban foresters claim the best way to avoid this problem is to be able to present solid cost versus risk analyses for all proposed changes to maintenance schedules. Successful municipal programs use street tree inventories, including pruning rotations, to help in discussions about the cost-effectiveness of certain maintenance strategies—especially at budget-time. For example, being able to prove that a pruning rotation of five years results in less lower limb damage and falling deadwood, increased health and longevity for the tree, improved public safety, and reduced replacement costs, than a ten-year rotation, helps to garner government financing for the highest quality maintenance programs.

In order to generate data-rich inventories, a growing municipal program needs computerized programs, all foresters agreed. The Street Tree Division of the Department of Parks, Recreation and Street Trees, in Santa Maria, California, was one of the first street tree programs to adopt computerized inventorying. That inventorying has enabled it to develop a complete programmed service approach to maintenance, as well as keep track of government funds spent on each tree in the city.

Figure 5-2.
Street Construction Dollar: For every dollar spent on city streets, trees generally are allotted only slightly more than two cents (AFA National Street Tree Survey).

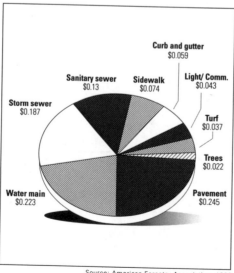

Source: American Forestry Association, 1990

SMUD/Sacramento Tree Foundation Shade Tree Program

As a key component of its Conservation Power Program to cool urban heat islands by shading homes, schools, and places of business, the Sacramento Municipal Utility District (SMUD) has sponsored over a million dollars annually to the Sacramento Tree Foundation for tree planting activities. In 1990, a team of SMUD "Energy Advisors" and Tree Foundation "Community Foresters" conducted energy audits in the SMUD service area to determine the need for shading. Community Foresters coordinated the location, selection, delivery, planting, and stewardship of shade trees with citizen volunteers.

The Tree Foundation, a citizen-volunteer planting and stewardship program, met its short-term goal of 3,000 new tree plantings for homes, businesses, and schools during fall and winter of 1990. To date, the program also is successfully meeting its 1991 objective of 25,000 trees planted by the end of the year. Over the long term, the Tree Foundation plans to increase the number of plantings each year to reach its goal of 500,000 new shade trees in Sacramento by the year 2000.

Specific goals of this program include:

1) Create a citizen tree planting and stewardship program with the ability to meet the tree demand from up to 40,000 residential, commercial, and school audits per year.

2) Establish a shade tree inventory and delivery system to meet the planting demands of the program.

3) Educate and promote awareness among area residents on the energy-saving benefits of planting and caring for shade trees.

Trees For Public Places

Trees For Public Places, a community tree grant program, is designed to plant new shade trees at parks and schools and along neighborhood streets. The program's record of accomplishments includes:

- Funded planting of over 13,000 trees
- Co-sponsored over 345 community tree planting projects
- Sponsored several large oak grove plantings
- Has provided urban forestry training in a 10-week Summer Youth program since 1983
- Receives continuous support of dedicated community groups

Support for the program primarily consists of grants from the County and City of Sacramento, along with an Urban Forestry Grant from the California Department of Forestry.

Fall 1991 activities underway include community groups and neighborhood volunteers representing nine schools, three parks, and ten residential and business streets who intend to plant 1,500 trees.

Trees For Public Places provides trees, educational materials, and technical assistance to each tree planting project. A designated volunteer "Tree Manager," who has been trained in a tree care and management workshop, follows up on each project for three to five years to ensure the healthy establishment of new trees.

—Sacramento Tree Foundation, Sacramento, California

Figure 5-3.
Breakdown of costs involved in city tree planting programs: Generally speaking, labor costs are actually greater than material costs in tree-planting programs. Using volunteers can reduce initial labor costs (AFA National Street Tree Survey).

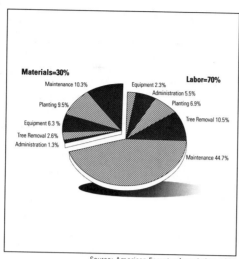

Source: American Forestry Association, 1990

Inventories can be instrumental in making a case for established pruning rotations—even in times of municipal financial woes. As pruning rotations are lengthened to save money, trees begin to develop more problems, prompting hazard and emergency calls from cities. It is more expensive and less efficient for emergency crews to answer random calls over a large territory than it is to conduct regular maintenance. When a city's complete tree care activities have been logged into a computerized inventory, such data is extremely accessible to urban foresters.

Inventories can also provide the information for analyses of the costs of caring for one species compared to another, or the varying costs of maintaining a particular species in different planting sites. This reveals which species are most cost effective in different urban sites.

Complete inventories, with all maintenance noted in each tree's file, also can offer proof that a city has not been negligent in its maintenance if it is sued over a tree care issue.

Forestry divisions that lack the inventory information to generate such figures and information themselves often can make persuasive arguments based on figures from comparably sized cities.

Private Programs

There are no easy funding answers for private programs either. Most programs mix funding from governmental and foundation grants, and corporate and private donations. Analysis shows that membership strategies take several years to pay for themselves, because members have to be serviced by newsletters, educational opportunities, and other amenities. Still, many groups swore by their members, saying they were the most loyal givers.

NeighborWoods in Chicago, IL, was very successful in securing corporate underwriting for projects which promised good publicity for both the funder and the program. Edith Makra credits the nationwide publicity of Global Releaf with attracting some short-term corporate givers, and she counsels fundraisers to watch for such tie-ins to larger issues. She also notes that a program needs general operating funds before it can pull together these high-profile plantings.

Fundraising tends to create its own momentum. The relationship between operating funds and corporate donations is important. Well-received, special projects create the kind of publicity that heightens public awareness and educates people about the urban forest. Increased public awareness, in turn, creates increased opportunities for general fundraising, as well as new opportunities to put together special events.

The Dallas Parks Foundation

The Dallas Parks Foundation is a non-profit organization that was established in 1982 to privately identify resources and build partnerships to develop new parks and greenspaces, support existing park systems, encourage public arts uses, and educate the public about local natural resources. The Parks Foundation has planted more than 18,000 trees in Dallas County over the past three years and plans to plant over 38,000 more trees during 1991 and 1992.

Past accomplishments include:

Treescape Dallas, Inc.: An urban treeplanting project of the *Dallas Junior League* and the *Central Dallas Association* from 1982 to the time it merged with the Dallas Parks Foundation in 1987, Treescape successfully completed 28 landscaping projects in downtown Dallas at a cost of $890,000. Over 32 percent of this total came from volunteer support and in-kind donations.

Woodall Rodgers Freeway: By September 1989, 570 trees were planted along the access road from North Central Expressway to Stemmons Freeway in a joint project with the *Texas Department of Highways and Transportation.* The total cost exceeded $200,000 in plant and irrigation materials.

Cityplace Tree Moving: The Parks Foundation transplanted over 80 trees and shrubs from the Cityplace construction area to sites throughout Dallas.

Oak Lawn Master Plan: The Parks Foundation facilitated a Master Plan for the major streets in Dallas' Oak Lawn neighborhood. The work was completed by teams of landscape architects and other design professionals. Prepared in conjunction with the *Oak Lawn Forum*, the Parks Foundation published the plans to encourage consistency in streetscape design in the Oak Lawn district.

Median Tree Plantings: Planted over 75 trees on major Dallas thoroughfares.

James Surls Sculpture: The creation of the Robert Buford Fund in 1990 allowed the Parks Foundation to meet its objective of acquiring public art for city parks.

Current programs include:

MKT Trails: The *Union-Pacific Railroad* plans to donate a 3.7-mile section of the Missouri-Kansas-Texas line to the Parks Foundation. This right-of-way will be developed as a hike-and-bike trail which will connect a number of neighborhood parks. Completion of design and commencement of fundraising is anticipated by the end of 1992.

Pioneer Plaza: Under a special agreement with the *Dallas City Council,* the parks Foundation will design and build a new park at the Dallas Convention Center adjacent to Pioneer Cemetery, and will present it as a gift to the people of Dallas. Anticipated construction is June 1993, completion expected January 1994.

Treeplanting: The Parks Foundation is actively involved in planting trees in parks, along boulevards, in school yards, and on other public lands throughout Dallas County. With the sponsorship of *Fina, Trees for Dallas* installed over 5,300 trees during the 1990-1991 planting season.

— Dallas Parks Foundation

A program with a proven track record always has an easier time fundraising than a new organization. So, it's a good strategy for new programs to seek heightened visibility through corporate-sponsored special event plantings. The problem is that many would-be funders, drawn by the chance for publicity, aren't interested in contributing toward general operating expenses. They want to be assured that all their money buys trees. In such cases, the program must try to insist on receiving an absolute minimum for its expenses. For the long haul, a program must have in place a solid funding base for its core program.

One of the most effective ways to defray costs for private organizations is also one of the best ways to assure successful plantings. Many of the programs we surveyed have adjacent property owners pay for the trees, or at least a portion of their costs. Citizens with a monetary investment in trees tend to be more actively interested in their welfare. In San Francisco, for instance, Friends of the Urban Forest subsidizes about half the cost of having a single tree planted. In an ordinary neighborhood, the cost to each participant is $135, part of which is earmarked for organizational costs. In low-income neighborhoods, where plantings are financed through various special grants (frequently governmental), there is nominal cost to the individual.

Most programs cannot afford to rest on their laurels; they have to get out and hustle every year for every donation and every corporate grant they get. This is why fundraising is such an important and time-consuming part of street tree planting. Indeed, sometimes groups get into financial trouble because they assumed certain corporate donations were guaranteed for an additional year, and then found out that the corporation gave the funds to other, seemingly "hotter" causes. In New York City, for instance, the New York Street Tree Consortium had a financial crisis when a change in tax laws in 1987 meant that several major corporate funders withdrew their support.

Fundraising is time consuming, but it works best when requests for support are linked to specific programs and events. General operating monies (salaries, rent) are harder to raise and frequently come from the operating allowance the IRS allows non-profit organizations to keep from membership fees, planting fees and certain other donations.[1] In general, program planning, budgeting, and fundraising are linked together, looking at least a year ahead.

Most groups constantly search for new ways to raise money, including staging annual benefits. However, most towns don't need another ball, home tour, or craft show. Developing unusual, effective fundraising activities is something the emergent tree-planting movement must address. Perhaps some inter-city networking and brainstorming between creative volunteers will generate some concepts that will work. In the meantime, several programs are undertaking major fund drives to establish legal trusts to generate ongoing funding.

---

[1] The IRS allows organizations to keep 25 percent of donations of this sort for overhead costs. Many trees organizations keep that percentage closer to 10 percent, to assure people their money really goes toward planting trees.

The Twin Cities Tree Trust

The Twin Cities Tree Trust, a private non-profit corporation, was established in 1976 to employ and train disadvantaged youth to reforest public and low-income properties devastated by Dutch elm disease. The mission of Tree Trust has expanded to include employment of disadvantaged adults and more projects of lasting community value such as tree plantings and landscape construction. Over 15,000 youth and 3,000 adults in government service and private employment programs have completed hundreds of landscaping and construction projects throughout metropolitan St. Paul and Minneapolis, Minnesota. Annually, Tree Trust employs over 800 disadvantaged youth from five metropolitan counties—in the Summer Youth Employment Program (SYETP)—and over 900 adults from Hennepin County in Minneapolis—in the Hennepin County Community Investment Program (HCCIP).

The unique Twin Cities Tree Trust program, blending the employment of disadvantaged youth with environmental improvement projects, consists of two basic goals:

1) To provide employees with a meaningful and challenging work experience.

2) To provide communities with a low cost quality product.

The state, counties, and municipalities request projects and provide all necessary materials. Tree Trust designs and implements the projects and supervises the crews. Contributions from the private sector provide ongoing support services including recruitment, supervisory training, transportation, equipment, tools, supplies, and administrative support. Funding is received from both the public and private sectors and from philanthropic support. Tree Trust believes that this combination of varied funding sources enables the program to succeed in meeting both goals, an outcome referred to as "Everyone Wins."

SYETP: Tree Trust trains the youth for future employment, stressing a positive work attitude and basic job skills such as attendance, teamwork, safety, proper use of equipment, working to exacting standards, and the importance of doing a job well. Because of the wide range in ability and skill level of the youth workers, Tree Trust encourages individuality and mutual respect. Individual accomplishments are recognized, including an Award Ceremony and picnic at the end of the ten-week program. Everyone receives an Environmental Service Citation from their respective County Commissioner and a Tree Trust T-shirt. The Governor signs a Commendation for youth who have shown outstanding effort.

HCCIP: Since 1988, Tree Trust has provided employment for economically disadvantaged and hard-to-employ adults who are receiving general assistance. Basic skills training is modeled after the youth program because most of the adults who come to the program have not worked in several years. During the week crews work for an average of twenty hours and attend classroom training sessions or seek unsubsidized employment during the remainder of the week. This program rewards good work attitudes and attendance with pay increases. It also allows participants to stay in the program for a maximum of thirteen weeks until they secure other employment.

Projects include public service and assistance to low-income handicapped residents in Hennepin County such as mowing and snow removal at no charge to the residents.

Tree Trust maintains a carefully trained staff of forty-five people, including a core staff of five professionals experienced in directing training and employment programs for disadvantaged youth and adults. Summer supervisors are hired on a seasonal basis and trained in supervisory, construction, landscape, planting, first aid, and other critical skills.

— Twin Cities Tree Trust

Getting Trees In The Ground: What Works Best?

The most successful plantings with private organizations are those in which citizen volunteers contribute financially and then take part in the actual plantings. This method may take more time than either hiring for the job or having mass plantings with seasoned volunteers. But it works over the long term, because it inspires a personal investment in the tree. It also helps educate the public. Learning how to plant and care for a tree is a far more effective educational tool than reading brochures or sitting through lectures.

This approach isn't practical in all areas, of course. Trees Atlanta's downtown planting areas, for example, are adjacent to corporate property owners who probably are not enthusiastic about getting their hands in the dirt. But where using local residents is practical, it needs to be seriously considered.

Friends of the Urban Forest, for instance, has used Community Block Grants from the U.S. Department of Housing and Urban Development (HUD) to plant trees in low-income neighborhoods in San Francisco. Gradjansky has found that the plantings are unsuccessful when FUF does most of the work, because the residents do not get interested in the trees. When the planting is done in conjunction with redevelopment projects—where citizens really want the trees—it works better. The most successful plantings are ones where the neighborhood takes the initiative from the beginning.

Maintaining The Trees: Can You Afford To Be Unconcerned?

Maintenance is the most ticklish issue in the current street tree and urban forest planting boom. The trouble is that maintenance seems rather dull and routine. It is not at all as engaging as the effort to get trees planted. And it is hard to convince average citizens—who look around and see apparently healthy trees—about the importance of pruning branches for strength, pruning roots to forestall sidewalk and curb damage, thinning foliage to allow wind passage, and other necessary tasks.

For reasons of public health and safety, maintenance standards have to be higher for street trees planted on public property than for those planted on private property. Both citizens and their government representatives have to understand these issues and be willing to fund them. As we have seen, however, regular maintenance usually gets neglected when money runs low.

The most promising plan for lessening the maintenance funding burden seems to be to have private groups (whether a street tree program or a developer) plant trees,

Urban tree planting is widely recognized today as being one solution to the global warming problem. But there is a catch to this "solution." The "technology" is a living one which requires extensive ongoing care if it is to work. That is, tree planting is not a technical "fix" that will handle a problem regardless of human action. It mandates an ongoing partnership between people and their environment.

— Andy and Katie Lipkis, TreePeople

and then have the city take care of them. In many cities, adjacent property owners, who have access to the trees, as well as program support and training, maintained the trees during the establishment period—which can be up to five years. When a tree has reached a certain size, and its care demands expertise and equipment that most homeowners don't possess, government has agreed to take over the maintenance, having saved the cost of planting and initial care.

Some cities, however, refuse to care for trees planted by volunteers. San Francisco, for instance, makes the property owners, who are permitted to plant trees, responsible for maintenance. The city maintains only the right to cite property owners and to demand tree care if a tree becomes a nuisance or a liability. In most cases, this does not deter planting in neighborhoods committed to having trees.

City foresters, however, do not like arrangements where citizens are completely responsible for street tree maintenance, because that maintenance is usually not guided by professional foresters. Too much bad maintenance—including inappropriate pruning and tree topping—undermines the appearance and health of individual trees, and reduces the value of the urban forest as a whole. Additionally, the foresters become like law enforcers with the unpleasant task of forcing residents to maintain trees on public property.

The Fort Collins program provides a good example of what can happen when citizens are held responsible for too much maintenance. Beginning in 1969, a large number of that city's trees became infected with Dutch elm disease. The property owners—who were primarily responsible for their trees—could not take care of them. Many of them did not recognize

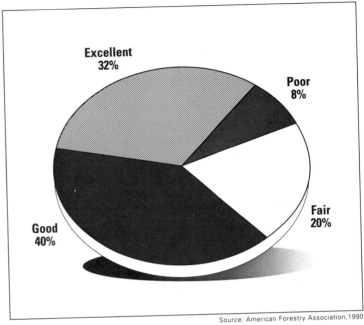

Source: American Forestry Association, 1990

Figure 5-4.
Percentage of trees in good condition: Almost three quarters of the nation's trees are in excellent to good condition. This record could be continued with proper maintenance from urban forestry programs (AFA National Street Tree Survey).

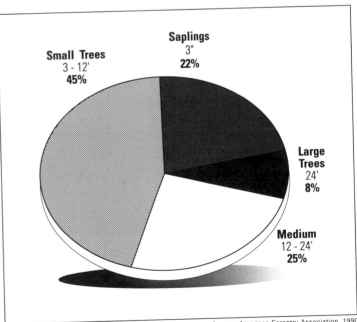

Source: American Forestry Association, 1990

Figure 5-5.
Tree size distribution: Today's urban forest contains many young or small-sized trees. It is important to plant more mature trees and trees that will grow large enough to provide adequate shading. Larger trees tend to be hardier and require less maintenance (AFA National Street Tree Survey).

the severity of the problem and simply assumed the trees would regain their vigor. Others could not afford either remedies or removal. Consequently, property owners neither treated nor removed their trees quickly enough to prevent contagion. Faced with the depletion of its urban forest, the Fort Collins government had to step in and take over all maintenance.

Of course, waiting for a crisis to develop is not a particularly effective strategy for forcing a city to sort out its priorities and take charge. Without adequate maintenance, our urban forests become run-down, and then move gradually from being a nuisance to being a threat to safety. Unfortunately, once the public has a negative association with the urban forest, it is hard to build a more positive image.

In general, the foresters we surveyed agreed that the urban forest receives the best maintenance and is healthiest when it is managed as a whole, from planting through removal, by a professional staff. The problem for cities is that the money is not usually available for the street tree program to go first-class.

Ideal Components of an Urban Forest Management System

City Forester
    City or government agency with planting, management, and maintenance responsibility and funding

Ordinances
Citizen tree commission or board
Citizen and youth involvement
Private contributions
General Public education
Neighborhood-level outreach
Tree Inventory
Tree or Forest Master Plan

Local Government
can be responsible for:
Ordinances
Maintenance
Specifications
Master planning

Tree inventory
Coordination of efforts

Private citizens
can take care of:
Fundraising
Community organizing
Small tree care

Either or Both
can promote:
Youth involvement
Public Education
Training
Planting
Tree Care Activity
Public celebrations
Citizen tree commission
Neighborhood planning

Andy and Katie Lipkis

Other maintenance strategies developed by private groups include the New York Street Tree Consortium's citizen pruning corps which consists of over 1500 citizens who are certified by Parks and Recreation. Residents who need help the city cannot provide can call someone from the Consortium's directory of citizen pruners. The organization also holds periodic Tree Care Days, on which groups of pruners gather to tend trees in a particular neighborhood. In Houston, some citizens commit to caring for the trees with the help of periodic maintenance workshops provided by Trees for Houston. Some neighborhoods have organized to do yearly tree assessments and purchase professional maintenance. At the same time, the program is developing a volunteer maintenance corps. Trees Atlanta includes three years of professional maintenance in the $2000 per tree charge. After three years, the city assumes responsibility.

Other cities use a combination of strategies. Friends of the Urban Forest, for example, has given maintenance workshops with neighborhoods a year after their plantings. That organization is also forming a corps of citizen pruners similar to the New York corps. There has been some experimentation with collecting a fee at planting to contract out for professional maintenance for at least the first year.

The truth is, however, that private planting groups, in general, have inadequate plans for maintenance. They admit this. If they waited to plant until they had lifetime maintenance for each tree assured, they say they would never plant. Even in cities where government crews are slated to take over maintenance after citizens have planted and established trees, there is concern that the money to actually do this won't be there as the trees come on line.

In the final analysis, of course, it may be the courts that determine who is ultimately responsible for trees planted on public property. Cases that question whether or not cities can legally assign responsibility and liability to adjacent property owners are beginning to work their way through the judicial system even now.

About Community Forest Planning
First Steps

Whether you are part of a private or a governmental program, you must first pick viable species for your area, and then plant them in appropriate sites. All of the planting programs we looked at have developed approved species lists for their areas. These lists emphasize natives where possible, but because they must consider urban growing conditions as well, they often include well-adapted, robust exotics. Lists usually include species approved for small, medium, and large planting sites.

Citizens generally want to have some voice in deciding what kind of tree will be planted in front of their property—even if they don't have to care for it. Most citizens are quite happy to choose from a short, approved list, and are generally receptive to tree program advice about design elements. Still, it is important to fully explain why there is a list of approved species, so residents understand why their choices are limited.

Citizen Foresters

One example of citizen involvement is TreePeople's Citizen Forester™ Program . We developed it when our grassroots operation began taking on the dimensions and problems of a centralized organization.

Two things happened. As the demand for tree planting increased, neither TreePeople's budget nor human resources (staff or volunteers) could meet the need. Of even greater concern, neighborhoods were planting trees, but then neglecting them.

As funds were tight, we were no longer able to do fundraising and get permits, nor were we able to do planning, organizing, or planting for community groups. Instead, we began to guide them through the process. And as they struggled to obtain planting permits and money, they galvanized extraordinary community commitment.

Even in very poor neighborhoods, families began realizing what they could contribute. On planting day, people would turn out to plant "their" trees. Even more important, they seriously adopted their role as tree guardians. One group built its own water wagon, by strapping two 55-gallon oil drums to a trailer pulled by various neighborhood cars. In one area, as we helped restake trees after a windstorm, confused neighbors drove by shouting, "Don't hurt our trees!"

The Citizen Forester training currently includes more than 30 hours of classroom time, plus practical field experience planting and teaching others. Citizen Foresters also learn tree care, fundraising, community organizing, how to work with government agencies, and more. Participants actually go through the government permit process and "graduate" with the planting permit in hand and their project well on the way to fruition. TreePeople is always there as back-up: It can provide logistical support, tools, trucks, pooled wholesale purchasing of trees and supplies, and hordes of "roving" volunteers to ensure a planting's success.

Regardless of the form your urban forestry project will take, you should ascertain whether or not you are duplicating the work of an existing or planned program. Time and energy have been devoted to such projects, and lessons may already have been learned. Moreover, community efforts require, above all else, cooperation, trust, and good will. Avoid unintentional offence by announcing a project that apparently ignores what already exists.

— Andy and Katie Lipkis, TreePeople

Basic components of an urban forestry program:

A truly successful urban forestry program includes a dynamic combination of roles for the community and government agencies. Maintenance costs today are far beyond that which most cities can afford; the cost of public education and training is beyond that which most believe is necessary. Even with sufficient funds, it's simply no longer possible to establish trees in most large cities without an extraordinary level of public involvement.

People who can get involved in tree-planting programs fall into a number of different categories:

- Individual Citizens
- Youth
- Politicians
- Organizations (churches, clubs, homeowner groups, etc.)
- Government Agencies, including:
    - City Forester
    - Public Works Department
    - Road or Highway Department
    - Parks Department
    - Fire Department
    - Other Forestry agencies (county, state, and federal)
    - Environmental Quality Board or Department
    - Planning, Building and Safety, Engineering Departments
    - Agriculture Commissioner
- Citizen Commissions (Trees, Public Works, Parks)
- Urban Forestry Professionals
    - Arborists
    - Landscape architects
    - Landscape maintenance firms
- Telephone and Electric Utilities (line clearance)
- Businesses
- Environmental organizations

Many or all of these players are already involved with trees in your community. Historically, they have acted independently, but with the rise of Urban Forestry as a profession, cities are increasingly making an effort to coordinate them.

— Andy and Katie Lipkis, TreePeople

Master Planning

The majority of the programs surveyed do little master planning. Urban foresters who had good communication with planning and public works departments did not feel a need for more formal master planning.

Even in these cases, however, an approved master plan would bring increased consistency and continuity to plantings throughout the city, which would provide an opportunity for creating some broad planting themes. In cities previously lacking inter-departmental communication, master planning can initiate contact between departments by bringing plant experts, planners, and planters together. A master plan certainly is advantageous in bureaucracies hindered by continual personnel changes.

In the absence of a master plan, a number of cities have established standards and specifications for tree planting by ordinance (See Chapter 7). This can also give cities some control over the shape of an emerging urban forest.

Not all master plans are created equal, however. Santa Maria, for instance, ran into problems when it adopted a master plan that was too specific about street tree species. Where the city was seeking elegance and uniformity, it ended up with trees being planted in inappropriate sites. Some trees had to be removed; others just never thrived. Today, the master plan has been more or less abandoned, and replaced by a program which matches trees from a selected palette to specific site situations after it had become obvious how certain sections of town would be developed. Property owners in the area are given a choice of 10 different trees that will perform within site constraints and have similar maintenance requirements.

It's important for a private organization to keep in step with a city's street tree strategy, whatever its state of organization. One good way to initiate cooperation is to have the city forester, a city planner, or perhaps a council person on the board of directors for the tree group. This provides an opportunity for developing at least informal guidelines for street tree planting.

Relationships With City Government

For a private planting organization, the group's relationship to the city, which usually issues the permits to plant trees on public property, is extremely important. On a day-to-day level, too, maintaining a good working relationship pays off in the long run.

The people surveyed indicated that while the mechanics of getting tree plantings planned and approved by the city may seem labyrinthine at the start, the process quickly becomes familiar. Planting coordinators usually work with the same city employees on project after project. It is important that these employees perceive the planting coordinators and the tree organization as professional and directed, because it makes them feel they are contributing to a meaningful movement. This will make their input more timely and professional.

In the highly charged political atmosphere of Chicago city government, NeighborWoods' Edith Makra learned that nothing elicited cooperation like writing to the supervisor of someone who has been particularly helpful. Makra was also quite politic about inviting bosses to the celebrations of high-profile plantings so they could receive public acknowledgment. Complaining to authorities about less than cooperative behavior, however, usually just makes things more difficult.

How Political Do You Have To Be To Survive?

Survey contacts, both in and out of government, felt strongly that street tree planting and maintenance was a highly political issue because of the funding allocations necessary for a viable, managed urban forest.

Successful tree politics depends on constantly remembering the importance of building a broad-based constituency that supports an integrated urban forestry program. Contacts noted again and again that taking the time to educate the public about street trees and the urban forest pays. Groups that work hard to attract media attention can reach numerous and diverse audiences simultaneously.

No matter how popular the program, however, a change from a supportive to non-supportive city government, whether or not the city funds the program, can mean progress or closure regardless of the program. "You can always envision upheaval at the top that could put you back in the Stone Age," said Cor Trowbridge of TreePeople.

Grassroots support from the community ultimately insulates a program from political tinkering. When the public vocally supports a program, it gets funded. When the public does not care, the program is propped up by a few people who have vision, but are constantly seeking funding and friends in high places. The lack of an integrated and broad-based support network can make a program extremely vulnerable in times of financial stress or political change.

Contact With The Public
Education

Contact with the public is inevitable because people live in the urban forest and see the day-to-day operations of street tree programs. Many people, however, can walk by a tree every day without it being meaningful to them, so most of the surveyed programs continually seek other opportunities to educate the public about tree and environmental issues. In other words, once a tree program is established, the next challenge is mounting a formal education component.

These education programs frequently target grade-school children to instill in them an environmental awareness. In general, these education projects include both classroom curriculum and a hands-on planting project at the school to give students a more lasting connection with trees and the idea of an urban forest. TreePeople has the largest such program, receiving 30,000 school children a year at its hilltop site, where some trees are planted and others are distributed to take home. Other successful educational programs include a city park/arboretum tour offered in Fort Collins and the use of rope and saddle maintenance crews in Santa Maria. This old-fashioned method of tree climbing—in which the climber shimmies up the trunk by wrapping a rope around the trunk and using a small saddle as a brace—draws daily crowds and provides crews with the chance for some impromptu public consciousness-raising.

Making literature available to people who seek it can also be a useful part of an integrated educational outreach program. Seeking exposure at appropriate community events, such as flower shows or Arbor Day-type celebrations, can be another useful way to reach large numbers of people.

Promotion

In addition to publicity resulting from day-to-day activities, many programs specifically plan special events targeted to call attention to their activities. Such events frequently fall on Arbor Day. Successful ones involve more than ceremonially planting a tree at an isolated site. High exposure plantings should have a real impact on the community in the days following Arbor Day, and should involve as many people as possible. Ft. Collins, Albuquerque, Colorado Springs, and a number of other communities around the country stage mass plantings with the cooperation of citizen volunteers and city forestry departments.

Both private and governmental programs have good luck with memorial and other dedicated plantings. One city has a grandparents' grove, where trees are planted for grandchildren. In all these situations, the individual pays for the planting and a plaque goes up with the tree or group of trees saying, for instance, "This tree planted in memory of...," or "These three blocks planted by Twelfth National Bank."

Inspiration

TreePeople is the group that takes a very inspirational approach to the work of street tree planting. Group leaders talk openly about involvement and empowerment, about teaching people to use their personal power as a force for positive change. "We've learned a lot about the power of inspiration," Trowbridge says, "about how far it can take you, about the power you have alone, but also about personal limitations. I think we show people what a force for change they can be when they work with other people and think big."

Deeper Roots Into The Community

Environmental groups around the country have begun reaching out to minority and working class groups, and street tree planting organizations are no exception. There's a strong feeling in the cities that a tree-planting program is more successful when a city's trees are truly for all citizens. There are, however, problems with follow-up care, especially for the private programs.

San Francisco's Friends of the Urban Forest, as noted earlier, has had less than sterling success with plantings in low-income areas because the program has had to take too much of the initiative in getting the trees in the ground. Gradjansky feels that the key to better success in such neighborhoods is to involve residents more. This is sometimes easier said than done in areas where trees are not a top priority.

Within Philadelphia Green, which works exclusively with moderate to low income neighborhoods in its city, no staff consensus has been reached over the organization's 14 years of existence as to whether community involvement is paying off and planting trees yields better results. The reality, according to Jonathan Frank, a program coordinator, is that most of the organization's plantings disappear within a few years.

It would seem that city governments will have to take a leadership role in providing street tree maintenance in these situations.

Plant the Future, Inc., in Griffin, GA, has reached out to the minority community in an unusual way. It has entered into a partnership with a local program providing vocational training to retarded citizens. Tree seedlings, available free from the state department of forestry, are raised by the training program participants to a size useful to Plant the Future, which then buys them. The vocational program makes money. The planting program saves money, and has received positive publicity about the arrangements.

In Minneapolis/St. Paul, MN, the Twin Cities Tree Trust is based on the 1930s Civilian Conservation Corps concept and uses trained crews of disadvantaged youths and adults for municipal planting and construction projects. As in Griffin, this approach involves minorities in the process without asking them to expend their possibly limited resources on maintenance in the future.

Landscape Ordinances

All in all, landscape ordinances greatly help the cause of trees in the cities we surveyed. There were a few complaints about what were viewed as excessively rigid ordinances forbidding tree planting under various circumstances, especially at city centers. Generally speaking, however, programs are anxious to work with the city, and glad to have formal guidelines, rather than bureaucratic whim, shape their relationships.

Marcia Bansley of Trees Atlanta spoke compellingly about the good that had been accomplished in her area through the passage of landscape ordinances to protect existing trees and assure replanting when trees are removed. By being identified as a force in the successful lobbying for such ordinances, Trees Atlanta has received wonderful publicity in instances where there have been dramatic preservation of huge old trees. "We've saved more trees through these ordinances than we could ever have planted," Bansley said.

As already indicated, landscape ordinances requiring tree plantings with new construction are the basis in many cities of a partnership with developers that helps the city grow the way residents want it to. These ordinances acknowledge that trees are as valued as street lights and other infrastructure that are also required. Certainly from a planning point of view, making way for trees from the beginning makes more sense than retrofitting a street with trees years later. (See Chapter 7 for more information about developing effective ordinances).

Keeping The Program Alive

Many of the contacts surveyed told tales of tree programs that had died. Most often, the reason was simply, "They just got tired."

How to keep from getting tired? In Los Angeles, TreePeople fights burn-out with new campaigns. Organizations need to change to reflect the changing needs of the

Synopsis of Fulton County (Rev. 11/88)
Tree Preservation Ordinance and Administrative Guidelines

ADOPTED: January 30th, 1985 by the Board of Commissioners

INTENT: To provide standards for the preservation and replacement of trees as part of the land development and building construction process in unincorporated Fulton County. Benefits derived from the protection and replacement of trees include: 1) Improved control of soil erosion; 2) Moderation of storm water runoff and improved water quality; 3) Improved air quality; 4) Reduction of noise and glare; 5) Climate moderation; 6) Improvement of urban wildlife habitat; 7) Increased property value; and 8) Aesthetics, scenic amenity.

OVERALL OBJECTIVE: To maintain a functional volume of trees to ameliorate stresses associated with the urbanization process.

ACCOMPLISHMENTS: To date over 60,000 trees will be or already have been planted as a result of this program, and over 2000 acres of trees have been actively protected—approximately an 11 percent reforestation of land developed in Fulton County since 1985. On the average, developers have exceeded our requirements by 50 percent.

Provisions of the Ordinance apply to all activity which requires the issuance of a land disturbance permit within unincorporated portions of the County. The Ordinance required the creation of administrative standards for the identification, preservation, and protection of specimen trees and trees outside the buildable areas of lots (within setbacks), as well as landscaping standards for properties with no trees and situations where tree protection is not feasible.

The Administrative Guidelines were written subsequent to filling the County Arborist position. A phased in implementation of the tree preservation program began with the approval of the Board of Commissioners. These guidelines became the substance of the program.

Tree protection during land development is difficult in the Piedmont region due to hilly topography associated with heavy soils, often resulting in necessary grading through shallow root systems. Given these complexities of land development juxtaposed with the specific biological needs of trees, it became evident that an approach towards education and flexibility was necessary in the administration of the program.

Applicants for land disturbance permits are required to submit tree protection/landscape drawings as part of the total development package. These drawings indicate limits of site disturbance, tree protection area, specimen trees, areas of landscaping and revegetation, methods of tree protection, and utilities, site design factors, and construction activity layout. The guidelines provide general information to assist the design professional in tree protection plan preparation. Every site is walked by the County Arborist, project engineers, and landscape architects to discuss planning considerations, and encroachment techniques, in terms of the existing on-site resources. Further support for the tree program is provided through conditional zoning (landscape strips, buffers, parking islands, etc.).

An innovative approach was taken in the prescription of replacement trees on developing properties. To ensure an environmentally functional urban forest for the future, a minimum density of trees is required per acre developed. This density (based upon tree size), can be satisfied with existing (protected) trees on the site, replacement trees, or a combination of both. This formula is effective because it recognizes variability in the extent of land disturbance between types of development projects, and thus affords the developer some flexibility. The formula does allow clearing where necessary for site preparation, but also provides a cost savings incentive to keep existing vegetation wherever possible. Requests for information on this formula have come from jurisdictions nationwide, and from abroad.

—Edward A. Macie, USDA Forest Service

people who run them, notes founder Andy Lipkis. His program recently switched from a campaign to plant one million trees for the Olympics to its current campaign to promote energy-efficient plantings. Other cities are often finding that variety is the spice of successful programs. In San Francisco, for instance, Friends of the Urban Forest is planning to become involved in more massive plantings outside the city to fulfill staff and contributor desires to make a greater environmental impact. In Atlanta, the fight for and passage of landscape ordinances in the suburbs has heightened feelings of empowerment and accomplishment. In the Twin Cities, Tree Trust crews moved from simple maintenance jobs into substantial building projects. In New York, the Street Tree Consortium will begin offering consulting services.

The programs surveyed have all evolved over the years as they have embraced new issues and new ways of getting the job done. Allowing a program to evolve while meeting the needs of the people and the city seems key to running a successful program.

A Checklist To Consider When Initiating Or Evaluating Programs

1. To develop your program's niche, investigate what other planting programs in your area are and are not doing with tree planting on private and public property. Begin working where genuine need exists and where there is a legitimate chance of success. Concentrate on doing one or two things well to start. You can take on additional campaigns once you are established.

2. Put together a board of directors with an eye toward building coalitions. Here is a chance to begin forging important partnerships with local businessmen, community leaders, politicians, planners, forestry, horticultural, and design experts, service organizations, and individual volunteers. All these sectors should be represented in planning programs. When it comes to implementation, be specific about the tasks the board will undertake (fundraising, promotion, education, special events) and for how long. From the beginning, plan toward hiring at least a paid executive director.

3. Always have a clear picture of how the talents and enthusiasm of volunteers can best be put to use. At first, volunteers will probably be doing everything. Later, the most successful tree programs continue to depend on volunteers as cornerstones of their efforts. These people serve as one-on-one ambassadors of the program in the community.

4. Pay people to do the routine work. Have volunteers do the inspirational work, such as planting, educating, organizing neighborhood committees, and special project planning.

5. The best way to guarantee money for programs is to mix sources. Successful programs mix funds obtained from memberships, corporate and business donations and grants, foundation grants, and governmental funds and grants.

6. Successful programs don't necessarily do everything. They provide timely assistance to citizens who have their own motivations for implementing improvement projects. Experience suggests that the long-term tree planting success is related to the extent of the involvement of those who directly benefit from the trees. Develop a planting strategy with this in mind.

7. To be a success over the long term, programs need plans for monitoring tree health and providing regular maintenance. A fruitful partnership grows when street trees are planted and initially monitored and maintained by adjacent property owners. As trees become more of both an asset and a potential liability, the municipality assumes more of these duties.

8. Lists of recommended trees for different types of planting sites are extremely valuable, as are training and literature on the proper way to plant and maintain young trees. This much planning is absolutely essential.

9. Successful tree planting programs are usually involved in lobbying for the passage of landscape ordinances in their communities, especially street tree, tree preservation and new construction planting ordinances. This gives trees legal status.

10. Successful programs are continuously fundraising, educating, promoting, recruiting, politicking, organizing, and inspiring the public. They are pragmatic, but innovative; stable, but dynamic. They evolve with time. Most importantly, they are visionary.

Some Individual Examples

Throughout this chapter, we have used a number of different tree planting programs to illustrate successful (and not so successful) strategies. Here are some fuller descriptions of some programs and their histories.

Chicago, IL: NeighborWoods
Population: 8,130,000
Program type: Private, apparently to be absorbed by government.

NeighborWoods was launched in 1987 as an auxiliary program of Open Lands Project, a non-profit open space preservation group operating in the Chicago metropolitan area. At that time, the city's Bureau of Forestry faced budget cuts that seemed destined to accelerate tree losses running three to one over replacement.

NeighborWoods focused on working with community groups that wanted to undertake planting projects. Each group was asked to submit a project proposal. Community members were required to pick up at least 25 percent of the cost of the trees and to participate in the actual planting of them. Planting projects included residential and commercial district street trees, park and school-yard plantings and planting buffers in railroad right-of-ways. They were targeted to include different socio-economic and geographic areas of the city, but they also were chosen to bring visibility to the program through their impact on the neighborhood. As the program matured and corporate sponsors became interested in backing high-profile plantings, city government began to take more and more notice, in many cases offering behind-the-scenes help with projects. Nearly 1,000 trees were planted in a two-year period.

As NeighborWoods developed, it took on a more and more important advocacy role, working to raise the public's awareness of the need for healthy, well-maintained plantings in the city. All the while, it continued planting trees, considering this advocacy by example and hands-on education. The organization was increasingly able to lend important support to attempts by the Bureau of Forestry to stabilize its budget and improve its service, many times by mobilizing community groups to attend budget hearings.

The organization was funded by a combination of government and private foundation grants and corporate donations. Fundraising was handled by Open Lands.

When Richard Daley became mayor, he lured NeighborWoods' creator and its single staff person, Edith Makra, to his office to run the new GreenStreets program. As of this writing, it remains to be seen what role NeighborWoods will fashion for itself, with GreenStreets committed to planting 450,000 trees, saving 50,000 trees in imminent danger of destruction, and providing funding to upgrade maintenance of trees. NeighborWoods has not hired a replacement for Makra, but has indicated a commitment to continue community education through planting trees.

Colorado Springs, CO
Population: 393,000
Program type: Governmental Forestry Program, within Natural Resources Division, of the Parks and Recreation Department

Colorado Springs' commitment to urban forestry was codified into ordinance as early as 1910, and older parts of town are forested with large, old trees. An ordinance specifically mandating that developers plant street trees during new construction, with the city picking up a portion of the cost, has been on the books since 1976.

As it developed, the New Homes Tree Fund, created by the ordinance, has become a boon to the city. In the early years of its existence, the fund—a repository for developer portions of new home tree fees—was allowed to build up without being spent because builders preferred to plant their own trees, rather than involving the city. By the time the city disallowed this practice, enough money was on deposit that today the fund generates sufficient interest to cover the city's portion of all new home tree planting costs.

Colorado Springs also has a variety of other planting programs. In 1977, the city forester initiated a program called Decade of Trees conceived to help reforest parts of town where losses to Dutch elm disease were heavy. Today, this program is used wherever fill-in street tree planting is requested by citizens whether a removal has taken place recently or not. The city pays up to $50 for trees planted under this program, with adjacent property owners also contributing. The city's portion of this program comes from funds generated by the Damaged Tree Fund, the repository for assessments and fines leveled against people who have damaged city trees.

The city finances an arterial street tree planting program and a park planting program, always emphasizing the right tree in the right place. It also automatically replaces any trees it removes of 8-inch caliper or more where room allows. The city requires adjacent property owners to fertilize and water street trees. City crews provide disease control, pruning, and removal until trees reach an 8-inch caliper. Care for large trees is contracted out at a cost of approximately $200,000 per year.

The city's inventory of over 70,000 street trees is computerized, with scheduled maintenance at least every eight years. Maintenance is also provided upon request.

A community forest master plan is in the works and is considered a major priority. The Forestry Program has 13 full-time employees. Its work is funded through the city's general fund.

Several private groups interested in civic beautification and tree planting are expected to have a significant impact on tree planting in the city. One, Trees for the Future, aims to become a funding source for both city and privately sponsored tree planting projects. Another, Greensprings, plans a major volunteer planting project once a year with the help of the Forestry Division. Hundreds of volunteers are involved in the projects, which have included placing seedlings at freeway interchanges.

Los Angeles, CA: TreePeople
Population: 13,770,000
Program Type: Private

TreePeople began in 1973, when founder Andy Lipkis began to dream of saving the smog-damaged San Bernadino National Forest. His idea was to plant millions of smog tolerant seedlings in the mountains surrounding the Los Angeles metropolitan area. Today, the organization's primary concern is for the urban forest in the Los Angeles Basin. But the organization is planting fewer trees itself, and diverting more energy toward training what it calls "Citizen Foresters," who are community organizing specialists capable of organizing whatever sort of planting program (or presumably any other sort of program) a neighborhood wants.

The current goal is to create a body of 500 to 1000 Citizen Foresters and to provide them with a variety of expert support services. Because of its longevity, the organization has a stable corps of trained volunteers that it can mobilize for worthwhile projects. Historically, a great many of the Citizen Foresters and neighborhood groups that have taken on projects through TreePeople have been interested in planting street trees because the permitting procedure is quite straight forward and planting is done according to the city's street tree master plan. The organization asks trained Citizen Foresters to take on at least one new project per year. To date, it has had mixed results with people keeping to this commitment.

"We've learned you don't have to plant every tree yourself," says Cor Trowbridge, director of the Citizen Forester program. "We're really becoming known as environmental problem solvers. We want to offer tools and expertise and show people their personal power as a force for positive change."

The organization, which currently boasts a staff of 23 full-time and 10 part-time employees, is divided into many different units and is administering a broad range of programs. It recently entered into an agreement with the city of Los Angeles to direct a campaign highlighting energy savings through the planting of shade trees. Its first shared project with the city was to help develop a city-wide recycling program. TreePeople's continued role in the recycling program has been incorporated into its educational endeavors. Every year, 60,000 grade school children visit the TreePeople site (a retired 1920s mountain fire station on 12 acres of wooded land along a mountain ridge in Beverly Hills, donated by the city, and dubbed Coldwater Canyon Park) for a tour and lessons about trees and recycling. Each child plants a seedling while there and is given a seedling (grown by the TreePeople nursery program) to take home. The purpose is to inspire environmental leadership in young people.

TreePeople's move away from staff-initiated planting projects and toward community group projects was based primarily on concerns over maintenance. The group's well-published campaign to plant one million trees in L.A. for the 1984 Olympic Games ended in fairly heavy losses in some areas because there was not enough follow-up maintenance. Although public support engendered in part by TreePeople's activities seems to be helping the funding situation for the L.A. Division of Street Trees, trees are visited only about once every six years. Without neighborhood groups committed to caring for trees during establishment years, TreePeople found many tree plantings were unsuccessful.

TreePeople is funded through its memberships (7,000 members), individual and corporate donations, foundation grants and a major grant, now in its second year, from the City of Los Angeles. The grant from the city has spurred a considerable staff expansion. TreePeople charges for its Citizen Forester training programs and for other training programs, such as the one to educate plant supervisors, who will be able to assist homeowners in the plantings for energy conservation, among other things. There is a $90 charge per tree to property owners for all neighborhood plantings.

The organization's board of directors makes important financial decisions and acts essentially in the capacity of a steering committee, as it makes decisions about what sorts of outside groups and activities TreePeople will get involved with. Because the TreePeople concept has been exported as far away as Australia as a model for environmental action through planting trees, the organization is increasingly approached to enter into partnerships for action of one kind or another.

Philadelphia, PA: Philadelphia Green
Population: 5,963,000
Program Type: Private

Philadelphia Green was established in 1976, as a special undertaking of the Horticultural Society to provide education and practical development in moderate-to low-income communities within the city. The intention is that community organization point the way toward stabilizing and revitalizing neighborhoods that are frequently in blighted areas. The organization emphasizes both street tree plantings and "lot-scapes," or gardens created where buildings have been razed, frequently as a consequence of fire. There are some 17,000 vacant lots in the city.

The organization is well-established and frequently publicized, and has no lack of requests for help. Typically, once Philadelphia Green begins working with a neighborhood, the process is to identify important community leaders and create a program plan in accordance with what the community seems to want and need. Lot-scapes can be strictly ornamental or they can include vegetable gardening and play areas. Philadelphia Green (financed by the Horticultural Society, foundation grants and corporate funders) pays for plantings. It has fluctuated back and forth over the years between requesting that community volunteers help plant projects and simply requiring that communities attend an educational workshop before qualifying for a planting.

There is still no staff consensus as to which is most appropriate, considering the lack of resources apparent in many project communities.

The tree planting arm of the program will expand in the near future, under the auspices of a local foundation, as the organization joins forces with the city to coordinate the planting of 4,000 trees in four years in neighborhoods where redevelopment projects have been completed.

The city's parks department, called Fairmont Park, after the city's largest park, usually regulates the tree planting activities of Philadelphia Green. The department, to the extent of its limited budget, plants street trees throughout the city and does what it can to maintain them. Philadelphia Green, for its part, tries to maintain trees during establishment years with a summer program of inner city youth trained as pruners. Then, it educates communities through workshops and printed material about the need to care for trees in the absence of regular city maintenance.

"The life expectancy of street trees in this sort of urban setting is seven to ten years," said Jonathan Frank. "It may be that maintenance over the long term is not the issue we tend to think it is. These may become disposable trees."

The organization includes a paid staff of 35. Hundreds of volunteers have been involved over the years in planting and caring for trees and gardens. The staff mounts a Junior Flower Show program in schools throughout the city each year. It also organizes a Harvest Show each fall to show off produce and flowers grown in its own community gardens.

6

Susan Davis
Phil Martien
Neil Sampson

Planting and Light-Colored Surfacing for Energy Conservation

People have been using trees and light-colored surfaces to cool their houses and communities for hundreds of years. That doesn't mean we all know how to do it, however. In the industrialized world, especially, we have come to rely more and more on mechanical cooling systems—including fans and air-conditioners—to counter high temperatures. Traditional methods have been forgotten, and others simply are not applied.

This chapter is designed as an introductory guide to the basic steps of planning strategies for landscaping and light-colored surfacing for homes, neighborhoods, or communities. It includes discussions of both street trees for communities and neighborhoods, and single trees for residences. Again, the dearth of practical experience with light-colored surfacing strategies means that the emphasis in this chapter is, by necessity, on trees.

Figure 6-1.
City streets: Planting more trees on the streets could supplement our mechanical cooling systems.

Landscaping For Energy Conservation

Regardless of species, size, or age, all trees depend on soil, water, and space for survival. Proper planting requires detailed species selection, careful site selection and preparation, and continuous maintenance.

With proper planning and knowledge, planting trees to reduce energy needs can be a fairly smooth operation. But the emphasis needs to be on "planning" and "knowledge." Creating an efficient urban forest takes more than digging holes in the ground and plopping in young trees. Trees are living things. As such, proper planting requires detailed species selection, careful site selection and preparation, and continuous maintenance. Each of these, in turn, requires time, effort, attention, and, of course, funding.

This is especially true for trees in the city. Trees in the wilderness grow fairly easily, impeded mostly by disease, pests, and dramatic climatic events. Urban trees, by contrast, suffer from a number of human-caused stresses. Air pollution, water pollution, soil compaction, and space confinement all make it difficult for a city tree to grow as well or as long as its country cousin.

What Trees Need

Regardless of species, size, or age, all trees depend on certain elements for survival. They need soil for mechanical support, nutrients, and moisture. They need the heat and light provided by sunlight. They need sufficient amounts of air, which supplies oxygen and carbon dioxide. They need space above-ground, so their trunks and crowns can grow. And they need space below-ground, so their roots can grow to find air and water.

Figure 6-2.

Sample guidelines for planning tree planting: The American Forestry Association proposes new tree planting techniques that allow roots to expand beneath pavement and water to drain properly.

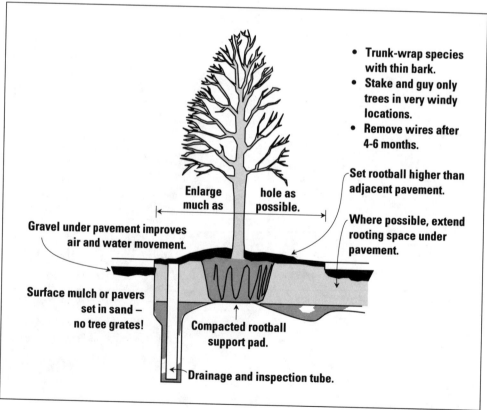

- **Trunk-wrap species with thin bark.**
- **Stake and guy only trees in very windy locations.**
- **Remove wires after 4-6 months.**

Set rootball higher than adjacent pavement.

Where possible, extend rooting space under pavement.

Enlarge **hole as**
much as **possible.**

Gravel under pavement improves air and water movement.

Surface mulch or pavers set in sand — no tree grates!

Compacted rootball support pad.

Drainage and inspection tube.

Source: Moll and Ebenreck, 1989

These needs seem basic. But in an urban environment, each can come in short or faulty supply. Soil is often compacted, contaminated, or has poor drainage. Sunlight can be blocked by tall buildings. Air supplies can be so polluted that the trees, while they do us the favor of absorbing particulate matter, begin to wither and die. Above-ground space can be reduced by buildings and utility lines, and below-ground space can be reduced by underground wires, building foundations, compacted soil, and retaining walls. In addition, damage caused by vandalism or accidents can hurt a trees' chances for survival.

Cities are cities regardless of our good intentions. It is impossible to mitigate these basic urban conditions. But with proper species selections, and with proper site selection and preparation, you can make a match that is more viable than planting a fragile tropical tree in Chicago's busiest downtown intersection, and then hoping it will survive unattended.

In addition to design considerations (including crown shape, blossom and foliage color, scent, and cluster density), we need to consider soil conditions, water quality, and space availability during plans for planting. Throughout the process, we must also consider the needs of the ultimate mature tree, rather than those of a seedling or sapling. A mature tree has different needs than its youthful predecessor.

Soils

Soils need to be clean from toxic substances, and fairly uncompacted. In many instances, you may have to mix in soil that is looser than what exists on site. The ideal soil is deep enough and drains well enough to prevent rapid changes in temperature, oxygen, and water content. It is also stable enough to support your tree. In addition, it may help to erect barriers around the tree to prevent pedestrians from walking or sitting on the soil. Any barrier, however, must be placed so that it damages neither the roots nor the trunk of the tree.

Water

Water needs are a serious consideration in any tree-planting program. Many cities have serious water shortages for much of the year. Most cities have problems with drought in a tree's microclimate, for compacted soil, sidewalk, and pavements all resist water absorption, thereby depriving a trees' roots of much-

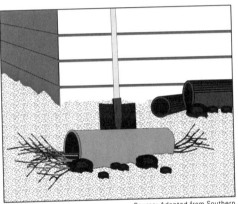

Figure 6-3.
Avoid planting trees right next to drainage pipes.

Source: Adapted from Southern California Edison Company, 1990

Figure 6-4.
Trees need to be placed a good distance away from concrete sidewalks.

Source: Adapted from Southern California Edison Company, 1990

Source: Moll and Ebenreck, 1989

Figure 6-5.

Improper tree planting: The planting procedure used in most cities today entombs tree roots and contributes to the tree's early death.

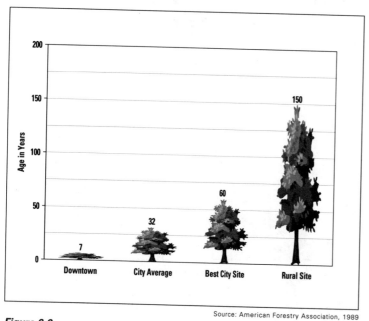

Source: American Forestry Association, 1989

Figure 6-6.

Comparison of tree longevity relative to location: In general, urban trees have not lived as long nor grown as tall as their rural cousins. Careful planting and maintenance, however, can help our urban trees flourish.

needed moisture. Using loose soils, instead of compacted ones, and using brick, instead of cement, can help alleviate this problem. So too can using any one of a number of "injector" irrigation technologies, which get the water right down into the roots of a tree. (See Chapter 4 for a more thorough discussion of balancing water needs with energy conservation.)

Space

Space considerations reign pre-eminent among the obstacles faced by urban foresters. Trees have to compete with buildings and utilities above ground, and with utility lines, building foundations, and sidewalks below-ground. Planting trees with the proper crown shape can help with above-ground concerns. Planting trees in containers can help with below-ground difficulties, but trees can become root-bound that way, and in colder climates, they lose the thermal heat of the earth. This can be crucial to their survival in winter months. Again, it is best to confer with a horticulturist on these matters. He or she will know what is best for your city trees in general, and for selected sites in particular.

General Planting Guidelines
Finding A Site

Generally speaking, three kinds of trees are available for planting: rural trees, street/park trees, and shade trees. Rural trees sequester carbon dioxide, a greenhouse gas said to contribute to ozone depletion. Street and park trees help cool communities through evapotranspiration. Shade trees, in addition to evapotranspiration, can reduce air-conditioning needs for an individual building by shading roofs, walls, windows, and air conditioners. Both shade trees and street/park trees also help reduce the amount of carbon dioxide in the atmosphere by lowering electricity demand.

The following guidelines were compiled from work by John Parker of Florida International University, E. Gregory McPherson of the U.S. Forest Service, Gordon Heisler of the U.S. Forest Service, and researchers at Lawrence Berkeley Laboratory. These can be included in city ordinances, or distributed as public information.

Shading The Air Conditioner

1) Air conditioning is the primary component of electrical peak demand. The single most cost-effective way to reduce your cooling needs is to shade the building's air conditioner and the immediate area around it. Air conditioners become less efficient as temperatures get higher. Preliminary measurements show that planting trees or erecting a trellis covered with vines around an air conditioner can reduce air temperatures around it by 6 or 7°F. This can increase the efficiency of the air conditioner by about 10 percent during peak periods (Parker, 1983).

2) To cool your air conditioner, plant several trees, so that after a five-year growth their canopies will completely shade the air conditioner and the adjacent area during mornings and afternoons throughout the entire cooling season.

Shading The Building And The Adjacent Ground

1) Because heat transfer through walls (particularly concrete and brick walls) causes a delayed impact on air conditioners, plant trees so they will shade the east- and south-facing walls to reduce peak period consumption. Plant other

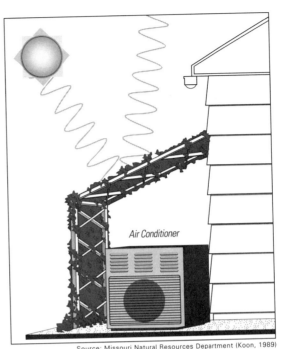

Source: Missouri Natural Resources Department (Koon, 1989)

Figure 6-7.
Shading the air conditioner with a vine-covered trellis or trees can provide enough shade to make a noticeable difference in temperature.

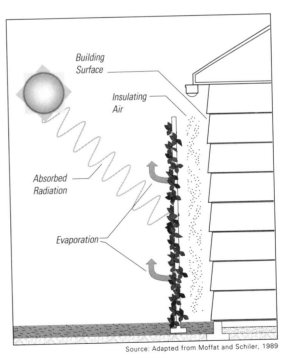

Source: Adapted from Moffat and Schiler, 1989

Figure 6-8.
Vines provide shade and evapotranspiration benefits. Use them while young trees and shrubs mature.

A few tips on space:

1) Increasing the size of the initial hole dug for a tree benefits its health throughout its entire lifetime. No studies have determined the ideal size. But a number of studies have shown that holes of less than 100 cubic feet cannot sustain long-term growth for mature trees 10-15 feet tall.

2) In general, the branches of trees need to be ten feet higher than sidewalks and fourteen feet higher than streets to maintain space for passersby.

3) Studies have shown that trees planted in open lawn areas which are *near* to paved areas, rather than *in* them, fare better than trees planted in constrained tree pits.

4) Similarly, trees protected by tree grates and tree guards tend to be less healthy than those standing free. Not using these protectors saves considerable amounts of money—and the lives of a considerable number of trees.

trees along the west wall to reduce air-conditioning needs during the late afternoon and evening after the period of electrical peak load. Air-conditioning energy use can be reduced 40 or 50 percent, or even more, by shading windows and walls.

2) The ideal pattern for shading walls is to plant trees so that, near maturity, the limbs reach within five feet of west or east walls and overhangs, and three feet of south walls or overhangs. Carefully placed trees provide optimal shading patterns and create cool microclimates directly adjacent to the house. Beware of planting trees too close to the building. Roots can damage the foundation, and large limbs can cause severe damage if they fall.

3) Similarly, place tall shrubs within four feet of west, east, and south walls, so that the inside edge of the hedge will reach within one foot of the walls within four years. While your trees and shrubs are still young, consider planting vines along the walls for direct shading. While less effective than trees or shrubs, they are a worthwhile substitute while those are coming of age.

4) To further optimize cooling, plant an understory of shrubs and groundcovers, especially if the trees are already surrounded by concrete and asphalt. Similarly, planting trees in clusters helps them keep each other cool.

5) If you have a solar collector on your house, try not to shade it during the day, even by deciduous trees.

Influencing Wind Movement

You also can plant trees to influence wind movement around and through a residence. The idea here isn't so much to reduce winds, as they can help cool your home, as to influence the wind's circulation patterns.

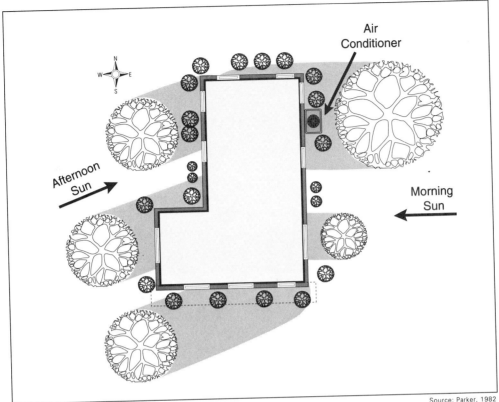

Air
Conditioner

N
W   E
S

Afternoon
Sun →

← Morning
Sun

Source: Parker, 1982

Figure 6-9.
Sample residential land-scape: Large trees are planted on the west and south sides to cast the maximum shadows and on the east side to shade the air conditioner. Shrubs planted on all sides of the house help to reduce wall and soil temperatures.

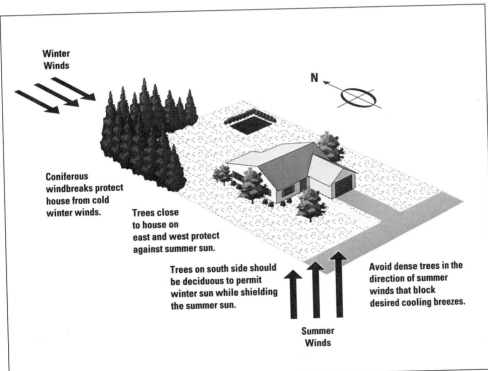

Winter
Winds

N

**Coniferous
windbreaks protect
house from cold
winter winds.**

**Trees close
to house on
east and west protect
against summer sun.**

**Trees on south side should
be deciduous to permit
winter sun while shielding
the summer sun.**

**Avoid dense trees in the
direction of summer
winds that block
desired cooling breezes.**

**Summer
Winds**

Source: Huang, 1990

Figure 6-10.
Strategic planting dia-gram: Trees in temper-ate climates must be chosen and planted to shield a house from both the hot summer sun and the cold winter winds.

Planning Shade

A simple tool for shade planning that arborists might use is the "solar path diagram." These are available for each four degrees of latitude. The diagrams provide a general sense of how to manage trees for shading and the times when a tree will shade a particular point of a house.

Shade on windows is especially important. Determining how a window is shaded by an existing tree throughout the year can be done by standing at a point near the middle of the window and sketching in the tree outline on a copy of the solar diagram. Angles can be estimated or measured with a compass and clinometer.

Plastic overlays for the diagrams are available to indicate amounts of radiation from the sun at different points in the sky for clear days. Data from the diagrams can also be used to find the length and direction of tree shadows on the ground.

Scale models of buildings and trees with a small sundial and a map to represent the sun also can be useful in shade planning.

—Gordon Heisler

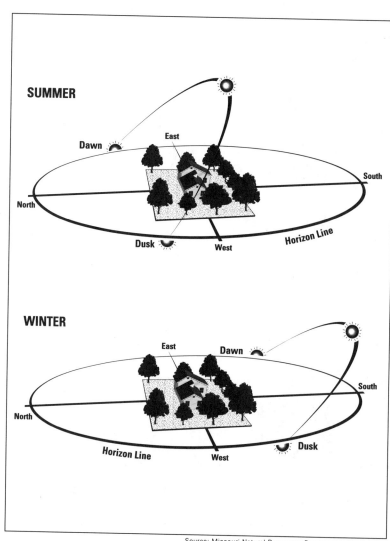

Source: Missouri Natural Resources Department (Koon, 1989)

Figure 6-11.

Solar path diagram: Shade diagrams such as this one can help homeowners plan the optimal energy-saving landscape.

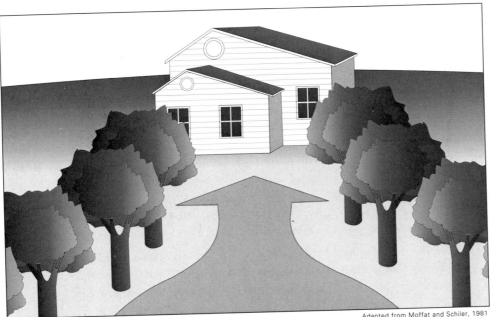

Figure 6-12.
Trees channel breezes: Homeowners with a good deal of land can plant trees so they will channel naturally cooling breezes.

Adapted from Moffat and Schiler, 1981

1) If you use minimal air conditioning in your home, you can position trees and shrubs so they funnel breezes into the windows, thereby maximizing natural cooling. First, determine the prevailing wind directions. Then prune back the low branches of surrounding trees to allow prevailing summer breezes to pass through the house.

2) If you use a lot of air conditioning, however, creating winds with tree position can actually increase air conditioning use, because warm breezes increase warm air infiltration and heat the interior. (This is generally only a problem in the Southwest). You can avoid this by placing shrubs and trees so winds are channelled into the dwelling when the windows are open, but away from it when the windows are closed.

In south Florida, for example, where Parker conducted his study, the prevailing summer winds are from the southeast. Consequently, air infiltration through the windows can be reduced by locating tall shrubs close to and on the north sides of east-facing windows and the west sides of south-facing windows. When the windows are opened during mild periods, these same shrubs will facilitate natural ventilation through the windows.

Choosing Species

The species you choose have to be appropriate both for the general climate of the city and for the microclimate of the exact site you select. Both of these factors are far too variable for this guidebook to tell you exactly which species to choose. A number of groups and software programs exist to help you match your criterion with what is available. Your local nursery, extension service, or university forestry department also can help you decide which species are most appropriate for your needs. The following, however, can give you a rough idea of what criterion to consider.

The species you choose have to be appropriate both for the general climate of the city and for the microclimate of the exact site you select.

1) Hardiness: Be sure to choose a plant that can survive the extremes of hot and cold in your city. The U.S. Department of Agriculture has a number of maps which delineate plant hardiness zones for the entire country. Be sure also to choose trees which resist disease and insect pests and which are fairly drought-tolerant.

2) Tree shape has a direct bearing on how well a tree grows in a selected site. *Oval* or *columnar* trees fit well in narrow spaces, often close to buildings, because they generally grow upward, rather than outward. They are not, however, a good choice for spaces near utility lines. *Round* trees with descending branches demand considerable amounts of space, but are beautiful to look at and play in. Round trees with ascending or lateral branches work well in spaces where trucks, pedestrians, and other traffic needs to pass beneath the tree. *Vase-shaped trees,* like elm and zelkova, are particularly well-suited to city streets because they grow up and out, while forming a shady canopy over streets, walls, and sidewalks.

3) Tree shape also directly affects how well a tree will shade a building. Generally, a canopy that is moderately thick is ideal. A very thick canopy blocks sunshine effectively, but it may make the interior of your building too dark.

4) If you are planting trees on the east and west sides of the building, plant trees that will grow tall if you are planting at a distance, as they will create a nice long shade in the early morning and late afternoon. If you are planting up close to the building, plant broad-canopied trees.

Figure 6-13.
Plant lines and plant forms: This figure illustrates vertical, weeping, and horizontal plant lines (above); and pyramidal, spherical, vertical ellipse, and horizontal ellipse plant forms (below). It is helpful to consider the lines and forms of trees in landscape design. Some plants may change as they mature: Crowns may spread or open, and limbs may be lost.

Source: McPherson and Sacamano, 1989

5) If you are planting along the northwest or northeast corners of the buildings, also use tall-growing species. In the late afternoon and morning, these trees will cast a long shadow along the north face of the building, thereby helping to cool it.

6) For trees on the south, southeast, and southwest corners of the building, plant deciduous species trees. In the winter season, these species will allow more sunlight to reach windows and walls than will evergreens. Be sure not to create a shade across south-facing windows as well, as this will block desired sunlight. In some northern areas, you may want to avoid planting trees on the south side altogether. That way, you will have access to as much winter sunlight as possible.

7) If you are planting in a parking lot, broad canopies are most effective as their shade covers the larger areas. It is also important to choose species with leaves, berries and blossoms that do not drip and stain. When you are planning the planting design, try to create islands of trees, rather than planting individual trees across the area. Trees clumped together share soil, help keep each other cool, and create a broader shade shape than do isolated trees. Such islands need to be curbed to protect the trees from bumper damage, soil compaction, and oil runoff.

8) Try to find out how much maintenance different trees require. The American Forestry Association has estimated that, on average, maintenance takes 40 percent of a tree program budget, 80 percent of which goes for trimming. Choosing trees that are vulnerable to disease and pests, or that require frequent pruning, can make your maintenance costs soar needlessly. Again, your local nursery or horticulturist can help you with this.

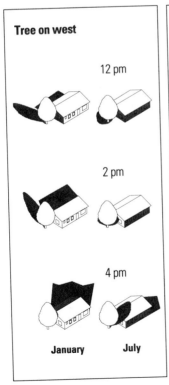

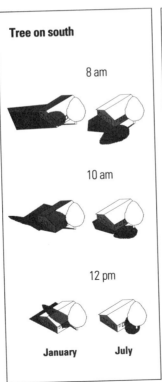

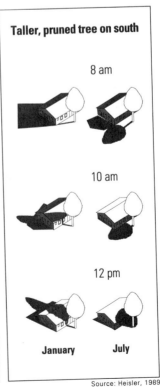

Source: Heisler, 1989

Figure 6-14.
These figures give a rough estimate of the ways in which shade patterns change on both a daily and seasonal basis. Be sure to correlate these with local conditions.

■■■■■■■

It's important to encourage community leaders and developers to save existing trees and include landscaping in any development plan.

Cooling A Neighborhood Or City

To help lower an entire city's temperatures through evapotranspiration, you need to plant as many street trees as possible in public as well as private spaces. Parking lots, plazas, street meridians, sidewalks, residential yards, corporate lawns, parks, shopping plazas, and many other niches are currently full of empty tree spaces.

New developments—which spring up constantly in many communities—are an excellent place to begin planting for heat-island reduction. Too often, however, these developments are just bulldozed in as quickly as possible, rather than being environmentally landscaped. Existing trees often are plowed under in this process, leaving a landscape bereft of their cooling and aesthetic benefits.

The difference between the two approaches reflects the attitude of city leaders, planners, and citizens toward the relationship between cities and nature. It's important to encourage leaders and developers to keep existing trees in developments, to plant replacement trees whenever the existing ones are destroyed, and to include landscaping as part of any development plan.

Unfortunately, many of our older cities were built with the latter attitude. But if new communities and developments learn from the mistakes of older cities, we can utilize the opportunities of the natural environment right from the outset. The result will be a better urban environment, at a lower long-term cost to the citizenry.

The best time to make a city fit into the natural environment, of course, is during the planning and development phase. For instance, new subdivisions in treeless areas can be required to plant large-growing trees as part of their development plan. Even very large trees can be transplanted into new urban development sites through skillful planning and execution. Proper placement of trees in new construction is as logical a part of development as locating streets and sewers and isn't overly expensive. In Milwaukee, WI, studies have shown that trees cost only about 2.2 cents of each construction dollar.

Obviously, that time is long past in many urban places. The best strategy, then, is to improve planting and management programs so as to mimic the natural world as closely as possible.

Significantly improving the ecology of the urban community calls for large trees, not small ones. The cooling of the urban heat island, the reduction of air and water pollution, the provision of wildlife habitat, and the visual impact breaking up the urban scene requires trees that can grow large and live long lifetimes. Rather than designing trees to fit inadequate urban spaces, we must design urban spaces to fit trees.

■■■■■■■

The single most effective way to reduce your cooling needs is to shade the building's air conditioner.

Parking Lot Tips

Parking lots can be shaded with little or no reduction in parking capacity. Extra planning to coordinate tree locations with lighting facilities, however, is needed. Adequate night-time lighting can be provided with 14-16 foot high light poles that are located at least 16-18 feet from trees. Tree planting space at least 5 feet wide can be borrowed from paved areas between rows of cars by allowing car bumpers to overhang planter space.

Source: Adapted from Parker, 1982

Figure 6-15.
(above) Parking lots without vegetation for shading are extremely vulnerable to the penetrating solar heat.

Figure 6-16.
(Below) Trees planted throughout a parking lot are far more effective "coolers" than those planted around the edges only.

Source: Adapted from Parker, 1982

Rather than designing trees to fit inadequate urban spaces, we must design urban spaces to fit trees.

Designs of streets should change to allow more greening. Modern engineers could use techniques like boulevards, that create a green path down the middle of the street and double the potential planting space for trees. Each street boulevard mile can handle about 400 trees rather than the 200 average of a normal street because the linear curb area is doubled. Unlike the business side of the street, which presents restrictions for trees ranging from sidewalks to power lines, the boulevard can concentrate on landscaping.

One example is the Pennsylvania Avenue Redevelopment effort in downtown Washington, D.C. Here, in the midst of an intensively developed urban area, the "nation's main street" has been landscaped with a variety of large street trees, in addition to landscaped parks and plazas in the middle of the boulevard. The development has converted a blighted urban street into a beautiful, tree-shaded boulevard.

This accomplishment is no accident. Specific tree spaces were created both above- and below-ground. Sidewalks and plazas were covered with blocks and bricks to allow water and air to enter the soil below. Aeration was provided by a tile system. An underground irrigation system was built to provide water when needed, and soil moisture monitoring to tell when the water should be turned on. The underground was opened up to allow tree roots to grow, rather than being tightly compacted.

Communities, in other words, have options. They are not without costs, but sound investments that result in long-lived, healthy forests are nearly always more cost-effective than their alternatives.

Figure 6-17
On Pennsylvania Avenue in downtown Washington, D.C., pedestrians enjoy a changing landscape featuring boulevards lined with trees.

Resources

There are many resources that can help to guide you through an urban tree-planting program. The American Forestry Association's Global Releaf program provides guidance on site selection and species selection to groups wanting to up the arboreal ante in their community. Los Angeles' TreePeople has a plethora of resources to help citizens start their own programs. Two California utilities, Pacific Gas and Electric and Southern California Edison, have developed planting guidelines (Appendix F includes an excerpt of a pamphlet by SCE on tree planting). There are also a number of governmental and private tree-planting programs that can help you get started. Refer to Chapter Five for a listing and analysis of tree-planting programs all across the country.

In addition, there are several computer inventories available. These all-in-one services analyze your street tree needs, develop preliminary plans for your city, and create planting and maintenance programs. Some services also provide planting and maintenance services.

Extending tree lifetimes five to ten years can more than double the value they bring to the community.

Plant New Trees, But Keep The Old

Planting young trees in your community can be an inspiring task. But preserving old ones is an equally inspiring—and more lucrative—strategy. Although tree care funds are most effective when spent on young and middle-aged trees, in actual practice, removing and repairing dying or damaged trees often soaks up most of the city budget. Indeed, one researcher estimates that of the average $10.62 forestry programs spend per tree per year, trimming amounts to about 30 percent of the budget, tree removal about 28 percent, and planting about 14 percent.

The economic value from an urban tree rests largely in its shading, cooling, and pollution-reducing effects. That means an urban tree continues to gain in value so long as its crown continues to grow and spread. New trees cannot develop these beneficial environmental effects for decades. This means that cities that can extend life spans of urban trees through improved care programs may find that urban forestry budgets are more effectively used and that total values from the forest are magnified. Indeed, extending tree lifetimes five to ten years can more than double the value they bring to the community.

Successful preservation will depend, in part, on local legislation governing development and re-development activities. For instance, in forested areas, developers can be required to preserve trees, and to protect them from harm during development due to machine damage, soil compaction, root cutting, or over-filling soils that smother tree roots. But legislation doesn't cure all ills. Citizens have to take an active part in ensuring the survival of their city's older trees.

—*Neil Sampson*

Finally, while we cannot tell you how to plant trees in this manual (it's a subject on which volumes have been written), we have included a short article from the American Forestry Association at the back of this manual to act as a primer (See Appendix E.)

Choosing Places For Light-Colored Surfacing

At present, there is little public awareness of the benefits of albedo modification. Although most people are aware that dark colors absorb more solar heat, there is little understanding about what constitutes high-albedo surfaces, and virtually no awareness that massive albedo changes can affect the temperatures of entire cities or neighborhoods. Similarly, few people realize that simple changes in albedo levels can reduce home energy use by 10 to 50 percent (see Chapter Three). The lack of public awareness of the benefits of increased urban albedo is reflected in the absence of research into the long-term characteristics of high-albedo materials, or the development of alternative building materials with higher albedo. Nevertheless, we can begin to identify surfaces, methods, and potential problems with some degree of accuracy.

Walls

Some surfaces are easier to modify than others. Building walls are the simplest and cheapest surfaces for albedo modifications. Since many buildings are routinely painted every 10 years or so, changing the albedo of walls is simply a matter of substituting a high-albedo paint for a darker one during repainting. Moreover, some paint companies are now beginning to list reflectivity on their product labels.

Changing the albedo of roofs and paved areas can be more costly because it may require the use of more expensive materials. In addition, the energy benefits may not continue over time due to product degradation or dirt accumulation. These questions are addressed in Chapter Four.

Roofs

For the purposes of this section, we divide roofs into those with steep or gentle pitches. The most common materials used for steep roofs are shingles made of asphalt, wood shakes, or concrete tile, and usually left unpainted and dark. The albedo of a shingle roof can be changed by either painting, which is uncommon but certainly possible, or replacing it with lighter-colored tiles during re-roofing.

Some of these options incur no additional costs. For example, installing a light-colored shingle roof is no more expensive than installing a dark-colored one. Some options, however, do cost more. A concrete tile made of white cement, for instance, is considerably more expensive than a tile made of normal cement, because the white tile is a specialty material.

Other options are expensive because they require otherwise unnecessary modifications. For example, painting a roof only to improve its albedo would cost at least an additional 20 to 30 cents per square foot. This obviously wouldn't be as cost-effective as changing color in the course of normal re-roofing.

Gentle-pitched roofs (with slopes of less than 4 inches per foot) are generally made of tar, bitumen, or asphalt. The costs for increasing the albedo for such roofs are about the same as those for dark roofs. Since it is common practice to protect the roof membrane with a protective coating, it is possible to increase the albedo by simply using lighter-colored roofing gravel or reflective paint. If this is done during re-roofing, increasing the roof's albedo would incur no additional costs.

Changing the albedo of a roof gives other benefits besides reducing cooling energy consumption. First, high-albedo roofs can protect an asphalt roof from the damaging effects of ultraviolet (UV) radiation. Second, because the high-albedo surface keeps the underlying roofing materials cooler, the roofs will tend to slide less.

Changing the albedo of a roof gives other benefits besides reducing cooling energy consumption. First, high-albedo roofs can protect an asphalt roof from the damaging effects of UV radiation. Second, because the high-albedo surface keeps the underlying roofing materials cooler, the roofs will tend to slide less.

Roads And Pavements

Paved surfaces like roads, playgrounds, and school yards can be lightened either by resurfacing or repaving. Resurfacing uses an asphalt mixed with aggregate, and typically adds only an inch or so to the existing surface. Many cities are resurfaced periodically to extend the life of a street or parking area. If the added aggregate is light, a thin layer of asphalt or a chip seal is a good way to increase the albedo of a paved surface.

Slurry seal, an aggregate of fine particles mixed with asphalt, is also often used on paved surfaces. Slurry seal typically has low cost and low albedo, because of its dark materials. Lighter-colored slurry seals are manufactured in Europe and have been used on tennis courts, plazas, and road shoulders, but the costs of such seals in the United States have not been investigated, nor have their albedos been measured.

If a paved surface is structurally damaged and must be replaced, or if a new surface is being constructed, either asphalt or concrete can be used at equivalent costs. Replacing asphalt with concrete, called "whitetopping," results in a slight increase in albedo. Rolling a light-colored aggregate onto the top few centimeters of an asphalt cement is slightly more expensive, but produces a higher albedo, especially after the surface has been slightly worn. The most expensive option for increasing albedo is to use white cement for the top inch or so of a cement pour.

Summary

A variety of measures can be taken to increase the albedo of a city, including:

For Walls :

1. Use light-colored paint during routine painting.

For Roofs:

1. Replace dark-colored shingles with light-colored shingles.

2. Paint dark shingles with a lighter color.

3. Add light-colored rocks to gently-sloped roofs.

4. Add light-colored aggregate to the roofing material. This extends the life of the roof by protecting it from UV radiation and preventing membranes from slipping.

For Paved Surfaces:

1. Use a light-colored aggregate in the asphalt. After weathering and road wear, the aggregate will be exposed.

2. Use a light-colored slurry or chip seal when resurfacing, if such materials can be found for reasonable prices.

3. Use a concrete surface with a light-colored aggregate, instead of asphalt.

Conclusion

While vegetation and light-colored surfaces are cleaner, cheaper, and more attractive than a mechanical cooling system, they do require more forethought before being used. This chapter has given enough guidelines to begin preliminary planning. If we are to successfully cool our communities, however, we need also commit ourselves to communicating with other residents and business owners about vegetation and light surfaces on a broader scale.

 Further Reading

There are many resources available to help citizens plant both on their private lands and in their communities. The American Forestry Association, the U.S. Forest Service, state Cooperative Extension Services, and local nurseries, horticulturists, and universities can all help you choose species and sites wisely. For specific information on landscaping to save energy and reduce heat islands, see the following works by Heisler (1984 and 1986), Meier (1987), Moffat and Schiler (1981), and Parker (1982). For general information on urban forestry, see AFA publications, Moll (1989), and publications from TreePeople, Lipkis (1990), and other local groups. In addition, the Proceedings from the Urban Forestry Conferences of the AFA are excellent collections of writings on the physical, social, economic, and political aspects of urban forestry.

7

Fred Patterson

Ordinances

Why Ordinances

Once it has been determined that an urban community's temperatures are rising, the next obvious question is "What can we do?" Heat islands are exacerbated, however inadvertently, by the actions of thousands of homeowners, landlords, and business owners. That means any remedy must be far-reaching to be effective. However, because most actions that cause increased temperatures originate on private property, policy makers need to consider issues of privacy and freedom of choice. This can be a difficult balance to find.

In general, a strategy for lowering temperatures by planting trees and lightening surfaces could be based on an overall plan which ensures public support and understanding. Education programs about the costs of increased temperatures and its possible solutions can inspire people to participate. Education alone, however, does not guarantee action.

Ordinances can lend guidance and authority to broader surfacing and planting programs. By providing a legal framework for action, setting consistent standards, demonstrating community support (if it was put to vote), and enforcing compliance, ordinances are effective in ways that even the best educational programs cannot be. In addition, a well-written municipal ordinance applies to all parties equally—even those like large, out-of-town developers with no incentive to cooperate—while taking issues of private property and freedom of choice into consideration.

An ordinance is only useful when it complements a broader plan by providing a legal framework for mitigation and by demonstrating community support. An ordinance which is highly intrusive, difficult to comprehend, or difficult to follow works against the overall program by provoking resentment and resistance. For this reason, ordinances should mandate only those steps which the majority of citizens consider acceptable. More intrusive or complex measures would be encouraged through education. After citizens are familiar with the issues and stakes involved, ordinances can be expanded to become more comprehensive.

Education alone does not guarantee action. Ordinances can lend guidance and authority to broaden heat-island programs.

Using Existing Ordinances

Questions of standards, flexibility and penalties are the foundations of any ordinance, and must be clearly resolved before putting the ordinance before the public.

Existing urban forestry ordinances provide both legal frameworks and ethical precedents for regulating vegetation on private property. Ordinances regarding trees have existed since the industrial revolution. Today, 70 percent of incorporated Californian cities have some kind of tree ordinance. None are designed specifically for the mitigation of urban heat islands, but many provisions in these ordinances apply exactly to heat-island reduction—or could complement that reduction.

For example, many ordinances preserve existing trees and require that a minimum number of trees be planted in each parking lot for aesthetic reasons. These trees undoubtedly prevent some warming of the city, even though that is not the purpose of the ordinance. Similarly, the Model Energy Conservation Landscaping Ordinance (shown in Appendix D), developed by Dr. John Parker, at Florida International University, and directed primarily towards energy conservation through landscaping, contains all the provisions necessary for reducing the urban heat-island effect. Since any heat-island mitigation strategy will involve trees, it is a good idea to place an ordinance targeted at reducing heat islands within an overall municipal tree ordinance.

As of today, few, if any, albedo ordinances exist in the United States. Because of this lack of precedent, the first mitigation step probably should not be a comprehensive ordinance. Albedo restrictions are an unusual reduction in the rights of property owners. Whereas tree ordinances require property owners to take action that beautifies and adds value to their property, albedo restrictions require homeowners to take actions that might lessen the aesthetic value of their holdings. Such programs engender opposition. On the other hand, an educational program encouraging albedo modification can alert property owners to the monetary and health benefits of reducing individual energy use and mitigating heat islands.

Elements Of A Heat-Island Ordinance

An ordinance designed to lower urban temperatures would do the following. It would set explicit standards for buildings and landscaping and provide for penalties to property owners and developers who violate these standards. It would designate or establish an agency which will be responsible for interpreting and enforcing the ordinance. It would provide explicit definitions of what is and is not acceptable for use by the executing agency. It would also state the motivations and guidelines for such standards for interpretation by courts, affected parties, and the executing agency in cases where the standards cannot be applied literally. The ordinance may also designate or establish a citizen group to oversee the design of the plan which the executing agency will implement, and it may explicitly establish a city-wide heat-island mitigation program.

General Issues

Several general issues should be kept in mind during the development of this type of ordinance. Questions of standards, flexibility, and penalties are the foundations of any ordinance, and must be clearly resolved before putting the ordinance before

Sample Revised Existing Ordinance
Oak Lawn Special Purpose Zoning District—Excerpts
City of Dallas, Texas (1985)

Purpose:

To permit the establishment of development standards specifically tailored to meet the needs of this unique urban environment—an area recognized as having cultural and architectural importance and significance to citizens—standards designed to achieve buildings more urban in form, with an attractive street level pedestrian environment, with continuous street frontage activities in retail districts, with hidden parking, and with scale and adjacency standards appropriate to character of adjoining neighborhood development; to restrict future use of property from some less compatible uses; to use the existing zoning density as a base from which to plan development and to provide for increased density as a bonus for the inclusion of residential in mixed-use projects in commercial zones; to discourage variances or zoning changes which would erode the quantity or quality of the single family neighborhoods, or would fail to adhere to the standards for multifamily neighborhoods and commercial areas or would fail to contribute to the overall objectives of the plan; and to require more extensive landscape/streetscape with new construction.

Sample provisions in the revised standards:

For Multifamily—1 Standards:

Provision requiring parkway/streetscape improvements: trees planted, minimum 3-1/2 inch caliper, 25 feet on center within first 5 feet back of curb; with 20 percent of areas, curb to property line, designated parkway planting area and available for growth of vegetation; and with a minimum 4 feet width sidewalk between tree plantings and lot line. (Parkway Landscape Permit required from the Director of Public Works)

For Multifamily—2 and 3 Standards:

Provisions requiring front yard and total site landscaping, parkway/streetscape improvements, parking screens, and landscape plan submission same as Multifamily—1 Standards.

For Office—1 and 2 Standards, General Retail and Light Commercial Standards, and Heavy Commercial and Industrial—2 Standards:

Provisions requiring parkway/streetscape improvements: minimum 3-1/2 inch caliper trees planted 25 feet on center within first 5 feet back of curb and with a minimum 6 feet width walk requirement. (Parkway Landscape Permit required from the Director of Public Works)

—City of Dallas, Department of Planning and Development

the public. The manner in which these issues are resolved will largely determine the effectiveness and intrusiveness of the ordinance. Therefore, the following issues must be resolved, while providing local citizens with as much flexibility and privacy as they require.

Performance Standards Versus Prescriptive Standards

Ordinances generally set standards for minimal performance using one of two methods. Performance standards specify what level of performance (e.g., shading) is required to satisfy the ordinance. One ordinance in Sacramento, California, for example, requires tree planting that will shade 50 percent of a parking lot within 15 years. Prescriptive standards require a simple method to achieve a minimum level of performance to satisfy an ordinance. One Los Angeles, CA, ordinance requires that one tree be planted for every four parking spaces in a parking lot.

An ordinance need not rely exclusively on one method. Developing standards that can be satisfied by following either a prescriptive or a performance track allow flexibility to home owners and builders. By allowing mitigation by various strategies, affected people can choose the method most appropriate to their circumstances.

Figure 7-1.

Ordinances set standards for a minimum level of performance. In parking lots, for example, an ordinance could establish guidelines for the number of trees to be planted relative to the number of parking spaces.

Required methods would also give benefits other than heat-island reduction. A regulation requiring certain numbers of trees in every parking lot, for example, keeps cars generally cooler. This reduces energy use, hydrocarbon emissions from heated gasoline tanks, chlorofluorocarbon emissions (by alleviating the need for air conditioning within the car), and occupant discomfort.

Private Rights Versus Public Responsibility

City governments have the authority to set standards designed to protect and enhance public health, safety, morals, convenience and welfare, and they have police powers to enforce these standards. With the exception of restrictions on noxious plants and those constituting a fire danger, little precedent exists for intrusive regulation of vegetation on private property. Furthermore, except for some beautification ordinances, there is little precedent for the regulation of building color. Nevertheless, because much of the problem of rising urban temperatures originates on private lands, some intrusion may be necessary if a mitigation program is to be successful.

If a proposed ordinance is perceived as an unwarranted interference with a citizen's privacy and property, it will generate intense opposition. Designing an ordinance to fit the local temperament and to include measures which are easily followed helps reduce that resistance. It also may help convince residents that the city has their best interests in mind.

A good strategy in drafting provisions is to carefully select desirable measures, and then divide them into groups, depending on how intrusive the measures are. Very intrusive measures need not be mandated at all. Instead, they can be part of an educational program and offered as suggestions to the public. Municipal agencies could implement the most intrusive measures of the ordinance, such as extensive planting requirements, or prohibitions of dark-colored roofs and parking lots. Current residents should be subject to the least intrusive measures, such as limited planting requirements on resale, prohibition of tree removal without a permit, and albedo restrictions on flat, non-visible roofs. Planned developments and existing businesses fall somewhere in between on the spectrum and could be subject to extensive planting requirements and some restrictions on visible roofs. Such a division will encourage maximum reduction in the heat island, while minimizing the negative effects on unwilling citizens, thus minimizing opposition.

Flexibility Versus Effectiveness

An ideal ordinance gives citizens a choice of strategies, while remaining effective. Programs with a sophisticated array of options offer great flexibility, but they are sometimes hard to understand and implement. Programs that are easy to understand, however, may be too loose and therefore ineffective.

For instance, one way of ensuring flexibility is to use a point system. In both California's energy conservation building code and Parker's Model Energy Conservation Landscaping Ordinance, any action taken to save energy earns a certain number of points, based on the effectiveness of that strategy. The ordinance requires a minimum number of points before a building is given an occupancy permit. This is a good system for new buildings. But the sophistication and complexity of the point system makes it difficult to understand, which does not help the overall program.

On the other hand, if homeowners are required to plant a given number of trees (based on house size), but not told where to put them, the trees may end up only shading other trees and empty lots, instead of roofs, walls and air-conditioners.

One alternative to this dilemma is to require a given number of trees or shrubs on the east, south, or west sides of a house. Property owners can pick species and locations—within stated limits. An ordinance requiring, for example, that three trees, chosen from a list of appropriate species, be planted anywhere within ten feet of the east, west, or south sides of the house would be fairly simple to implement. Giving residents the opportunity to substitute several shrubs for one tree increases the number of choices available to residents. In general, this system allows maximum flexibility and ease of interpretation and compliance. Any reduction in effectiveness could be mitigated by simply requiring that more trees be planted at each household.

The costs of such a program would be minimal when compared with the total cost of constructing a new building. However, if such plantings were required at existing structures, the financial impact could be substantial on low-income home

Figure 7-2.
Flexibility may be one of the most appealing features of a good ordinance. When citizens can exercise choice about the types of trees or colors of paint, they are more likely to be enthusiastic about meeting the requirements of the ordinance.

owners. The expense of planting several trees may total more than a month's income for the elderly or others on fixed incomes. This is another indication that ordinance writers must be cautious when regulating the landscaping of existing houses. If such landscaping is required, a process for community-supported plantings or special exemptions for low-income property owners must be developed. One criteria listed in the ordinance for the granting of variances must be extreme financial hardship to the property owner.

Citizens feel less threatened by an ordinance with more latitude, because they retain the right to choose the manner in which they will live. Generally speaking, if community support is less than complete, it is better to design an ordinance that is flexible. Policymakers may find they have no choice in this matter, as people will accept nothing less. Effectiveness will be less than complete, but it is better to have a weak ordinance that has community support — and is part of an overall mitigation program designed to build public awareness — than a stringent ordinance that is unlikely to be followed—if it even gets passed.

The most effective ordinances will reduce heat islands by encouraging right actions, not by punishing wrong ones.

Positive Versus Punitive Ordinances

An overly punitive ordinance also is not effective. Cities may need ordinances to enforce heat-island reduction plans, but the most effective ordinances can reduce heat islands by encouraging right actions, not by punishing wrong ones. For example, an ordinance should emphasize tree planting, and not financial penalties for something like a dark roof. Similarly, the emphasis of heat island reduction programs and ordinances need not be enforcement. Instead, it could be the establishment and maintenance of a program that reduces the heat island with the enthusiastic cooperation of the public, not its coerced participation.

Key Items For An Ordinance

If you have never developed an ordinance before, the next section provides a good basic guide. But you should seek other guidance as well—either from more experienced people in your city government, or from various planning services currently available.

If you already have experience with ordinance development, this section gives

Figure 7-3.
The effectiveness of ordinances may be assisted by generating enthusiasm to co-participate.

you some ideas on viable—and sometimes necessary—provisions. Parker's ordinance developed for southern Florida (Appendix D), also provides excellent examples of possible provisions for a temperature reduction ordinance. Since every city has different climatic conditions, statutory limitations and traditions, however, all examples should be liberally interpreted and adapted to local conditions.

1. Long and short title.

"The Tree Planting and Light-Colored Surfacing Ordinance of the City of Anytown," or "Tree and Surface Ordinance."

2. Purpose.

States the intent of the ordinance for interpretation by the voters and the courts. For example, "To improve the health and welfare of the citizens of Anytown by reducing the summer heat island."

3. Findings of fact (optional).

For example: "The importance of energy conservation, the effect of the heat island on health and energy use, the possibility of energy shortages and the certainty of energy price increases, and the effect of light-colored surfaces and trees on the heat island."

4. Definitions.

Any and all terms used, including albedo (how it's measured and what standard is used); size of protected trees; condition of trees; protected, encouraged, and prohibited trees, etc. When defining a parking lot, include access roads and turnarounds and any other area of asphalt that is exposed to sunlight. If a point system is used, terms like "cooling trees" and "cooling bushes" (that is, those that are accepted as cooling a structure) should be clearly defined, based on minimum height and proximity to the surface to be shaded.

5. Establishment of authority.

Establishes or designates the authority(s) that will design and/or implement the city's program to reduce the summer heat island. Alternatively, the ordinance could merely designate several agencies, each responsible for implementing part of the program.

For example, the department responsible for building inspections may be designated as responsible for inspecting shading and roof albedo, while the Parks and Recreation Department is given the task of planting and maintaining trees on city property.

If the ordinance establishes a new authority, such as a Shade Tree Board or a City Forester, the ordinance could set qualifications for membership (e.g., "one botanist or horticulturist, one lawyer, one architect, one builder, one forester with five years experience, and two citizens of the community") and provide for their selection and replacement. It would set their compensation (usually none or car fare), and also set the pay and qualifications of any position established—or delegate these decisions to the shade tree authority or other authority.

The ordinance should discuss the authority of the executing agency (whether it is a Shade Tree Board and a City Forester, or any other city agency) to issue permits for planting and stop-work orders, withhold occupancy permits, and to enter private property to determine compliance with the ordinance and to remove hazardous trees.

If a master plan for heat-island reduction is not explicitly included in the ordinance, then authority to develop one can be delegated. In this case, the ordinance would include specific guidelines for such development, including acceptable and unacceptable measures for mitigation and stating what levels of intrusion onto private property are acceptable; criteria deemed sufficient to justify variances such as extreme economic hardship or unusually shaped property; and a discussion of to whom the ordinance will apply.

6. Definition of responsibility.

The ordinance must define the responsibilities of the agency(s) and property owners who participate in the mitigation program or who are otherwise subject to the ordinance. These responsibilities may include, for instance, the planting, maintenance, pruning, and removal of trees on municipal, public agency, and private lands. Similar issues must be covered for albedo, if it is addressed in the ordinance, including the installation and cleaning of light-colored surfaces.

In general, a municipal tree ordinance should establish title to and responsibility for all trees on public lands and for trees planted on private land to satisfy municipal requirements. An ordinance designed solely to reduce heat islands will have a similar scope.

Liability for damage due to tree planting, including vehicles hitting trees, pedestrians tripping on cracked sidewalks, injury to body or property from fallen limbs or trees, fires, and damage to sewers or utility lines is a very important issue. If it has not been addressed by an existing municipal tree ordinance, it must be addressed by the heat island ordinance.

7. Minimum standards.

The ordinance should set minimum requirements and specify when they must be met. The basic purpose of the ordinance is to facilitate management of city trees to minimize a heat island. But the ordinance need not be so restrictive that it makes

> **Note:** Establishing a new agency is rarely easy. Legal, procedural, and political problems can be daunting, especially for those who are inexperienced. The experience of those who have worked in tree-planting programs or who have set up other agencies will be vital to the creation of a shade tree or other type of tree-planting authority.

compliance difficult and thus lowers public support and participation. Nor should the ordinance be used to micro-manage the actions of the agencies' responsible for implementing it.

Instead, it can set broad policy aims and give an outline of acceptable methods of mitigation. Day-to-day management must be done according to the professional opinion of the person given the responsibility of carrying out the program mandated, who should be guided by the ordinance, and by any other authorized agency such as a Tree Board. Standards specific to trees can include:

a. Species restrictions/requirements/suggestions.

A general municipal tree ordinance may include restrictions on noxious species, species vulnerable to disease, or tall species beneath utility lines. A heat-island ordinance may further restrict species by requiring that trees used to meet its requirements grow to a minimum height—if the only requirement is that a given number of trees be planted. It also should list protected species if they are given special consideration in the ordinance.

If any of the provisions of the ordinance are based on shading, then the ordinance should list, or designate a resource that lists, the crown diameters of desirable species so that citizens can plan their landscaping. The ordinance lists recommended species along with characteristics.

b. Planting requirements.

The ordinance can specify which types of property are subject to particular provisions and where plantings must be made on each property. The ordinance also can specify whether existing structures are subject to its provisions, or only new construction and remodeling. In most cities, new construction will contribute only a small part of the problem, and so, unless existing structures are targeted, little will be done to alleviate the problem.

As discussed above, measures such as shading air conditioners that have the largest benefits at the least cost, should be applied to existing structures. More restrictive measures should be applied to businesses and new construction. If a system similar to the Model Energy Conservation Landscaping Ordinance is used, then this section should state the minimum number of cooling trees and bushes, or the minimum number of points, that are required for a building or a piece of property of a given size and type.

c. Prohibitions on planting.

The ordinance should prohibit planting where it blocks view of signs or natural scenery, and where it restricts access to solar radiation, including sunlight falling on solar collectors, on another property. Restricting solar access should be defined explicitly as shading a given percentage of a solar collector at a given time on a given day.

d. Protection of trees.

This area is generally a function of standard municipal tree ordinances, as are prohibitions on planting. However, the protection of existing trees is a valuable tool in the prevention of further urban warming. Existing trees are often large and effective shade trees, even if they are not ideally placed, historically significant, or locally endangered.

Provisions of an ordinance that prevent significant tree clearing during development and tree damage during construction are especially valuable. Such provisions include a prohibition of grading beneath the canopies of desirable trees, and a requirement that no trees be removed, topped, or severely pruned without a permit. Nurseries, silviculture, nuisance trees, emergencies, and utility work should be discussed and granted limited exemptions.

Since utility workers have no incentive to preserve existing trees, an explicit standard of tree pruning (no topping, for example, and no cutting of branches over 2 inches in diameter) should be part of the exemption.

Los Angeles county has adopted a weak prohibition against clearing historic trees. When developers clear oak trees, which the county is trying to preserve, they are required to make a contribution to a fund that supports the planting of oak trees elsewhere in the county. Although mature oak ecosystems are lost, the ordinance attempts to preserve the overall amount of trees. The heat-island ordinance should include criteria to be used in the evaluation of exceptions to such restrictions.

No Net Loss of Forest

The "no net loss of forest" idea has been suggested in connection with urban and community forests, where it is entirely possible to think about protecting, replacing or improving forests as a part of normal community growth and development. Clearly, some forest will be lost in the process. That is to be expected. But when development takes place on formerly open land, there is also the opportunity to convert such land into a community forest with a 50 percent or higher canopy cover. The result would be a net gain of forest cover for the region. So the question is logical: Can development ordinances in a growing region attempt to achieve a "no net loss" goal?

One region grappling with such a question is the Chesapeake Bay Region, where it has become widely recognized that many of the water quality problems afflicting the Bay are really land-based problems. The watershed, previously forested, now harbors millions of people, and the growth rate continues to climb. Can the Bay Region, with better growth management controls, support this growth without completely wrecking the Bay's aquatic ecosystem? That question is high on the priority list of regional leaders, and the "no net loss of forest cover" idea may be one aspect that gets a thorough testing in the process.

—Neil Sampson

e. Minimal standards for plantings.

The ordinance can contain a provision stating that all trees must be planted according to specific standards of size and grade if they are to be used to satisfy the ordinance's planting requirements. One example of such standards is the International Society of Arboriculture's Standard Municipal Tree Ordinance. But many local ordinances have more explicit and restrictive standards.

Responsibility for watering and other maintenance can be assigned in Section 5 of the ordinance. This section should set minimal standards for this care.

The ordinance can also define the minimal acceptable size of the planting area for one tree. That is, building and landscaping codes may need to be modified so that each tree has enough root space to survive. Constricted root spaces are a common cause of illness and death in urban trees. Standards specific to albedo modification include:

a. Surfaces to be modified.

As discussed above, if albedo modifications are required by ordinance, then they should be limited in scope because of their unusual nature and the potential for opposition. If you decide to include albedo measures in the ordinance, two areas that should be considered are asphalt coverings for flat roofs, and parking lots.

Flat roofs are not very visible, so little aesthetic harm can result from an ordinance that requires a final coating of light-colored sand. Light-colored materials are commonly used as the final layer on roofs because they save energy and because the roofing materials last longer when more light is reflected away from them. An ordinance would simply require that this practice be universal. It would affect a relatively small number of builders and business owners, since few single family homes have flat roofs.

Similarly, a surfacing requirement for parking lots would impact relatively few property owners, while providing a benefit for many. Parking lots should be an early target of an energy conservation program, because they make up a large area of many city centers.

Developing albedo ordinances is slightly more complicated than developing tree ordinances. Tree planting requirements for parking lots are quite common. Surfacing requirements designed to reduce heat buildup are not. Modified surfaces will be more obvious—and less aesthetically pleasing—to the general public than increased tree cover. Businesses may oppose such a provision if they think people will not like it (due to increased brightness or increased visibility of dirt, oil and trash), or if they anticipate increased maintenance costs on new or modified city-owned parking lots. This way, problems can be solved, and fears allayed, before the provision is forced on businesses.

b. Initial albedo required.

The ordinance can specify a range of acceptable values on a specified scale and the method used to determine compliance.

c. Minimal maintenance.

Since light-colored surfaces inevitably get darker as they weather and get dirty, the ordinance may specify what level of maintenance (such as cleaning) is required or the required level of albedo which must be maintained. Note that policing continued compliance adds a great deal to the cost of implementing the program.

d. Material restrictions.

Alternatively, the ordinance can restrict the materials and techniques that can be used to satisfy the ordinance. For example, if albedo is never checked after initial installation and no maintenance is required (which reduces the cost to the administering agency as well as to the business complying with the ordinance), the ordinance should prevent businesses from using materials with a short life-time.

8. Procedure and criteria for variances.

As previously discussed, the ordinance can set up a process in which variances can be granted by the administering agency and list the criteria to be used in granting them. This process will help to ensure that the aim of the ordinance is accomplished while preventing avoidable harm.

For example, variances could be granted for landscaping that approximates a natural ecosystem, regardless of the number of trees, since such ecosystems have value beyond their potential to reduce the heat island. In many areas, for example, native vegetation is locally endangered.

9. Process for appeals.

The ordinance can specify a procedure whereby anyone unhappy with the analysis done by the administering agency can appeal the decision. If a shade tree board or other citizens group is established, it can serve as a reviewing body.

10. Penalties for violations.

Penalties will vary depending on which provision is violated.

If planting is required during construction, then an occupancy permit can be denied until the administering agency is satisfied.

If existing trees are illegally removed, then replacement should be required, along with a fine sufficient to prevent illegal tree removal from becoming routine. A mandated replacement policy can stipulate that several trees replace each one illegally removed, for example by requiring that the cumulative circumference of the replacement trees be equal to the circumference of the tree removed.

A system that is easier to administer, especially if the diameter of the original tree is unknown, is to require that a given number of trees of a minimum size be planted for each one removed. Fines for illegal removal also encourage compliance.

If the ordinance requires a re-inspection to determine tree health, a daily fine can be levied when required plantings are removed, dead, or dying.

Any provisions concerning the albedo of construction materials can be implemented in the same way. For example, occupancy permits can be denied if required steps are not taken, and fines levied and replacement mandated if light surfaces are removed or darkened.

11. Provision for feedback and modification of regulations.

A reduction in urban temperatures is dependent on the public performing a variety of unaccustomed actions.

A shade tree plan, or other regulations derived from the ordinance, should be modified periodically, as experience is gained, and as the public becomes more educated about the issue. This allows adaptation to change in the community, and permits the regulations to be updated as needed. The ordinance should specify a procedure, and possibly a timetable, for such changes.

Public input is vital at this stage. Public hearings should be held by the administering agency or, preferably, by the group established to guide implementation of the ordinance such as the Shade Tree Board.

12. Effective date.

Many actions required by an ordinance for tree planting and light-colored surfacing require considerable advance warning (for example, planting trees in parking lots), since they must be included in construction plans from the beginning. Other actions, such as using light-colored surfaces on roofs, can be done with little advance notice. If a single implementation date is specified, it must be far enough in the future that projects that already have detailed construction plans are not affected.

Alternatively, the effective date could be set earlier, with exemptions provided to any project that has submitted detailed architectural or landscape plans for approval, or that submits them within a given time limit such as one month.

13. Severability.

The ordinance should state that each section is independent and if any section is found by the courts to be invalid, other sections are not affected.

Other Implementation Issues

1. Published information on albedo and plantings.

Ideally, the administering agency should design a workbook that is made available to the public, and which contains the criteria and standards which the agency inspectors will use to determine compliance.

A reduction in urban temperatures depends on the public performing a variety of unaccustomed actions. This means the public needs access to information which enables them to perform these actions: including the expected height, crown diameter, growth characteristics, water needs, and other facts about trees. Without this information, residents cannot choose the correct species for their needs.

In addition, those home and business owners who wish to comply with a heat island ordinance must have a way of determining whether specific measures will be satisfactory.

The ordinance or the administering agency can designate a resource which discusses all the issues involved in activities for reducing urban temperatures. That resource must be complete enough to serve as the sole information source for residents planning their compliance.

Ideally, the administering agency could design a workbook for the public that contains the criteria and standards which the agency inspectors will use to determine compliance.

For instance, when the city of Davis, California, implemented its energy conservation building code, it published a workbook with numerous examples, completed forms, lists of materials and their color value or insulative properties, and other information to help builders comply with the code.

Software designed to aid the selection of appropriate vegetation can also be made available in city offices or public libraries. Another method of assisting compliance is the labeling of building materials and paint according to albedo, and the labelling of nursery trees according to their expected height, crown shape, and other characteristics. This enables members of the public who do not have a workbook (for example, because they are not required to comply with any ordinance) to consider the issue and make an informed decision.

Figure 7-4.
The public needs access to information that clearly explains compliance criteria and standards.

Common Problems with Ordinances

1. No maintenance required.

After trees are planted, they require systematic follow-up care and watering—often for several decades. Without such care, a tree may not live to maturity or may only be a nuisance by interfering with utility lines, dropping limbs, or cracking sidewalks. No trees should planted as a part of a program to mitigate a heat island until the person responsible for follow-up care is designated. Often, this designation should be done through the ordinance.

2. Trees too small at maturity.

If inappropriate trees are planted, they will be too small at maturity to provide much shade, although they benefit the utility by not interfering with its lines. In addition, trees that are too small at the time of planting may not be able to survive the rigors of the urban environment. An ordinance should always specify the minimum size (at maturity) of acceptable trees, either by specifying species or crown diameter and height.

3. Trees too small at planting.

The ordinance also can set a minimum acceptable size at planting. If trees are too small, they will not provide continuous benefits. A related problem is that the

Figure 7-5.
Trees require systematic care and watering in order to reach maturity. The individuals responsible for follow-up can be designated in the ordinance.

minimum size of trees protected by ordinance is greater than the minimum size of tree required to be planted. An ordinance that requires new trees be planted to replace mature trees removed during construction may not actually protect those new trees. In other words, a developer can remove these new trees during later construction, since they are too small to be protected by the ordinance. This has reportedly occurred in southern California.

4. Landscaping is required, but not shading.

Landscaping must be designed to provide shade if it is to prevent a significant amount of warming. Many ordinances require plantings of various kinds, but even when ordinances require that trees be planted, they don't require that they be positioned in any particular way and they seldom require that enough be planted to make much of a difference.

5. Single-family homes are exempted.

It may be tempting to exempt single-family homes from a heat-island ordinance to garner public support. This is not a particularly effective strategy, however. Single-family homes consume a significant proportion of the electricity used for air conditioning. They also make up a large fraction of a city's area. If an ordinance is so unpopular that it will not be passed unless most citizens are exempted, then it is poorly written.

6. Community support is not achieved.

Community support is critical to the passage and acceptance of any new, unusual, and far-reaching ordinance.

Community input is required at the planning stage so that potential problems are discovered, and provisions inappropriate for the particular location are removed or modified. All affected parties should be consulted, and the more participation a group has in the process, the less likely it is to object to the results. If certain people are affected by the ordinance but have not been consulted about it and do not understand its specific provisions, they will, quite reasonably, feel threatened by it and oppose it.

Finally, community support is required after approval so that compliance and cooperation is achieved. The wide-spread adoption of non-mandated measures, such as those promoted by an educational campaign, are wholly dependent on community support.

The administering agency has a great deal of impact over how the ordinance is viewed by the community. Consistent enforcement, sincere attempts to explain ordinance requirements to the affected parties, and a reasonable delay period before implementation all will encourage support, or at least reduce opposition.

Figure 7-6.
Community input at the planning stages of ordinances is invaluable to both the community and the administering agency.

7. No review by legal council.

A legal review can trouble-shoot problems of legality specific to a particular city, such as separation of powers and improper delegation of funding decisions.

8. No long-range plans.

Urban temperatures have risen over decades as the result of thousands of individual actions. A single ordinance will not correct this problem overnight.

The mitigation of heat islands will require a community-supported program which includes an ordinance or two and an educational program. Such a program takes time to set up and more time before it shows success. Many strategies for mitigation are based on vegetation that takes years to mature and requires years of care. For these reasons, a program of tree planting and light-colored surfacing requires that plans be made further in advance than is typical in most city governments.

 Further Reading

Parker and Panzer's MECLO (shown in Appendix D) is very useful as an example of one method of implementing the points discussed above. While it is targeted at energy conservation, its provisions are equally useful in reducing a summer urban heat island. Again, like any model ordinance, it must be extensively modified to meet the needs of any particular location.

Since this ordinance does not discuss albedo, it may be used as part of a comprehensive heat island ordinance, or it may stand alone if albedo modification is encouraged through education, but not mandated in an ordinance. MECLO is not a standard municipal tree ordinance, and some concerns, such as explicit standards for tree planting, are not discussed.

For an example of a concise, standard municipal tree ordinance that addresses many urban forest issues, including issues of tree survival, but does not address heat islands or energy conservation, see Neely's work for the International Society for Arboriculture's model.

Vine's report on Davis discusses the implementation of a number of ordinances dealing specifically with energy conservation. For descriptions of ordinance implementation in general, see Parker, Weber, and Beatty.

8

Conclusions
And Recommendations

Trees And Light-Colored Surfaces Can Reduce The Impact Of The Heat-Island Effect

Actions by citizens to strategically plant trees and lighten building and pavement surface colors have the potential to reduce energy use for cooling and lower electrical bills. This may also help lower summer temperatures in our communities, thereby reducing the production of tropospheric ozone and improving the quality of our environment. By reducing the generation of electrical power, these actions also decrease the emission of carbon dioxide (CO_2), the most important greenhouse gas, and may help lower the risk of global climate change.

The Economic And Environmental Benefits Of These Strategies May Be Significant

We are confident of the ability of trees to provide cooling benefits, but know less about the potential value of light-colored surfaces. Likewise, we know little about the savings produced by the two in combination, but it seems that they may offer significant benefits at low cost or with net gains. The relative cost effectiveness of these strategies will differ by type, region, building stock, and current conditions. For example, planting trees for energy conservation will probably have the highest return when applied to older homes in the Sunbelt. The single most effective improvement that can be made is shading air conditioners.

If implemented, these activities may have large impacts on energy savings and pollution abatement at the national scale. A study by the National Academy of Sciences (NAS, 1991) indicates that planting trees and lightening the color of our urban surfaces may be able to save 50 billion kilowatt hours, or 25 percent, of the 200 billion kilowatt hours spent annually in the United States for air conditioning. Energy conservation at that scale would prevent the emission of 16-18 million tons of carbon (in the form of carbon dioxide) to the atmosphere. Lastly, successful implementation may also slow the rise in temperatures of our urban areas, which have been experiencing a steady rise over the last few decades.

Future Urban Scenarios
From One Scientist's Point of View

We can speculate briefly on how much we could cool a city if we really became concerned about the multiple and cumulative threats of local heat islands, global warming, smog, and expensive air conditioning derived from fossil fuel. Let's look at three possible scenarios for the Los Angeles metropolitan area over the next fifty years:

Status Quo

We continue development as usual, replacing orchards and fields with blacktopped roads and parking lots, building homes with dark colored roof tiles, and increase our fossil fuel use by 1 to 2 percent per year. By the year 2050, the local heat island will further intensify by 6°C, while global warming will have added another 1-4°C (Line A on graph). This will make the city warmer than any tropical city on the continent today.

Frozen Heat Island

In this scenario, the current inventory of trees and dark surfaces is held steady. No net loss of vegetation is permitted. All new roofs and roadways are light-colored. This halts the increase in the local heat island, but regional warming due to the greenhouse effect causes Los Angeles summers to grow increasing hot and smoggy (Line B in graph).

Heat Island Reduced to 1940 Levels

In this scenario, a concerted effort is made to reduce the local heat island

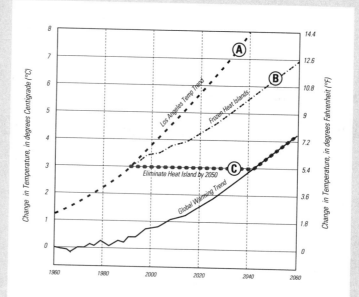

Figure 8-1.

Three scenarios of future Los Angeles temperatures, added to a forecast of global warming trend.

By 2050, under the business-as-usual "Los Angeles Temp Trend" (1° per decade growth in the heat island), downtown L.A. will be 18° hotter than it was in 1940 (A). With the L.A. heat island "Frozen" at its 1990 level, the city will still be 12° hotter (B). With a vigorous program of heat-island mitigation ("Eliminate Heat Island by 2050"), it's possible to entirely compensate for the effects of global warming in L.A. until somewhere around 2050 (C). Note: the global warming trend shown assumes an exponential greenhouse gas growth of 1.5 percent per year.

fast enough to compensate for global warming (Line C on graph). This will require large-scale planting of trees and vines, and not permitting the use of dark materials on either new construction or during resurfacing of roofs and roadways. The local heat island is reduced, but summer temperatures in Los Angeles stay constant because of global warming.

—Arthur Rosenfeld
Lawrence Berkeley Laboratory

Further Research Is Required To Quantify Benefits

Although preliminary measurements and computer simulations indicate significant potential for achieving many of the benefits we have described, more research is needed to confirm this. The Environmental Protection Agency, the Department of Energy, Lawrence Berkeley Laboratory, the Forest Service, the Department of Defense, and the American Forestry Association, together with other researchers and institutions, are beginning to measure these benefits, some of which have been difficult to quantify. As more results become available, it seems more evident that heat-island mitigation strategies such as trees and light-colored surfaces will significantly lower building cooling loads.

Even as this document goes to print, new data are becoming available that begin to quantify the effects that light-colored surfaces may have on energy use. Although a study by the Lawrence Berkeley Laboratory is preliminary and cannot be used to generalize about other types of buildings in other climatic situations, data show that one house in Sacramento, California realized a significant reduction in energy use for air conditioning when its dark roof was painted white. More work must be done before the results of this study are complete, and can be used to draw final conclusions about the value of light-colored surfaces.

As we have discussed throughout this guidebook, a number of aspects of energy use in communities and temperatures have yet to be explored. Following is a list of suggestions for in-depth research:

1) Direct Effects

Field measurements are needed on the direct effects of tree cover and light-colored surfacing in different climatic regions of the country, and on different types of buildings. These investigations should consider different types of trees and vegetation, and changes in the color and composition of roofs and walls. The primary focus of the measurements should be to document the direct energy savings, both for cooling and heating.

2) Indirect Effects

Field studies are needed to verify the indirect effects on air temperature at the neighborhood level of wide-spread planting and surface-color enhancement. A number of computer simulations have suggested that evapotranspiration from trees and the lowered temperatures on light-colored surfaces will produce lower ambient air temperatures, which will in turn result in lowered building cooling loads. Field studies would greatly assist in confirming these phenomena and quantifying the magnitude of the savings possible. Additionally, research is needed to determine the extent of changes in tree cover and surface colors that would be needed to lower temperatures in a given area by a given amount.

3) Potential Negative Effects

Research is needed on the possible detrimental effects of increased albedo, increased water vapor from evapotranspiration, and reduced natural ventilation potential caused by lowered wind speed. These evaluations must be carried out specifically for each weather type and for local conditions. The effects of increased emissions of volatile organic compounds (VOC's) from trees, such as monoterpenes and isoprenes, should be investigated.

4) Conflicting effects

Further research on the trade-off between heating costs rising as trees (both evergreen and bare deciduous trees) block winter sun, and cooling costs falling from increased summer shade would be helpful. Likewise, a determination should be made of where it is best, climatologically, to plant trees for wind-shielding to reduce heating-energy requirements. The balance between these effects will differ among different parts of the country. Finally, similar investigation is needed on the trade-off between light-surfacing for cooling benefits and retaining dark surfaces in areas where energy use is dominated by heating requirements.

5) Economic Analyses

Research is needed on the benefits and costs of tree planting and light-colored surfacing. Does landscaping and retaining mature trees increase the sales value of existing properties and new developments? Data are needed on the amount and type of vegetation required to influence values, and on the magnitude of value changes possible. We should investigate more precisely the magnitude of savings possible from tree planting and changing surface colors in different parts of the country. This should include quantification of the contributions of both direct and indirect effects towards reducing energy consumption. The goal should be to assemble national estimates, on a region by region basis, of the savings in energy, costs, and pollutants (and the attendant savings in health and welfare costs) of instituting these changes.

Specific information is needed on the cost of different types of planting stock, planting services, maintenance, and disposal in different parts of the country. Likewise, data are needed on the availability and cost of high-reflectivity paints, roofing materials, and paving materials. What is the trade-off between the initial cost, useful life, and maintenance cost of asphalt and cement surfacing for roads and other pavements. Are there similar trade-offs for dark and light-colored roofing materials and paints.

6) Long Term Concerns

Perhaps the single most important factor in the success of a community tree-planting strategy is whether or not the trees survive. Trees suffer the stresses of urban pollution, root compaction and insufficient root space, water stress, inadequate maintenance and care, and vandalism. Work is needed to develop ways to ensure tree health and survival. Strategies need to be developed to successfully implement the solutions, and to reduce stresses that contribute to or cause early mortality. Long-term concerns about light surfaces are whether they last longer than dark surfaces, whether the light surfaces degrade and get dirty, and what impact degradation has on reflectivity, and ultimately, on the reliability of this strategy.

7) Evaluation of Resources

In order to more precisely calculate energy savings and financial benefits, what mitigation strategies cost, and where they need to be done, data are needed on the current state of infrastructure, buildings, and landscaping in the United States. National inventories are needed of the condition of building stocks, roadways and pavements, and community trees, conducted on a community or regional basis.

8) Implementation

We need to know how best to motivate homeowners, businesses, utilities, and local and federal governments to establish implementation programs. What incentives are needed under varying demographic and regional conditions?

Citizens Can Affect Change If They Understand The Issues And Know That Opportunities Exist

Research on the effects of urban heat islands is coming at a time of great public concern about local and global environmental conditions. Air pollution, water pollution, and the possibility of global climate change all mandate that we decrease our energy use.

At the same time, our city sizes are growing at unprecedented rates. By the year 2000, 50 percent of the world's population will live in cities, where only 14 percent lived 100 years ago. Correlating population size to heat-island intensity is still inexact. It is clear, though, that heat islands intensify as urban areas grow. Already, urban temperatures in this country can be 8°F hotter than those in surrounding areas, and urban temperatures in tropical and sub-tropical countries are as much as 15°F higher than their surroundings. Furthermore, if global temperatures continue to rise as predicted by many scientists, the net increase in summer temperatures could be even greater.

A first step is to demonstrate the principles we have discussed here and prepare community infrastructures. We need to learn how best to develop light-colored roadways, to formulate and label high-reflectivity paints and roofing materials, and to organize massive tree-planting campaigns that stress tree health and survival through proper maintenance. Finally, the information has to be transferred to both private citizens and public officials who serve them.

Implementing These Strategies On a Large Scale Will Take Concerted Efforts By Many People

We can probably design programs to encourage implementation of these strategies in the places where they will accomplish the most at the least cost. Two approaches stand out as having particular promise.

1.) *Incorporate strategic tree planting and light-colored surfacing in new developments.* Design space for trees into all new construction, and design buildings and pavements with light-colored materials.

2.) *Plant trees strategically and use light-colored materials in retrofits and maintenance.* Building and home owners can probably use light-colored roofing and paints in the normal maintenance cycle with little or no additional cost, while street and highway departments can use light-colored paving materials when repaving roads. Similarly, property owners intending to plant trees can adjust their choice of planting stock and placement to optimize the energy benefits.

Ultimately, municipalities and their residents make the decisions and take actions to make these changes in their local environments. It is up to state and local governments to lead on finding the best ways to integrate energy saving techniques into land use, infrastructure investment, and zoning activities. Much work has already been done by professional foresters, tree-planting groups, and local governments. We have used the experiences of several of these tree-planting groups to show how other interested groups might undertake similar efforts. Municipalities, businesses, homeowners, developers, and state and local governments can all contribute to those efforts.

A Number of Activities Can Expedite the Adoption of These Strategies

Specifically, the following tasks could be undertaken to reduce urban temperatures and the attendant levels of energy use and smog production:

1) Undertake and expand community-wide programs for shade-tree planting and add albedo modification. These programs can consist of volunteer programs in conjunction with community tree planting and development groups, and public education. Information could be made available to the public on how to organize them.

2) Promote energy conserving activities by providing information on albedo of building products, suggestions for landscaping designs, and the energy savings possible—through retailers of building materials and trees, through forestry extension agents, city foresters, and contractors, and through utilities and municipalities.

3) Provide incentives for developers to build well-arbored, light-colored, energy efficient buildings and communities.

4) Encourage Public Utility Commissions to provide utilities with incentives to support tree planting and surface color enhancements. Also provide infrastructure and incentives for utility companies to promote heat-island mitigation strategies through the concept of shared savings.

5) Utilities can support these activities as a way to reduce demand for peak power and perhaps eliminate the need to build new power facilities.

6) Corporations can encourage energy conservation by sponsoring tree planting and light-colored surfacing programs among their employees and in the communities in which they and their employees reside.

7) Professional groups can create professional education materials so that their members are conversant with new techniques for community planning, tree planting, and other modifications to current practices.

8) Municipalities can pass tree ordinances, specify the use of light-colored paving materials in roads, buildings and renovations, provide financial incentives, or zone for light-colored building materials in commercial areas, strengthen the ability of roads and parks departments to plant new trees and maintain existing ones, and foster community efforts in these areas.

9) Professional schools and other educational programs could incorporate these principles in the training of builders, engineers, architects, city and urban planners and designers, arborculturists, foresters, and landscape architects.

Community Design: A Long-term Perspective

Making Space for Urban and Community Trees

Planting trees is one of the easiest and most effective ways to humanize our environment. Often, trees are quickly removed when they interfere with signs, billboards, and lights. Communities could seek other solutions first. The addition of trees not only makes an area more attractive, it also tends to raise property values. Perhaps the greatest hindrance to urban tree planting is inadequate planting space. One way to correct this problem is to "think trees" while planning projects and determine how they might best fit. Trees actually can be a welcome asset in housing developments, shopping centers, roads, downtown malls, parking lots, and parks. Tree planting is a cost-effective way of creating strong community identity and visual quality.

The densities of land development affect the amount of space available for urban and suburban trees. Densities over about three units per acre (net) may offer little space for effective tree planting. Clustered housing concepts are preferable, because exterior space is consolidated in amounts large enough to allow intensive tree planting to take place. Large lots, with two or less units per acre, are rare these days. However, where homes must be built in wooded or hilly areas, this density can preserve existing trees, terrain, and topsoil. Existing low-density residential development could be a good place to emphasize mass tree planting for carbon dioxide sequestering and aesthetic purposes.

Here are some general comments on considering trees in development projects:

Figure 8-2.
Planning room for trees: Including trees in the planning stages of development projects where trees are appropriate, could add to the immediate and long-term value of the projects. Most people enjoy trees and appreciate landscapes that feature trees.

- Undeveloped suburban open space provides an excellent site for significant tree planting. Ideally, open space should be preserved in direct proportion to the density of development. Open space is not necessarily synonymous with urban/suburban parkland.

- Parkland is frequently needed for recreational and sports purposes and requires a high degree of landscaped development and maintenance. Parkland is not necessarily a good place for trees or wildlife. Parkland and open space can exist side by side with careful planning.

Sewage treatment plants could be considered as potential sources of water for major tree planting projects.

- The present pattern of suburban development could leave more room for ecologically useful open space. Creeks, drainage areas, rugged terrain, and land poorly suited for building could be set aside during development as natural tree areas and managed as such after development. Such areas allow natural growth, death, decomposition, and regeneration of trees and enhance the restoration of natural plant and animal interrelationships. Linear open spaces are important as cover for migrating wildlife. Without it, animals cross streets and yards, and risk death by vehicles and domestic pets.

- Sewage treatment plants could be considered as potential sources of water for major tree planting projects. Although there are frequently problems associated with transporting and discharging effluent water, they are not insurmountable. Designs to capture street run-off and use for trees are also available.

Beginning To Implement Strategies for Cooling Our Communities

Early actions might include a review of all existing means, both public and private, to encourage planning and design that reduces fuel consumption, saves trees, provides adequate and suitable space to plant new shade trees, and encourages heat-reflecting surfaces. This review could cover public policies such as taxation and subsidies policies, development regulations, public works programs and education/research activities. Much could be learned from the private sector, including representatives of large development firms, their engineers, architects and landscape architects, developers of telecommunication systems, the transportation industry, environmental groups, and non-profit foundations and volunteer organizations.

Incentives

Following are ideas for providing incentives for individuals to participate in the community development efforts discussed in this guidebook:

Figure 8-3.
The value of incentives: People who do find creative, cost-effective ways to lighten surfaces and plant trees for shade could be rewarded for their efforts with conservation credits, for example, rebates, lower rates, and tax credits.

- Whenever they are applied, energy conservation credits could be provided to homeowners who plant urban shade trees and use light-colored surfaces.

- Credit could be given for homes that incorporate wide overhanging eaves and other passive design approaches which save energy.

- Incentives could be provided for new and retrofit work that incorporates these energy conserving strategies.

- Developers who create energy-efficient homes and workplaces could be allowed additional incentives for their effort.

- Power companies could provide credits, lower rates, or rebates for customers who incorporate these design strategies into their homes and businesses.

Development Standards

Modifications to laws governing highways, local roads, and private development could encourage more efficient land-use and transportation strategies. The revised standards would encourage pedestrian-oriented neighborhoods, allowing well-planned mixes of commercial, office, and residential uses and narrower streets. Higher densities of development would be placed around transit stations.

Revisions to public and private development standards also could encourage maximum space for planting new trees and preserving existing trees. Local government and federal lenders could require shade trees along streets and in parking areas for all new development within their control. Other recommendations include:

- Tree planting for new public roads and highways.
- Preservation of existing trees, forests, and wetlands.
- Light-colored pavement surfaces for new public roads.
- Light-colored overlays for road-resurfacing projects.
- Tree maintenance and replacement resources.

—Ralph Carhart
California Department of Transportation

Citizens Can Take Individual Actions to Improve Their Environments

As this century of rapid development draws to a close, people have become more and more concerned about the quality of their environment. Individuals in communities across the United States are planting trees and greening their homes and work places. Planting a tree or painting a building white is a powerful first step toward transforming our communities into a livable, enduring inheritance for our children. The activities we have suggested here are simple. They give people living in communities the opportunity to take individual actions to improve their environments in ways they will be able to see. We hope this guidebook will spur efforts by manufacturers and retailers of building materials, developers, city planners, urban and landscape designers, foresters, state and local officials, and the private sector to join with citizens in working toward that goal.

U.S. Department of Agriculture

Figure 8-4.
Thinking about the future: Planting a single tree today seems simple, but it is a powerful first step toward transforming tomorrow's cities into a livable, enduring inheritance for our children.

References

Acacia Software. "PlantMaster Professional Plant Selector." Santa Barbara, CA.

Aida, M. 1982. "Urban Albedo as a Function of the Urban Structure: A Model Experiment." *Boundary Layer Meteorology*. 23:405-413.

Akbari, H., H.G. Taha, Y.J. Huang, and A.H. Rosenfeld. 1986. "Undoing Uncomfortable Summer Heat Islands Can Save Gigawatts of Peak Power." *Proceedings of the 1986 ACEEE Conference Summer Study on Energy Efficiency in Buildings* (Santa Cruz, CA, Aug. 1986). Washington, D.C.: American Council for an Energy-Efficient Economy (ACEEE), 2:7-22.

Akbari, H., H.G. Taha, P.T. Martien, and Y.J. Huang. 1987. "Strategies for Reducing Urban Heat Islands: Savings, Conflicts, and City's Role." Presented at the First National Conference on Energy Efficient Cooling (San Jose, CA).

Akbari, H., H.G. Taha, P.T. Martien, and A.H. Rosenfeld. 1987. "The Impact of Summer Heat Islands on Residential Cooling Energy Consumption." Presented at the Eighth Miami International Conference on Alternative Energy Sources.

Akbari, H., H.G. Taha, and A.H. Rosenfeld. 1987. "Vegetation Micro Climate Measurements." Research report to Univ. of California/Universitywide Energy Resources Group.

Akbari, H., Y.J. Huang, P.T. Martien, L.I. Rainer, A.H. Rosenfeld, and H.G. Taha. 1988. "The Impact of Summer Heat Islands on Cooling Energy Consumption and CO_2 Emissions." *Proceedings of the 1988 Summer Study on Energy Efficiency in Buildings* (Asilomar, CA, August 1988). Washington, D.C.: American Council for an Energy-Efficient Economy (ACEEE).

Akbari, H., A.H. Rosenfeld, and H.G. Taha. 1989. "Recent Development in Heat Island Studies: Technical and Policy." *Controlling Summer Heat Islands: Proceedings of the Workshop on Saving Energy and Reducing Atmospheric Pollution By Controlling Summer Heat Islands* (Berkeley, CA, February 1989). LBL Report 27872, Berkeley, CA: Lawrence Berkeley Laboratory, pp.14-30.

Akbari, H., A.H. Rosenfeld, and H.G. Taha. 1990. "Summer Heat Islands, Urban Trees, and White Surfaces." *1990 ASHRAE Transactions* (Atlanta, GA, January 1990). Atlanta, GA: American Society of Heating, Refrigeration, and Air-Conditioning Engineers (ASHRAE), also LBL Report 28308, Berkeley, CA: Lawrence Berkeley Laboratory.

American City and Country. "Asphalt vs. Concrete." July 1986. pp. 31-38.

American Forestry Association. 1989. "Save Our Urban Trees: Citizen Action Guide." Washington, D.C.

American Forestry Association. 1990. National Street Tree Survey. Washington, D.C.

Ames, R.G. 1980. "The Sociology of Urban Tree Planting." *Journal of Arboriculture.* 6(5):120-123.

Anderson, L.M., and H.W. Schroeder. 1983. "Application of Wildland Scenic Assessment Methods of the Urban Landscape." *Landscape Planning.* 10:219-237.

Argento, V.K. 1988. "Ozone Non-attainment Policy vs. the Facts of Life." *Chemical Engineering Progress.* pp. 50-54.

Arnold, H. 1980. *Trees in Urban Design.* New York, NY: Van Norstrand Reinhold. pp. 167.

Asphalt Institute. 1978. "Slurry Sealing." Construction Leaflet No. 22.

Balling, R.C., and R. Cerveny. 1987. "Long Term Associations Between Wind Speeds and the Urban Heat Island of Phoenix, Arizona." *Journal of Climate and Meteorology.* Vol. 26: pp. 712-716.

Bartenstein, F. 1982. "Meeting Urban and Community Needs through Urban Forestry." *Proceedings of the Second National Urban Forest Conference.* Washington, D.C.: American Forestry Association. pp. 21-26.

Beatty, R.A. and C. Heckman. 1981. "Survey of Municipal Tree Systems in the United States." *Urban Ecology.* 5:81-102.

Bennett, M. and N. Saab. 1982. "Modeling of the Urban Heat Island and of its Interaction with Pollution Dispersal." *Atmospheric Environment.* 16:797-1822.

Bernatsky, A. 1978. *Tree Ecology and Preservation.* New York, NY: Elsevier Scientific Publishing.

Bornstein, R.D. 1975. "The Two-Dimensional URBMET Planetary Boundary Layer Model." *Journal of Applied Meteorology.* 14:1459-1477.

Bornstein, R.D., A. Lorenzen, and D. Johnson. 1977. "Urban-Rural Wind Velocity Differences." *Atmospheric Environment.* 11:597-604.

Bouza, A.V. 1990. "Trees and Crime Prevention." *Make Our Cities Safe For Trees: Proceedings of the Fourth Urban Forestry Conference.* Washington, D.C.: American Forestry Association. p. 31.

Brown, D.E. and A.M. Winer. 1986. "Estimating Urban Vegetation Cover in Los Angeles." *Photogrammetric Engineering and Remote Sensing.* 52(1):117-123.

Brown, L.R. 1987. *State of the World: A World Watch Institute Report on Progress Toward a Sustainable Society.* New York, NY: W.W. Norton. Chapter 3.

Brown, L.R. 1988. *State of the World: A World Watch Institute Report on Progress Toward a Sustainable Society.* New York, NY: W.W. Norton. Chapter 5.

Buffington, D.E. 1979. "Economics of Landscaping Features for Conserving Energy in Residences." *Proceedings of the Florida State Horticultural Society*. 92:216-220.

California Dept. of Water Resources. 1987. "California Water: Looking to the Future." Bulletin 160-87. Sacramento, CA: Dept. of Water Resources.

California Office of Conservation. 1986. "Urban Water Management in California: A Report to the Legislature in Response to the Urban Water Management Planning Act of 1983." Sacramento, CA: Dept. of Water Resources.

California Office of Conservation. 1989. *Annual Report*. Sacramento, CA: Dept. of Water Resources, Landscape Water Management Program.

Chameides, W.L., R.W. Lindsay, J. Richardson, and C.S. Kiang. 1988. "The Role of Biogenic Hydrocarbons in Urban Photochemical Smog: Atlanta Case Study." *Science*. 241:1473-1475.

Coate, B. 1986. "Water Conserving Plants and Landscapes for the Bay Area." Alamo, CA: East Bay Municipal Utility District.

Concrete Construction. 1983. "Concrete Tiles Put Color on Residential Roofs." pp. 750-754.

Cook, D.I. 1978. "Trees, Solid Barriers, and Combinations: Alternatives for Noise Control." *Proceedings of the Fourth Urban Forestry Conference*. Washington, D.C.: American Forestry Association. p. 31.

DeWalle, D.R., G.M. Heisler, and J.E. Jacobs. 1983. "Forest Home Sites Influence Heating and Cooling Energy." *Journal of Forestry*. 81(2):84-87.

DeWalle, D.R. 1978. "Manipulating Urban Vegetation for Residential Energy Conservation." *Proceedings of the First National Urban Forest Conference*. Washington, D.C.: U.S. Dept. of Agriculture Forest Service. pp. 267-283.

DeWalle, D.R. and G.M. Heisler. 1983. "Windbreak Effects on Air Infiltration and Space Heating in a Mobile Home." *Energy and Buildings*. 5:279-288.

DeWalle, D.R. and G.M. Heisler. 1988. "Use of Windbreaks for Home Energy Conservation." *Agriculture, Ecosystems and Environment*. 22/23:243-260.

Duckworth, F.S. and J.S. Sandberg. 1954. "The Effect of Cities Upon Horizontal and Vertical Temperature Gradients." *American Meteorological Society Bulletin*. 35:198-207.

Duffield, M.R. and W.D. Jones. 1981. *Plants for Dry Climates: How to Select, Grow, and Enjoy*. Tucson, AZ: H.P. Books.

Dwyer, J.F. 1982. "Challenges in Managing Urban Forest Recreation Resources." *Proceedings of the Second National Urban Forest Conference*. Washington, D.C.: American Forestry Association. pp. 267-283.

Dyson, F. and G. Marland. 1979. "Technical Fixes For Climatic Effects of CO_2." *Workshop on the Global Effects of Carbon Dioxide from Fossil Fuels*. Washington, D.C.: Dept. of Energy. pp. 111-118.

Federer, C.A. 1976. "Trees Modify the Urban Climate." *Journal of Arboriculture.* 2:121-127.

Feng, J.P. 1990. "A Synoptic Climatological Approach for Assessment of Air Pollution Concentration in Philadelphia, PA." *Air Pollution: Environmental Issues and Health Effects* (Majumdar, S.I., Miller, E.W., and Cahir, J., ed.).

Flemer, W. 1975. "Planting for Energy Conservation, Solar Radiation Consideration in Building Planning and Design." *Working Conference on Solar Effects on Building Design* (Washington, D.C.: no proceedings).

Flynn, J.J. 1979. "Point Pattern Analysis and Remote Sensing Techniques Applied to Explain the Form of the Urban Heat Island" (Ph.D. dissertation). Syracuse NY: State Univ. of New York, Syracuse College of Environmental Science and Forestry.

Foster, R.S. 1978. "Bio-Engineering for the Urban Ecosystem." *Metropolitan Tree Improvement Alliance Proceedings.* p. 15.

Freeman, D.L., R.T. Egami, N.F. Robinson, and J.G. Watson. 1986. "A Method for Propagating Measurement Uncertainties Through Dispersion Models." *Journal of the Air Pollution Control Association.* 36:246-253.

Fukui, E. 1970. "The Recent Rise of Temperature in Japan." *Japanese Progress in Climatology.* Tokyo: Tokyo Univ. of Education. pp. 46-65.

Garbesi, K., H. Akbari, and P.T. Martien, eds. 1989. *Controlling Summer Heat Islands: Proceedings of the Workshop on Saving Energy and Reducing Atmospheric Pollution by Controlling Summer Heat Islands* (Berkeley, CA, February 1989). LBL Report 25179, Berkeley, CA: Lawrence Berkeley Laboratory.

Geiger, R. 1965. *The Climate Near the Ground.* Boston, MA: Harvard Univ. Press.

Givoni, B. 1981. *Man, Climate, and Architecture.* New York, NY: Van Nostrand Reinhold Co.

Gold, S.M. 1977. "Social and Economic Benefits of Trees in Cities." *Journal of Forestry.* pp. 84-87.

Goodridge, J. 1987. "Population and Temperature Trends in California." *Proceedings of the Pacific Climate Workshop* (Pacific Grove, CA). U.S. Geological Survey. pp. 22-26.

Goodridge, J. 1989. "Air Temperature Trends in California 1916 to 1987" (personal manuscript). Chico, CA: J. Goodridge.

Gordillo, J. 1980. "Colored Slurry Systems." *Proceedings of the International Slurry Seal Association*, 8th Annual Convention.

Gray, G. and F. Deneke. 1986. *Urban Forestry* (second edition). New York, NY: John Wiley & Sons.

Griffin, C.W. 1982. *Manual of Built-Up Roof Systems* (second edition). New York, NY: McGraw-Hill.

Griggs, E.I., T.R. Sharp, and M.J. McDonald. 1989. "Guide for Estimating Differences in Building Heating and Cooling Energy Due to Changes in Solar Reflectance of a Low-Sloped Roof." ORNL Report 6527. Oak Ridge, TN: Oak Ridge National Laboratory.

Hansen, J., I. Fung, A. Lacis, D. Rind, S. Lebedeff, R. Ruedy, and G. Russell. "Global Climate Changes as Forecast by Goddard Institute for Space Studies Three-Dimensional Model." NASA Goddard Space Flight Center, Goddard Institute for Space Studies, New York, NY, from *Journal of Geophysical Research*, 93(D8):9341-9364, August 1988.

Harris, R. 1983. *Arboriculture: Care of Trees, Shrubs, and Vines in the Landscape*. Englewood Cliffs, NJ: Prentice-Hall.

Hartig, T.M., Mang, and G.W. Evans. 1987. *"Perspectives on Wilderness: Testing the Theory of Restorative Environments: Proceedings of the Fourth World Wilderness Congress* (Estes Park , CO).

Heisler, G.M., H.G. Halverson, and R.P. Zisa. 1981. "Solar Radiation Measurements Beneath Crowns of Open-Growth Trees." *15th Conference on Agriculture and Forest Meteorology and 5th Conference on Biometeorology*. Boston, MA: American Meteorological Society. pp. 162-165.

Heisler, G.M. and D.R. DeWalle. 1984. "Plantings that Save Energy." *American Forests*. September.

Heisler, G.M. 1986. "Energy Savings with Trees." *Journal of Arboriculture*. 12(5):113-124.

Heisler, G.M. 1989. "Effects of Individual Trees on Solar Radiation Climate of Small Buildings." *Urban Ecology*. (9) 337-359.

Heisler, G.M. 1989. "Site Design and Microclimate Research" (final report to Argonne National Laboratory). University Park, PA: U.S. Dept. of Agriculture Forest Service, Northeast Forest Experiment Station.

Hoyano, A. 1988. "Climatological Uses of Plans for Solar Control and the Effects on the Thermal Environment of a Building." *Energy and Buildings*. 11:181-199.

Huang, Y.J., H. Akbari, H.G. Taha, and A.H. Rosenfeld. 1986. "The Potential of Vegetation in Reducing Summer Cooling Loads in Residential Buildings." LBL Report 21291, Berkeley, CA: Lawrence Berkeley Laboratory.

Huang, Y.J., H. Akbari, and H.G. Taha. 1990. "The Wind-Shielding and Shading Effects of Trees on Residential Heating and Cooling Requirements." *1990 ASHRAE Transactions* (Atlanta, GA, January 1990). Atlanta, GA: American Society of Heating, Refrigeration, and Air-Conditioning Engineers (ASHRAE), also LBL Report 24131, Berkeley, CA: Lawrence Berkeley Laboratory.

Husband, T.P., J.M. Lawrence, and A.R. Knight, eds. *Street Trees: A Guide for Communities in Southern New England*. Bulletin 212: Univ. of Rhode Island, Cooperative Extension.

Hutchinson, B.A., F.G. Taylor, and the Critical Review Panel. 1983. "Energy Conservation Mechanisms and Potentials of Landscape Design to Ameliorate Building Microclimates." *Landscape Journal.* 2(1):19-39.

Intergovernmental Panel on Climate Change. 1990. *Integrated Analysis of Country Case Studies*; Report of U.S./Japan Expert Group to the Energy and Industry Subgroup. IPCC, Geneva, Switzerland.

Intergovernmental Panel on Climate Change, Response Strategies Working Group. 1991. *Climate Change: The IPCC Response Strategies.* Island Press, Washington, D.C. 273 pp.

Ivanyi, A., and I. Mersich. 1982. "Simulation of the Urban Air Pollution Based on the Numerical UBL Model." *Atmospheric Environment.* 16:1835-1849.

Jauregui, E. 1973. "Urban Climate Mexico City." *Erdkunde.* 27:298-307.

Johnson, C., E.G. McPherson, and S. Gutting. 1982. *Community Forestry Manual.* Logan, UT: Utah State Univ., Dept. of Landscape Architecture.

Johnson, C.W. and F.A. Baker. 1989. "Urban and Community Forestry: A Guide for the Cities and Towns of the Interior Western United States." Ogden, UT: U.S. Department of Agriculture Forest Service, Intermountain Region.

Jones, H.G. 1983. *Plants and Microclimate.* Cambridge, England: Cambridge University Press.

Karl, T.R. and N.C. Williams. 1987. "Data Adjustments and Edits to the U.S. Historical Climate Network." Asheville, NC: National Climatic Data Center.

Karl, T.R., H.F. Diaz, and G. Kukla. 1988. "Urbanization: Its Detection and Effects in the United States Climate Record." *Journal of Climate.* 1:11, p. 1099-1123.

Karl, T.R., C.N. Williams, F.T. Quinlan, and T.A. Boden. 1990. *United States Historical Climatology Network Serial Temperature and Precipitation Data.* ORNL Report ORNL/CDIAC-30. Oak Ridge, TN: Oak Ridge National Laboratory, Carbon Dioxide Information Analysis Center.

Kielbaso, J. 1988. "Trends in Urban Forestry Management." *Baseline Data Report.* Washington, D.C.: International Management Association. 20 (Jan/Feb):1.

Kielbaso, J., and V. Cotrone. 1990. "State of the Urban Forest. Make Our Cities Safe for Trees." Proceedings of the Fourth Annual Urban Forestry Conference. Washington, D.C.: American Forestry Association, p. 11.

Kiley, M.D. and W. Mosell, ed. 1989. *National Construction Estimator* (37th edition). Carlsbad, CA: Craftsman Book Company.

Kittredge, J .1948. *Forest Influences.* New York, NY: Dover.

Koon, C. 1989. "Grow Your Own Savings." *Missouri Research Review.* Jefferson City, MO: Missouri Dept. of Natural Resources. Vol. 6: 2, p. 14-19.

Kramer, P.J. and T.T. Kozlowski. 1960. *Physiology of Trees.* New York, NY: McGraw-Hill.

Kukla, G., J. Gavin, and T.R. Karl. 1986. "Urban Warming." *Journal of Climate and Applied Meteorology.* 25:1265-1270.

Kusuda, T. 1971. "Earth Temperatures Beneath Five Different Surfaces." NBS Report 10-373. Washington, D.C.: U.S. Department of Commerce, National Bureau of Standards.

Lashof, D.A. and D.A. Tirpak. 1991. *Policy Options for Stabilizing Global Climate: Report to Congress,* Executive Summary. U.S. Environmental Protection Agency, Washington, D.C. 45 pp.

Laechelt, R.L. and B.M. Williams. 1976. "Value of Tree Shade to Homeowners." Montgomery, AL: Alabama Forestry Commission.

Landsberg, H.E. 1981. *The Urban Climate.* New York, NY: Academic Press.

Lay, M.G. 1986. *Handbook of Road Technology* Vol. 2. New York, NY: Gordon and Breach.

Lee, D.O. 1979. "The Influence of Atmospheric Stability and the Urban Heat Island on Urban-Rural Wind Speed Differences." *Atmospheric Environment.* 13:1175-1180.

Linder, K.P. and M.R. Inglis. 1989. "The Potential Effects of Climate Changes on Regional and National Demands for Electricity." In J.S. Smith and D.A. Tirpak (eds.) *The Potential Effects of Global Climate Change on the United States.* Appendix H: Infrastructure. Washington, D.C.: U.S. Environmental Protection Agency.

Lipkis, A. and K. Lipkis. 1990. *The Simple Act of Planting A Tree.* Los Angeles: J.P. Tarcher, Inc.

Martien, P.T. et al. 1989. *"Approaches to Using Models of Urban Climates in Building Energy Simulation."* LBL Draft Report, Berkeley, CA: Lawrence Berkeley Laboratory.

McBride, J.R. and D.F. Jacobs. 1986. "Presettlement Forest Structure as a Factor in Urban Forest Development." *Urban Ecology* (R. Rowntree, ed.). 9(3/4):245-266.

McGinn, C. 1982. "Microclimate and Energy Use in Suburban Tree Canopies." Ph.D. Thesis. Davis, CA: Univ. of California.

McPherson, E.G., L.P. Herrington, and G.M. Heisler. 1988. "Impacts of Vegetation on Residential Heating and Cooling." *Energy and Buildings.* 12:41-51.

McPherson, E.G. and C. Sacamano. 1989. *Southwestern Landscaping That Saves Energy.* Tuscon, AZ: The University of Arizona.

McPherson, E.G., J.R. Simpson, and M. Livingston. 1989. "Effects of Three Landscape Treatments on Residential Energy and Water Use in Tucson, Arizona." *Energy and Buildings.* 13:127-138.

McPherson, E.G. 1991. "Economic Modeling for Large-Scale Tree Plantings." In E. Vine, D. Crawley, and P. Centolella (eds.) *Energy Efficiency and the En-*

vironment: Forging the Link, Chapter 19, 10pp. Washington, D.C.: American Council for an Energy Efficient Economy.

Means, R.S. Company Inc. 1989. *Building Construction Cost Data* (2nd annual western edition).

Means, R.S. Company Inc. 1989. *Means Site Work Cost Data* (8th annual edition).

Meier, A. and J. Friesen. 1987. "Strategic Planting." *Energy Auditor and Retrofitter Magazine*. July/August:7-12.

Meyer, J.L. and R. Strohman. 1989. *Handbook for Irrigation Evaluation and Scheduling*. Riverside, CA: Univ. of California Cooperative Extension, Univ. of California.

Mies, M. 1979. "The Climate of Cities" in *Nature in Cities* (I.C. Laurie, ed.). New York, NY: John Wiley pp. 91-115.

Miller, P.R. and A.M. Winer. 1984. "Composition and Dominance in Los Angeles Basin Urban Vegetation." *Urban Ecology* (R. Rowntree, ed.). 8(1/2): 29-54.

Miller, R.W. 1988. *Urban Forestry: Planning and Managing Urban Greenspaces*. Englewood Cliffs, NJ: Prentice Hall. pp. 386.

Moffat, A.S. and M. Schiler. 1981. *Landscape Design that Saves Energy*. New York, NY: William Morrow and Co., Inc.

Moll, G.M. 1985. "How Valuable are Your Trees?" *American Forests*. April, 1985. pp. 13-16.

Moll, G.M. 1987. "Improving the Health of the Urban Forest, Part I." *American Forests*. Nov-Dec, 1987. pp. 61-64.

Moll, G.M. 1987. "The State of Our City Forests." *American Forests*. 93:5-6.

Moll, G.M. 1988. "Improving the Health of the Urban Forest, Part II." *American Forests*. 94:1-2.

Moll, G.M. and Ebenreck, S., eds. 1989. *Shading Our Cities: A Resource Guide for Urban and Community Forests*. Washington, D.C.: Island Press. pp. 300.

Moore, E.O. 1981. "A Prison Environment's Effect on Health Care Service Demands." *Journal of Environmental Systems*. 11:7-34.

Morgenstern, R.D. 1991. Testimony of Richard Morgenstern, Acting Deputy Assistant Administrator for Policy, Planning, and Evaluation, U.S. Environmental Protection Agency, Before the Committee on Environment and Public Works, United States Senate, March 20, 1991. Washington, D.C.

Municipal Water District of Orange County, Dept. of Landscape Architecture, California Polytechnic University and EDAW, Inc. (no date available). "Landscape Water Conservation Guidelines for Orange County (California)." Prepared for the California Dept. of Water Resources.

Myrup, L.O. 1969. "A Numerical Model of the Urban Heat Island." *Journal of Applied Meteorology*. 8: 908-918.

Myrup, L.O. and D.L. Morgan. 1972. "Numerical Model of the Urban Atmosphere." *Contributions in Atmospheric Science.* Davis, CA: Univ. of California, Dept. of Agricultural Engineering and Dept. of Water Science and Engineering. No. 4.

National Aid Precipitation Assessment Program. 1990. *Acidic Deposition: State of Science and Technology: Summaries of NAPAP State-of-Science.* Technology Reports 1-28 (Irving PM, ed.). Washington, D.C.: Office of the Director.

National Academy of Science. 1991. *Policy Implications of Greenhouse Warming.* Report of the Mitigation Panel. Washington, D.C.: National Academy Press.

National Association of Home Builders. (NAHB) 1979. *Single Family Construction Practices.* Rockville, MD: National Association of Home Builders.

Neely, D.R., ed. 1988. *A Standard Municipal Tree Ordinance.* Urbana, IL: International Society of Arboriculture. 1988.

Nelson, J.O. 1987. "Water Conserving Landscapes Show Impressive Savings." *Xeriscape News.* Austin, TX: National Xeriscape Council, Inc. Jan/Feb.

Nunez, M. and T.R. Oke. 1977. "The Energy Balance of an Urban Canyon." *Journal of Applied Meteorology.* 16:11-19.

Oke, T.R. 1975. "Inadvertent Modification of the City Atmosphere and Prospects for Planned Urban Climates." *Meteorology as Related to Urban and Regional Land-use Planning* (Pub. No. 444). Geneva, Switzerland: World Meteorological Organization.

Oke, T.R. 1978. *Boundary Layer Climates.* London: Methuen.

Oke, T.R., ed. 1986. *Urban Climatology and Its Applications with Special Regard to Tropical Areas: Proceedings of the Technical Conference organized by the World Meteorological Organization and the World Health Organization.* Geneva, Switzerland: World Meteorological Organization.

Oke, T.R. 1987. "City Size and Urban Heat Island," *Perspectives on Wilderness: Testing the Theory of Restorative Environments*: Proceedings of the Fourth World Wilderness Congress (Estes Park, CO). 7:767-779.

Otterman, J., 1977. "Anthropogenic Impact on the Albedo of the Earth." *Climatic Change.* 1:137-155.

Ottman, K.A. and J.J. Kielbaso. 1976. "Managing Municipal Trees" (Urban Data Service Report). *Journal of Forestry.* Washington, D.C.: International City Management Association. 81(2):82-84.

Parker, J.H. 1982. "The Implementation of Energy Conservation Landscaping Through Local Ordinances." Miami, FL: Florida International Univ., Dept. of Physical Sciences.

Parker, J.H. 1983. "Landscaping to Reduce the Energy Used in Cooling Buildings." *Journal of Forestry* 81(2):82-83.

Parker, J.R. 1987. "The Use of Shrubs in Energy Conservation Planting." *Landscape Journal*. 6:132-139.

Perry, B. (no date available). *Trees and Shrubs for Dry California Landscapes: Plants for Water Conservation.* San Dimas, CA: Land Design Publishing.

Phillips, A., and D. Gangloff, eds. 1987. *Proceedings of the Third National Urban Forestry Conference.* Washington, D.C.: American Forestry Association. pp. 272.

Pitt, D. 1979. "Trees in the City" in *Nature in Cities* (I.C. Lau, ed.). New York, NY: John Wiley. pp. 91-115.

Rainer, L.I., P.T. Martien, and H.G. Taha. 1989. "Measurement of Summer Residential Microclimates in Sacramento, CA." *Proceedings of the Workshop on Urban Heat Islands* (Berkeley, CA, February 23-24). Berkeley, CA: Lawrence Berkeley Laboratory.

Reagan, J.A., and D.M. Acklam. 1979. "Solar Reflectivity of Common Building Materials and its Influence on the Roof Heat Gain of Typical Southwestern Residences." *Energy and Buildings*. 2:3, 237-248.

Reifsnyder, W.E. 1967. "Forest Meteorology: The Forest Energy Balance." *Reviews Forest*. Res. pp. 127-179.

Reisner, M. 1989. "The Next Water War: Cities vs. Agriculture." Bay on Trial. 1(1):8-10.

Ripley, E.A. and R.E. Redmann. 1976. "Grassland," in *Vegetation and the Atmosphere* (J.L. Monteith, ed.). London, UK: Academic Press. 2:349-398.

Rowntree, R. 1984. "Forest Canopy Cove and Land Use in Four Eastern United States Cities." *Urban Ecology* (R. Rowntree, ed.). 8(1/2):55-67.

Santhanam, K. 1980. "One-Dimensional Simulation of Temperature and Moisture in Atmospheric and Soil Boundary Layers." M.S. Thesis. San Jose, CA: San Jose State Univ.

Sayler, R.D. and J.A. Cooper. 1975. "Status and Productivity of Canada Geese Breeding in the Twin Cities of Minnesota." Presented at the Thirty-sixth Midwestern Fish and Wildlife Conference (Indianapolis), Lincoln, NE: Association of Midwest Fish & Wildlife Commissioners.

Schroeder, H.W. 1989. "Environment, Behavior, and Design Research on Urban Forests." *Advances in Environment, Behavior, and Design* (E.H. Zube and F.T. Moore, eds.). New York, NY: Plenum. 2:87-117.

Shigo, A.L. 1986. *A New Tree Biology.* Durham, NC: Shigo & Trees.

Smith, J.S. and D.A. Tirpak. 1989. *The Potential Effects of Climate Change on the United States.* (Appendix H: Infrastructure). EPA-230-05-89-058. Washington, D.C.: U.S. Environmental Protection Agency.

Smith, W.H. and S. Dochinger. 1976. "Capability of Metropolitan Trees to Reduce Atmospheric Contaminants." *Better Trees for Metropolitan Landscapes*. General Technical Report NE-22. Washington, D.C.: USDA Forest Service. pp. 49-59.

Sopper, W.E. and S.N. Kerr. 1978. "Potential Use of Forest Land for Recycling Municipal Waste Water and Sludge." *Proceedings of the First National Urban Forest Conference.* Washington, D.C.: USDA Forest Service. pp. 392- 409.

Southern California Edison Company. 1990. "Trees: Saving Energy Naturally." Reardon, CA: p. 1-5.

Spirn, A.W. 1984. *The Granite Garden.* New York, NY: Basic Books. pp. 334.

Summers, P.W. 1966. "The Seasonal, Weekly, and Daily Cycles of Atmospheric Smoke Content in Central Montreal." *Journal of the Air Pollution Control Association.* 16:432-438.

Swearengin, R. 1987. "Water Saving Flow with Efficient Irrigation, Good Practices." *Xeriscape News.* Austin, TX: National Xeriscape Council. Nov/Dec.

Taha, H.G. 1988. "Nighttime Air Temperature and the Sky View Factor: A Case Study in San Francisco, CA." LBL Report No. 24009. Berkeley, CA: Lawrence Berkeley Laboratory.

Taha, H.G. 1988. "Site-Specific Heat Island Simulations: Model Development and Application to Microclimate Conditions." LBL Report No. 26105. Masters Thesis, Univ. of California. Berkeley, CA: Lawrence Berkeley Laboratory.

Taha, H.G., H. Akbari, A.H. Rosenfeld, and Y.J. Huang. 1988. "Residential Cooling Loads and the Urban Heat Island Effects of Albedo." *Building and Environment.* 23(4):271-283.

Taha, H.G., H. Akbari, and A.H. Rosenfeld. 1988. "Vegetation Canopy Micro-Climate: A Field Project in Davis, California." LBL Report LBL-24593. Berkeley, CA: Lawrence Berkeley Laboratory.

Taha, H.G., H. Akbari, and A.H. Rosenfeld. 1989. "Heat Island and Oasis Effects of Vegetative Canopies: Micrometeorological Field Measurements." To appear in *Theoretical and Applied Climatology.*

Taha, H.G. 1991. Unpublished data.

Threlkeld, J.L. 1970. *Thermal Environmental Engineering* (2nd edition). New York, NY: Prentice Hall.

Ulrich, R.S. 1981. "Natural Versus Urban Scenes: Some Psychophysiological Effects." *Environment and Behavior.* 13:523-556.

Ulrich, R.S., R.F. Simons, B.D. Losito, E. Fiorito, M.A. Miles, and M. Zelson. (In press). "Stress Recovery During Exposure to Natural and Urban Environments." *Journal of Environmental Psychology.*

U.S. Council on Environmental Quality. 1984. *Environmental Quality-15th Annual Report of the Council on Environmental Quality.* Washington, D.C.: U.S. Government Printing Office.

U.S. Dept. of Agriculture Forest Service. 1985. "Using Trees to Reduce Urban Energy Consumption: Transferring Technology to Users." NE-INF-62-85. Brookman,

PA: U.S. Dept. of Agriculture Forest Service, Northeastern Forest Experiment Station.

U.S. Dept. of Agriculture Forest Service, Pacific States, Region 5 & 6. 1989. "A Technical Guide to Community and Urban Forestry in Washington, Oregon, and California." Portland, OR: World Forestry Center.

U.S. Dept. of Energy (DOE). 1988. "Energy Technologies and the Environment: Environmental Information Handbook." DOE/EH-0077. Washington, D.C.: Dept. of Energy.

Vine, E. 1981. "Solarizing America: The Davis Experience." *Public Policy Report No. 5*. The Conference on Alternative State and Local Policies.

Weber, C. 1989. "Developing a Successful Urban Tree Ordinance," in *Shading Our Cities* (G.M. Moll, and S. Ebenreck, ed.). Washington, D.C.: Island Press.

Zube, E.H. 1973. "The Natural History of Urban Trees." *Metro Forest, A Natural History*. Special Supplement 82 (9).

Appendix A

Haider Taha

Further Data on Heat Islands

C hapter 1 presented data on rising urban temperatures and energy use in a number of cities in the U.S. and abroad. This appendix presents similar data on five other cities. Their citations are found in the References section that follows Chapter 8.

Rising Urban Temperatures

Just as Los Angeles and San Francisco average temperatures are rising, so too are average temperatures in other California cities rising. Oakland, for instance, though only a few miles away from San Francisco but sheltered from cool ocean breezes, is warming at a rate of 0.4°F per decade. San Jose is warming at a rate of 0.3°F, San Diego by 0.8°F, and Sacramento, an inland city, by about 0.4°F per decade. Similarly, Baltimore is warming at a rate of 0.4°F per decade. Figures A-1 to A-5 illustrate the temperature increases in these cities.

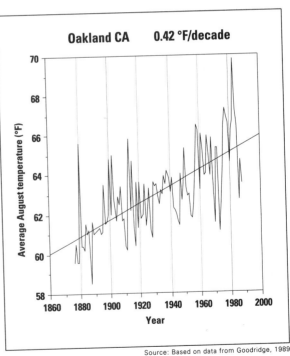

Source: Based on data from Goodridge, 1989

Figure A-1.
In Oakland, California, sheltered from ocean breezes, temperatures have increased 0.42°F per decade.

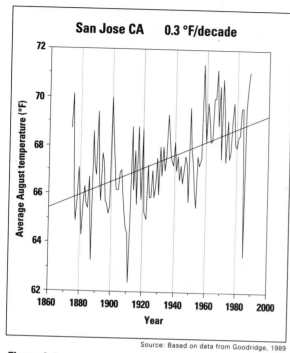

Figure A-2.
San Jose, California is warming at a rate of 0.4°F per decade.

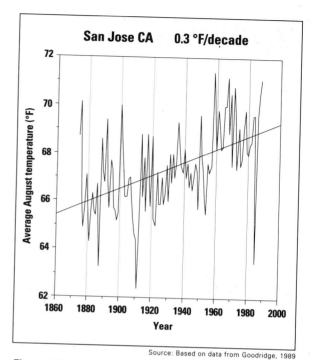

Figure A-3.
In San Diego, California, temperatures have been rising at a rate of 0.8°F per decade.

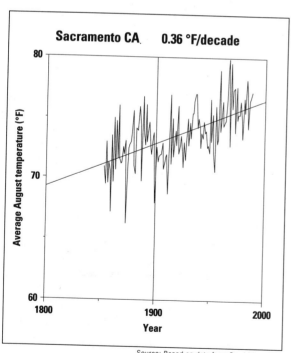

Figure A-4.
Sacramento, California, and inland city, is warming at a rate of 0.36°F per decade.

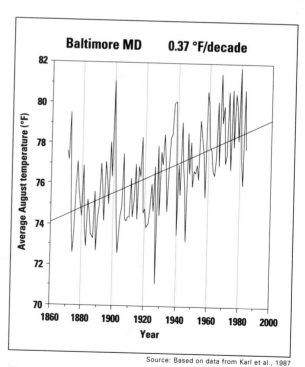

Figure A-5.
Temperatures in Baltimore, Maryland have been increasing at a rate of 0.37°F per decade.

Appendix B

Ronald Ritschard

The Costs of Conserved Energy

Policy makers interested in using urban trees and light-colored surfaces to mitigate urban heat islands and their detrimental effects will also be interested in the potential costs of that mitigation. Researchers have developed several formulas for calculating and comparing the costs of implementing necessary measures to save energy, to save carbon, or to save and sequester carbon. In general, they have found that using heat-island mitigation strategies such as planting trees is competitive with using energy efficient appliances. This appendix briefly reviews those formulas.

Saving Energy

The potential savings from investments in energy conservation are called the costs of conserved energy, or CCE. The formula for CCE was developed to express the economics of energy conservation and new energy supplies on a similar basis (Meier et al., 1983). To establish the unit of cost of conserved energy (dollars per kWh), the annualized cost of the conservation measure is divided by the annual energy savings. The formulation is:.

$$\text{CCE (\$/kWh)} = \frac{\text{Capital Cost x Capital Recovery Factor}}{\text{Energy Savings/year}}$$

where: capital recovery factor (CRF) is used to annualize the capital cost of the conservation measure.

CRF is equal to $d/1 - (1 + d)^{-n}$
d is the discount rate and n is the lifetime of the investment

Calculating the cost of conserved energy therefore involves four variables:

1. capital cost (investment cost) of the conservation measure;
2. annual energy savings expected from the measure;
3. amortized period of investment; and
4. discount rate of the investor.

Cost of Conserved Carbon

Akbari et al. (1988) modified the concept of cost of conserved energy and applied it to the carbon savings from efficiency improvements. This new relationship, cost of conserved carbon (CCC), is calculated by annualizing the total cost of the conservation investment, and dividing it by the amount of carbon saved annually.

$$\text{CCC (\$/Tons-Carbon, \$/T-C)} = \frac{(\text{Net CCE}) (1{,}000{,}000)}{\text{Carbon Burden}}$$

where: carbon burden (CB) is the amount of carbon saved in grams C/kWh and 1,000,000 is the number of grams per metric ton.

The value of this approach is that comparisons of quite disparate conservation strategies can be made using the CCE and CCC formulations. Planting trees, changing surface colors, using energy-efficient appliances and lighting fixtures, and insulating a building can be compared for cost, energy and carbon conservation efficiency. The estimates of CCE and CCC are only as good as the data used to make them. For example, there are many uncertainties in the costs of saved carbon and in the costs assumptions for urban trees in general. Some of these factors will be discussed later in this appendix.

Costs of Saved and Sequestered Carbon

The combined effects of direct carbon sequestering and the indirect fossil carbon savings from trees were recently calculated using a further modification of the methods described above (Krause and Koomey, 1989). The new formulation allows the comparison of trees which save energy and trees that only sequester carbon. If it is assumed that a properly placed urban tree can both save carbon through reduction in electrical energy requirements as well as by direct sequestration during tree growth, then a new formulation (cost of saved/sequestered carbon, CSSC) is possible. It is defined as:

$$\text{CSSC (\$/T-C)} = \frac{\text{Net (CCE)} (1{,}000{,}000)}{\text{SR/ER} + \text{CB}}$$

where: SR = carbon sequestration rate (g/tree-year)
ER = annual energy savings per tree (kWh/tree-year)
CB = carbon burden (gC/kWh)

The formulation of CSSC includes the net costs of conserved energy (i.e., difference between the costs of conserved energy and avoided energy costs), carbon sequestration rate (SR), energy savings (ER), and carbon burden for those savings (CB). For a tree which does not contribute to energy savings, the formulation is somewhat different because the main net benefit is through the sequestering of carbon for plant growth. The cost of sequestered carbon (CSC) is thus given as:

$$\text{CSC (\$/T-C)} = \frac{\text{Capital Cost x (CRF)}}{\text{C sequestered/year}}$$

where: CRF = capital recovery factor, as given above.

Factors Affecting Unit Cost of Saved Carbon

There are many factors that influence the cost of sequestered carbon from tree planting. They include seedling price, planting cost, maintenance cost (watering, fertilizing, and protection), survival rate, soil quality and climate (which determines the range of available species and growth rates). Trees in communities generate costs for leaf and branch disposal, pruning, and eventually, removal and disposal. Other important variables are the type of species planted, location (urban vs. rural), labor costs and overhead, land cost, economic benefits other than carbon saving, i.e., soil conservation, and energy conservation, etc., and the discount rate used in calculating the unit costs.

For trees which contribute to energy savings, the factors affecting the cost of sequestering carbon are the same as for trees that do not. However, since the former both sequester carbon as part of their growth and development and save carbon indirectly through reductions in energy use, the relevant cost factors also include other parameters affecting energy savings, such as site suitability and space conditioning efficiency.

Conclusions and Recommendation

In this appendix, we discuss the possible net benefits of trees for reducing energy, and saving and sequestering carbon. These benefits are described both from the overall perspective of the effects of trees on microclimate and mesoscale climate, as well as from the idea of reducing the release of carbon from trees and fossil fuel power plants. In both situations, a case can be made that trees offer many opportunities for cooling buildings, cooling cities, saving carbon that would ordinarily be released to the atmosphere as carbon dioxide, and maintaining the general well being of human inhabitants.

The appendix provides analytical methods that can be used to compare trees from the perspectives of conserving energy, conserving carbon, and saving and sequestering carbon. The difficulty in making specific estimates resides in the lack of credible data on the costs of planting and maintaining trees, tree survival rates, and the rate of carbon sequestering over the lifetime of the tree. Also, keep in mind that at this time we are unable to estimate a cost benefit of reducing stormwater or preventing soil erosion or other such benefits. Those wishing to use these equations should investigate the costs and biological factors applicable to their areas and use them in the calculations.

Future research on this topic seems highly warranted. Several research topics are recommended. First, there is a need for more precise information about the establishment costs of tree planting programs (e.g., planting and maintenance costs, soil quality, etc.). Second, the various limitations to massive tree planting programs need to be identified and evaluated. As examples, the spatial and water requirements and pollution sensitivities of different tree planting scenarios will require thorough and well documented assessments. Also, it has recently been reported by Chameides et al. (1988) that some tree species may affect urban air pollution in a more important way than previously thought by their emissions of reactive hydrocarbons. This finding needs to be included in any long-term assessment of tree planting programs. Third, case studies of tree planting programs need to be established that can lead to critical evaluations, including field based measurements, of the various different parameters described earlier. Finally, future work is needed to extend this methodology to consider the costs and benefits of urban trees to all sectors of the economy.

References

Akbari, H., J. Huang, P. Martien, L. Rainer, A. Rosenfeld, and H. Taha, 1988. "The impact of summer heat islands on cooling energy consumption and global CO concentration." *Lawrence Berkeley Laboratory Report No. (LBL-25179),* Berkeley, CA.

Akbari, H., J. Huang, P. Martien, L. Rainer, A.Rosenfeld, and H. Taha, 1988. "Saving energy and reducing atmospheric pollution by controlling summer heat islands." *Proceedings of the Workshop on Saving Energy and Reducing Atmospheric Pollution by Controlling Summer Heat Islands (LBL-27872),* February 23-24, 1989, Berkeley, CA. pp. 31-44.

Energy Information Agency (EIA), 1984. *Residential Energy Consumption Survey: Consumption and Expenditures,* April 1984 through March 1985, Part 2: Regional Data (DOE/EIA-0321). U.S. Department of Energy, Washington, D.C.

Krause, F. and J. Koomey, 1989. "Unit costs of carbon savings from urban trees, rural trees, and electricity conservation: a utility cost perspective." *Proceedings of the Workshop on Saving Energy and Reducing Atmospheric Pollution by Controlling Summer Heat Islands* (LBL-27311), February 23-24, 1989, Berkeley, CA. pp. 92-121.

Meier, A., J. Wright, and A.H. Rosenfeld, 1983. *Supplying Energy Through Greater Efficiency.* University of California Press, Berkeley, CA.

Appendix C

Karina Garbesi

Estimating Water Use by Various Landscape Scenarios

This appendix describes a plant water use system originally developed for agricultural crops, but now being used for urban landscape plants. This system was described briefly in Chapter Four. The appendix will also discuss the water-usage implications of changing the relative coverage of lawns, trees, and shrubs.

The Crop Coefficient System for Characterizing Water Use by Landscape Plants

Studies of the irrigation requirements of agricultural crops have provided a useful system for describing relative water use by plants, and for estimating their evapotranspiration (ET) in different environments.[1] In this system, a reference evapotranspiration (ET_0) is defined as the ET (in, for example, mm per day) of a 4 to 7 inch tall, cool-season grass that is not water-stressed, and that is in a large field, rendering boundary effects negligible. (UC Cooperative Extension, Leaflet 21426).

ET_0 data for California are available through the Department of Water Resources (DWR) in a number of forms: 1) monthly historic data are averaged and presented as ET_0 isolines superimposed on the state map; 2) tables of historic data are available for many regions; and 3) ET is calculated daily based on meteorological data collected at 90 weather stations throughout the state. This information, gathered and managed by the California Irrigation Management Information System (CIMIS), is accessible by computer modem and is used by some agricultural irrigators and large-turf managers to calculate deficit irrigation requirements (i.e., watering one week makes up for the water deficit due to evapotranspiration of the week prior, minus any contribution from precipitation).

Evapotranspiration for a particular crop (ET_c) is determined by multiplying a crop coefficient (K_c) by the reference ET:

$$(1) \quad ET_c = K_c \, ET_o \, .$$

In this way, crop coefficients give the relative water use of different crops.

A volumetric evapotranspiration rate (V_{ET}) can be determined by multiplying crop ET by crop area.

$$(2) \quad V_{ET} = ET_c \, A_c = K_c ET_o A_c \, .$$

For a single tree, the volumetric rate of water use is obtained by multiplying the crown area by ET_{tree}, representing the total water transpired and evaporated in the area covered by the tree.

From the perspective of an irrigator, the interesting quantity is the amount of water that needs to be applied to meet the ET demand of the crop. Losses due to runoff and percolation out of the plant root zone are incorporated by an irrigation efficiency term, η , indicating the fraction of applied water which remains in the plant root zone available for use. The irrigation requirement, I_r, for a homogeneous crop under constant environmental conditions is:

$$(3) \quad I_r \, \eta = K_c \, ET_o - P \, .$$

Where I_r is the irrigation water (mm/day) required to make up for ET losses from the previous period which were not replaced by precipitation (P).[2]

Changes in the irrigation requirement due to changes in vegetation type and cover can be calculated by taking the difference of the summed ET requirements of all crops:

$$(4) \quad \Delta I_r = (\sum_{i=1}^{n} K_{c, final\,i} \, f_{final\,i} \, - \sum_{i=1}^{n} K_{c, initial\,i} \, f_{initial\,i}) \, ET_o/\eta$$

where $f_{final\,i}$ and $f_{initial\,i}$ denote the final and initial fractions, respectively, of the total urban area covered by the ith crop. The precipitation term, assumed unchanged, drops out. Similarly, $K_{c, final\,i}$ and $K_{c, initial\,i}$ denote the final and initial crop coefficients of the ith "crop", allowing for changes in water use due to selection of either high- of low-water-use plants. And there are n total "crops", or plant classifications.

The summed terms can be thought of as a net crop coefficient for the region of interest:

$$(5) \quad K_n = \sum_{i=1}^{n} K_{c_i} \, f_i \, ,$$

for either the initial or final distribution. Finally, the percent change in water use may be determined by:

$$(6) \quad \Delta K_n(\%) = \frac{K_{n,\,final} - K_{n,\,initial}}{K_{n,\,initial}} \times 100 \, .$$

Irrigation efficiencies (h) have been measured for large turf areas. An efficiency of 65 percent is considered to be about the best attainable. Typically, irrigation efficiencies of large-turf areas are considerably lower, around 45 to 50 percent , the difference being lost to excessive runoff or percolation due to poor irrigation uniformity or overly rapid or lengthy irrigation.[3] Irrigation efficiency of small lawn areas such as on median strips or bordering streets can be considerably lower if sprinklers are not adjusted properly to limit spray area to the turf. Increasing irrigation efficiency from 45 to 65 percent corresponds with a water savings of 20 percent without any decrease in ET.

It appears that no studies have been made of irrigation efficiencies of urban vegetation types other than turf. Better figures are available for agriculture. In California about 60 percent of applied water leaves as ET[4] to groundwater; and most of the remainder is runoff (Cooperative Extension, Leaflet 21379). Note that a relatively small fraction of the water taken up by a plant is actually incorporated into plant matter. In the case of a tree, for example, more than 95 percent of water taken up is lost through transpiration (Kramer and Kozlowski, 1960).

Recent studies of the water requirements of landscape plants, which were motivated by water scarcity in the western United States have focused on *minimum* rather than optimal water requirements, while maintaining acceptable plant appearance. An *adjusted* crop coefficient (AK_c) was therefore developed for landscape plants, incorporating an allowable level of water stress. AK_c is used by the California Department of Water Resources for calculating turf irrigation requirements. In practice, this parameter is taken as:

$$(7) \quad AK_c = 0.8 * K_c \quad \text{(Walker and Kay, 1989).}$$

If low-water use management practices are adhered to and plants are watered according to an adjusted crop coefficient, then evapotranspiration rates and irrigation requirements would be calculated by equations 1 through 5 replacing K_c with AK_c.

While a huge lore on plant water use exists, little of it explores urban settings. Most studies of plant water-use are for agricultural crops, for which loss in yield due to water stress is not tolerated. Except for some studies of turf grass, researchers have only begun to investigate the water use of trees, shrubs, and ground covers in urban settings.

In addition to the scarcity of reliable data, our ability to quantify the water demand of urban landscapes is complicated by the large number of urban factors that can alter water use. These include:

1) The variety of plant species in urban areas (including large numbers of imported and exotic plants) makes calculations of total landscape water-use starting at the species level intractable.

2) Similarly, transpiration rates for an individual plant also vary with time of day, season, and the life cycle of the plant. Some cease transpiring in darkness, while others also stop in intense sunlight.

3) Variations in environmental and meteorological conditions strongly affect plant evapotranspiration. Changes in light intensity, temperature, humidity, wind, and water availability can drive plant transpiration rates from near zero to maximum levels that can exceed even pan evaporation rates. Urban soils are also often compacted by traffic or covered with pavement, which can affect transpiration rates by limiting the flow of water, oxygen, and nutrients to plant roots.

4) Variations in landscape maintenance practices can mean large variations in water availability, even when all other environmental factors are seemingly equal.

The sources of uncertainties outlined above make it clear that it is difficult to attempt to precisely quantify urban water usage. However, it is possible to estimate landscape water usage rates averaged over longer time periods—such as month—for broad plant categories. Such an approach is adopted here, following a system used by the California Department of Water Resources.

Data on Water Use by Landscape Plants

Table C.1 presents crop coefficients for April to October (the likely irrigation months) for some landscape plants for which measurements have been made. The data appear to indicate a trend that grass uses more water than trees and trees use more water than groundcovers.

Two studies currently underway will provide more data on water requirements of non-turf landscape plants. One project is investigating minimum water requirements of six mature shrubs and groundcovers common in urban Southern California: Hedera *helix* (English ivy), *Baccharis pilularis* (coyote bush), *Potentilla tabernaemontana* (cinquefoil), *Vinca major* (periwinkle), *Gazania rigens* (trailing gazania), and *Drosanthemum hispidum* (pink ice plant).[5] Preliminary results, based on the one year of data on mature plants collected thus far, indicate that minimum water requirements of at least two species are consistent with the low-end K_c's given for groundcovers in Table C.1, but that ice plant, at least, can tolerate a very wide range of applied water.[6]

Another project investigating the minimum water requirements of landscape trees[7], is studying eight tree species: *Liquidambar styraciflua* (sweet gum), *Quercus ilex* (holly oak), *Ficus microcarpus* (Indian laurel fig) *Cupaniopsis anacardioides* (carrot wood), *Pinus radiata* (Monterey pine), and one species of *Phoenix* and two of *Washingtonia* palm. The trees under study are not yet mature, but preliminary results are consistent with the data given above. Data from these studies should become available in the next few years and will be a significant contribution to our quantitative knowledge of water use by landscape plants.

Table C.1 Monthly and Averaged Crop Coefficients for Selected Plants.[a]

Month	Turfgrass Warm	Cool	Avocado	Citrus	Deciduous	Liquidambar	Groundcover Warm Cool
April	.72	1.04	.45	.52	.47	.45	
May	.79	.95	.50	.53	.66	.50	
June	.68	.88	.55	.53	.72	.55	.25 - .50
July	.71	.94	.55	.53	.72	.60	.25 - .50
August	.71	.86	.50	.53	.62	.60	.25 - .50
September	.62	.74	.45	.52	.40	.60	.25 - .50
October	.54	.75	.45	.51	.22	.55	
Average Kc	.68	.88[b]	.49	.52	.54	.55	.25 - .50
Average AKc	.55	.70	.39	.42	.44	.44	.20 - .40

Source: J.L. Meyer and R. Strohman, 1989

a. Data are presented only for months during which irrigation is likely.

b. K_c for a cool season grass is defined as 1.0 by the definition of ET_O given above, this is not to be confused with a cool season *turf* grass, given here. Turf grass has different water requirements because it is cut shorter, 1 to 2 inches rather than 4 to 7 inches as for the reference crop.

Based on currently available data and on discussions with horticultural researchers, we will take the following values as typical crop coefficients:

Table C.2 Average Summertime Crop Coefficients for Landscape Vegetation Classes. (Estimates are subject to change as new data become available.)

Vegetation Type	K_c	AK_c
grass[a]	0.8	0.6
trees	0.5	0.4
shrubs and groundcovers	0.4	0.3

a. K_c for grass was estimated as an average value available for cold and warm season turf grasses.

Although data on crop coefficients of landscape plants are limited, numerous observations by landscapers support the finding that grasses, in general, use more water than trees and shrubs.[8] In fact, the first principle of Xeriscape (low-water use landscaping) is to minimize turf area and replace it with low-water-use trees, shrubs, or groundcovers. Not only do grasses in general want more water than trees, but it appears that watering trees at the same level as grasses can be harmful to many trees. A report by the Municipal Water District of Orange County and the Department of Landscape Architecture at California Polytechnical University lists 44 tree species, their typical lifetimes in Southern California, and their estimated lifetimes if planted in lawns. On average, the lifetime of trees in lawn was 42 percent of their typical lifetimes. For one drought adapted species of eucalyptus (red-iron bark), the estimated lifetime in lawn was only 10percent of the typical lifetime (MWDOC, no date available).

The values in Table C.2 are useful for making first order estimates of water use in areas for which the study plants are representative. However, in areas with primarily high or primarily low-water-use plants, these data may be misleading. It is therefore important to account for the actual local distribution of plants.

Another drawback of using highly aggregated crop coefficients, such as those in Table C.2, is that they can obscure potentially important transpiration characteristics of individual plants. For example, some drought tolerant species like ceanothus and manzanita are dormant during the summer, during which time transpiration is minimized and over watering can actually be lethal. This characteristic could be useful for areas trying to reduce peak summertime water use.

Ideally, we would like to have crop coefficients for a wide range of species to determine, for example, the effect of switching from high to low-water-use plants. We would also like ET data for any given plant in various climates, so that problems of variable adaptations to new environments could be eliminated. Unfortunately, these data do not exist for many plants.

Until better data become available, the relative water needs of different species can be estimated from data on precipitation received in their native habitats. MWDOC (no date available) lists precipitation in their native habitat of 150 landscape plants present in Orange County. These data are reproduced in Table C.3, and crop coefficients are estimated using the crop coefficient of *Liquidambar styraciflua* (from Table C.1) as a reference point. The calculation assumes that runoff and percolation from the root zone are in the same proportion to precipitation in all habitats—so that if plant A lives in an area which receives twice as much precipitation as plant B, it is assumed that the water received and used in the plant root zone is twice as high.

At the end of Table C.3, the estimated crop coefficients are aggregated into average coefficients for groundcovers, shrubs, trees and palms, and vines. These estimates concur with the finding that trees use more water than shrubs and groundcovers. The range of estimated crop coefficients, 1.3 - 0.04, clearly illustrates the potential for altering landscape water needs through species choice. Note, however, that the aggregated crop coefficients given in Table C.3 are somewhat lower than those given in Table C.2. In fact the values are more similar to the *adjusted* crop coefficients of the latter. This result is to be expected, since the species listed in Table C.3 are all plants present in arid Orange County, California. It is likely, therefore, that many were chosen because they are low-water users indigenous to water stressed environments. In addition, the vegetation in Table C.2 cannot be as neatly classified as in Table C.1. Many of the listed species can occur as both trees and shrubs (trees/shrubs). But no distinction is made in the data. This tends to smear distinction among classes. Note that the average crop coefficient for shrubs plus trees/shrubs is somewhat higher than if shrubs only are included. Similarly, the value for trees, palms and trees/shrubs

Table C.3. *Estimated Crop Coefficients of 150 Landscape Plants Based on Annual Precipitation in their Native Habitats.*

(source of rainfall data: MWDOC, no date available)

Veg.* Class	Tree species and genus	annual precip. (inches)	relative water**	estimated Kc***
GC	Delosperma "Alba"	31.8	0.61	0.34
GC	Hedera canariensis	15.9	0.31	0.17
GC	Hedera helix	25.7	0.49	0.27
GC	Vinca major	25.7	0.49	0.27
S	Acacia cyclops	9.9	0.19	0.10
S	Acacia ongerup	18.7	0.36	0.20
S	Albelia gradiflora	43.1	0.83	0.46
S	Arctostaphylos densiflora	15.8	0.30	0.17
S	Arctostaphylos hookeri	29.8	0.57	0.32
S	Baccharis pilularis "Twin Peaks"	39.6	0.76	0.42
S	Baccharis pilularis "Pigeon Point"	39.6	0.76	0.42
S	Carissa gradiflora	39.7	0.76	0.42
S	Ceanothus "Concha"	14.2	0.27	0.15
S	Ceanothus "Joyce Coulter"	14.3	0.28	0.15
S	Ceanothus cyaneus	9.5	0.18	0.10
S	Ceanothus griseus horizontalis	12.3	0.24	0.13
S	Cistus crispus	25.4	0.49	0.27
S	Cistus ladanifer	16.5	0.32	0.17
S	Cistus pupureus	16.5	0.32	0.17
S	Coprosma baueris (C. repens)	60.5	1.16	0.64
S	Dodonaea viscosa	24.0	0.46	0.25
S	Echium fastuosum	21.5	0.41	0.23
S	Elaegnus pungens	42.5	0.82	0.45
S	Encelia californica	12.3	0.24	0.13
S	Escallonia rubra	14.1	0.27	0.15
S	Grevillia lanigera	26.8	0.52	0.28
S	Heteromeles arbutifolia	43.3	0.83	0.46
S	Jasminum humile	9.1	0.18	0.10
S	Lantana camara	71.3	1.37	0.75
S	Lantana montevidensis	53.1	1.02	0.56
S	Leptospermum scoparium	36.9	0.71	0.39
S	Myrtus communis	20.0	0.38	0.21
S	Pittosporum tobira	44.7	0.86	0.47
S	Plumbago auriculata	36.8	0.71	0.39
S	Psidium littorale	53.1	1.02	0.56
S	Rhamnus californica "Eve Case"	14.2	0.27	0.15
S	Rhus integrifolia	15.6	0.30	0.16
S	Ribes viburnifolium	15.6	0.30	0.16
S	Rosmarinus officinalis	23.2	0.45	0.25
S	Syzygium paniculatum	44.7	0.86	0.47
S	Tecomaria capensis	8.9	0.17	0.09
S	Viburmum japonicum	82.8	1.59	0.88
T	Acacia baileyana	23.0	0.44	0.24
T	Acacia melanoxylon	55.3	1.06	0.59
T	Acacia pendula	23.0	0.44	0.24
T	Agonis flexuosa	38.9	0.75	0.41
T	Albizia julibrissin	46.4	0.89	0.49
T	Alnus rhombifolia	42.6	0.82	0.45
T	Araucaria bidwillii	69.8	1.34	0.74
T	Arbutus unedo	23.3	0.45	0.25
T	Brachychition acerifolius	26.1	0.50	0.28
T	Brachychition populneum	23.0	0.44	0.24

Veg.* Class	Tree species and genus	annual precip. (inches)	relative water**	estimated Kc***
T	Carpobrotus chilensis	10.2	0.20	0.11
T	Carpobrotus edulis	20.0	0.38	0.21
T	Casuarina cumminghamiana	23.0	0.44	0.24
T	Casuarina equisetifolia	41.0	0.79	0.43
T	Casuarina stricta	23.0	0.44	0.24
T	Cedrus deodora	9.7	0.19	0.10
T	Ceratonia siliqua	25.7	0.49	0.27
T	Chorisa specios	65.8	1.27	0.70
T	Cinnamomum camphora	52.6	1.01	0.56
T	Cupaniopsis anacardiopsis	44.7	0.86	0.47
T	Eriobotrya deflexa	84.8	1.63	0.90
T	Erythrina caffra	8.9	0.17	0.09
T	Eucalyptus camaldulensis	21.1	0.41	0.22
T	Eucalyptus citriodora	39.6	0.76	0.42
T	Eucalyptus cladocalyx	9.4	0.18	0.10
T	Eucalyptus ficifolia	39.7	0.76	0.42
T	Eucalyptus globulus	24.0	0.46	0.25
T	Eucalyptus grandis	44.7	0.86	0.47
T	Eucalyptus lahmannii	22.4	0.43	0.24
T	Eucalyptus leucoxylon	17.7	0.34	0.19
T	Eucalyptus maculata	37.2	0.72	0.39
T	Eucalyptus nicholii	36.5	0.70	0.39
T	Eucalyptus polyanthemos	23.0	0.44	0.24
T	Eucalyptus robusta	59.3	1.14	0.63
T	Eucalyptus rudis	10.1	0.19	0.11
T	Eucalyptus sideroxylon	21.8	0.42	0.23
T	Eucalyptus viminalis	26.4	0.51	0.28
T	Ficus benjamina	63.0	1.21	0.67
T	Ficus macrophylla	40.0	0.77	0.42
T	Ficus rubiginosa	21.8	0.42	0.23
T	Fraxinus uhdei	39.5	0.76	0.42
T	Fraxinus velutina	21.9	0.42	0.23
T	Geijera parviflora	19.2	0.37	0.20
T	Ginkgo biloba	44.7	0.86	0.47
T	Gleditsia triacanthos	49.1	0.94	0.52
T	Grevillea robusta	46.5	0.89	0.49
T	Jacaranda mimosifolia	20.4	0.39	0.22
T	Koelreuteria bipinnata (elegans)	19.3	0.37	0.20
T	Koelreuteria paniculata	43.1	0.83	0.46
T	Lagunaria patersonii	52.4	1.01	0.55
T	Leptosperman laevigatum	46.5	0.89	0.49
T	Ligustrum japonicum	46.3	0.89	0.49
T	Liquidambar styraciflua	52.0	1.00	0.55
T	Magnolia grandiflora	50.8	0.98	0.54
T	Melaleuca linariifolia	46.5	0.89	0.49
T	Melaleuca quinquenervia	44.7	0.86	0.47
T	Olea europaea	23.3	0.45	0.25
T	Photinia serrulata	43.1	0.83	0.46
T	Pinus canariensis	3.9	0.08	0.04
T	Pinus halepensis	25.4	0.49	0.27
T	Pinus Pinea	35.6	0.68	0.38
T	Pittosporum phillyraeoides	9.7	0.19	0.10
T	Pittosporum viridiflorum	30.9	0.59	0.33
T	Platanus acerifolia	19.2	0.37	0.20
T	Platanus racemosa	14.1	0.27	0.15
T	Podocarpus gracilior	38.2	0.73	0.40
T	Podocarpus macrophyllus	124.8	2.40	1.32

Veg.* Class	Tree species and genus	annual precip. (inches)	relative water**	estimated Kc***
T	Pyrus calleryana	36.8	0.71	0.39
T	Quercus agrifolia	12.3	0.24	0.13
T	Quercus ilex	25.4	0.49	0.27
T	Quercus suber	23.2	0.45	0.25
T	Schinus molle	28.2	0.54	0.30
T	Tristania conferta	41.0	0.79	0.43
T	Ulmus parvifolia	15.9	0.31	0.17
T	Viburnum tinus	25.4	0.49	0.27
T(P)	Archontophoenix cunninghamiana	66.5	1.28	0.70
T(P)	Butia capitata	40.1	0.77	0.42
T(P)	Chamaerops humilis	15.4	0.30	0.16
T(P)	Phoenix reclinata	35.1	0.68	0.37
T(P)	Washingtonia filifera	3.3	0.06	0.04
T(P)	Washingtonia robusta	8.4	0.16	0.09
T,S	Callistemon citrinus	44.7	0.86	0.47
T,S	Callistemon viminalis	41.0	0.79	0.43
T,S	Feijoa sellowiana	65.8	1.27	0.70
T,S	Hakea suaveolens	11.4	0.22	0.12
T,S	Laurus nobilis	16.5	0.32	0.17
T,S	Melaleuca armillaris	29.5	0.57	0.31
T,S	Melaleuca nesophylla	26.4	0.51	0.28
T,S	Metrosideros excelsus	49.1	0.94	0.52
T,S	Myoporum laetum	35.1	0.68	0.37
T,S	Nerium oleander	23.2	0.45	0.25
T,S	Pittosporum crassifolium	35.1	0.68	0.37
T,S	Pittosporum undulatum	46.5	0.89	0.49
T,S	Prunus caroliniana	52.0	1.00	0.55
T,S	Prunus ilicifolia	14.2	0.27	0.15
T,S	Prunus lusitanica	32.3	0.62	0.34
T,S	Prunus lyonii	31.2	0.60	0.33
T,S	Psidium guajava	53.1	1.02	0.56
T,S	Schinus terebinthifolius	54.5	1.05	0.58
T,S	Xylosma congestum	42.2	0.81	0.45
T?	Acacia "Pecoffverde"	10.2	0.20	0.11
T?	Acacia rosmarinifolia	9.1	0.18	0.10
V	Bougainvillea glabra	53.1	1.02	0.56
V	Bougainvillea spectabilis	53.1	1.02	0.56
V	Cissus antartica	46.5	0.89	0.49
V	Lonicera japonica "Halliana"	43.1	0.83	0.46
V	Parthenocissus tricuspidata	52.6	1.01	0.56
V	Wisteria sinensis	27.3	0.53	0.29
	Average of all plants	32.96		0.35
	Max	124.80		1.32
	Min	3.34		0.04
	St. Dev.	18.50		0.20
	Average of GC's	24.775		0.26
	Average of S's and T,S's	31.99		0.34
	Average of T's, T(P's) and T,S's	33.82	0.36	
	Average of V's	45.95		0.49

*Vegetation Classes: GC = groundcover, S = shrub, T = Tree, T(P) = Palm, V = vine
**Water use is relative to that of Liquidambar Styraciflua.
***Kc's are calculated relative to Kc of Liquidambar Styraciflua (= relative water use . 0.55).

is somewhat lower than if trees alone are included. In other words, if only species known to belong to a given class are included, the values in Table C.3 diverge toward the values of the adjusted crop coefficients given in Table C.2.

ET in a Multi-layered Canopy

One final issue is worth examining—the potentially important contribution to water-use by grass growing beneath trees. In other words, real urban canopies are multi-layered. The assumption of a single-layered canopy implicit in the fore-going calculations might under-estimate net landscape water use. This section examines the effect on lawn water use of shading by trees.

We will assume that the environment seen by the tree is essentially unchanged and calculate the additional ET of the shaded lawn. A simple empirical model of potential ET (ET_p) of crops is used to estimate the change in grass ET.[9] The model, developed by Jensen and Haise (1963), is given as a function of dry-bulb temperature (T) and net short wave radiation (R_n) at the grass surface.

$$(8) \quad ET_p = (0.0252 \, T - 0.078) \, R_n$$

where ET_p is in cm of water per day, T is in degrees Celsius, and R_n is expressed in equivalent cm of evaporated water per day. Rewriting R_n in terms of the incident solar radiation I as I(1-a), where a is the albedo of the grass, and using an average value of a = 0.2 (Oke 1987, pg. 12):

$$(9) \quad ET_p = 0.8 \, (0.0252 \, T - 0.078) \, I \, .$$

Taking the total differential of ET_p and dividing by ET_p gives:

$$(10) \quad dET_p/ET_p = dI/I + (0.0252 \, dT)/(0.0252 \, T - 0.078) \, .$$

So, in order to estimate the effect of the tree on $ET_{p,grass}$ we need to estimate the attenuation of net short wave radiation due to the presence of the canopy and the change in air temperature under the canopy. Taha et al. (1988) measured daytime temperature suppression in an orchard. Within 5 m of the edge of the canopy they measured temperatures as much as 4.5°C lower than outside the orchard. Because we are interested in the effect of an isolated tree, under which air exchange with the surroundings should be considerably larger, we will use a smaller value of 1°C.

We will use a simple model of exponential attenuation of light as it filters down through the canopy (Jones 1983, pg. 31):

$$(11) \quad I/I_0 = e^{-kL} \, ,$$

where I_0 is the intensity of light at the top of the tree canopy, L is the leaf area index,[10] and k is an attenuation factor, dependent on canopy structure and sun angle. Observed values of k range from 0.3 to 1.5 (Jones 1983, pg. 33). Kittredge (1948) lists leaf area indices of 10 trees ranging from 2.8 to 10.7. Using even a modest leaf area index of

5 and a k of 0.5, the fraction of incident radiation which makes it through the canopy (I/I_0) is only 0.08. In other words, the short wave radiation the lawn sees is 92 percent lower in the shade of the tree ($dI/I = -0.92$). Using this value, $dT = -1°C$, and $T = 32°C$ in Equation 9, we get an estimated reduction in ET of grass of 95 percent !

We should interpret this result as an indication that suppression of lawn ET can be large as a result of shading. Indeed, the results suggest that the total water use of a fully shaded lawn covered by low-water-use trees might well be lower than water use of the unshaded lawn alone. We should not, however, put a lot of faith in the numerical result for a number of reasons. First, an isolated tree will not provide full shade under the canopy at all times of day. Second, vegetation might be shaded at certain times of day by buildings regardless of the presence of the tree.[11] Third, simple linear models like Equations 9 and 10 are not likely to be robust against large changes in the input parameters. This can be seen by using high K and L values which results in a reduction in ET of greater than 100 percent .

In conclusion, while planting trees above lawn is certainly not as effective in reducing landscape water-use as planting trees without lawn, lawn water needs can be reduced enough by shading to make planting worthwhile. The best tactic, of course, would be to either mulch beneath the tree or to plant low-water-use groundcover or shrubs.

Sample Calculations of Changes in Landscape Water Use and ET based on Different Planting Scenarios

In theory, changes in landscape water requirements for a given urban area can be estimated based on the surface areas covered by different plants species. However, few urban areas have extensive plant inventories which distinguish numbers of plants at the species level. Although most cities now have, or are in the process of creating, tree inventories for street and park trees, few are likely to gather a complete inventory of trees on other public and private lands.[12] Furthermore, statistics on these trees are not likely to be representative of the rest of the urban forest for two reasons. First, trees on streetsides and in parks which are managed by the city are likely to be chosen from a limited list of pre-approved tree species, whereas trees planted on private lands are not similarly controlled. Second, park and street trees make up only a small fraction of the total urban forest.[13]

More detailed biomass data is available for some areas. Miller and Winer (1984) used random sampling to quantify species composition and dominance in the Los Angeles Basin. The study identifies 184 species, and the number of occurrences of each, distributed among six structural classes: broadleaf trees, conifers, palms, shrubs, grasses, and ground covers. For 56 prominent species, total ground area occupied and total leafy crown volume are estimated (including the average area and volume per specimen). Others, for example Richards et al. (1984) and Dorney et al. (1984), have investigated the composition of vegetation of some subsection of a city in detail.

This lack of data on species present in urban areas parallels the lack of data on water use by individual species. The combination means that estimates of landscape water use for large urban areas must generally be based on estimates of occurrence and water use of broad classes of plants—such as grasses, trees, shrubs, and groundcovers. Different landscape types can then be represented by changing the relative areas covered by each plant class or modifying water use of a given class—which in practice corresponds with, for example, selecting low-water-use species within a class. This approach is taken below. Changes in water use due to changes in relative areas covered are calculated using Equation 7. And changes in landscape water demand due to selection of primarily low-water-use plants are estimated by modifying the crop coefficients.

The initial vegetation distribution (the base case) is assumed to be 13 percent turf, 10 percent trees and palms, and 4 percent shrubs and groundcovers. This distribution is the same as that given by Brown and Winer (1986) for the Los Angeles Basin and was chosen as representative of vegetation in an arid western city, not as an attempt to describe landscape water use in that city in particular. The total vegetation coverage 27 percent of the urban area) falls within the range found by Rowntree (1984), 24-37 percent, in his study of four eastern United States cities.

In the first analysis, the three vegetation classes are assumed to have the typical crop coefficients given in Table C.2. Table C.4 shows the estimated changes in landscape ET requirements due to changes in areal cover of the three vegetation classes. In Cases 1-4 total vegetation cover was held constant. In Cases 5-7 total vegetation cover was increased first to 33 percent, and later to 40 percent.

Table C.4. Calculated changes in plant ET requirements for different landscape scenarios based on crop coefficients in Table C.2. (Estimated changes are relative to the base case.)

| | K_c | % of urban area covered by vegetation type | | | | | | |
		Base Case	Case 2	Case 3	Case 4	Case 5	Case 6	Case 7
grass	0.8	13	8	3	4	5	3	0
trees and palms	0.5	10	15	20	15	20	30	20
shrubs and GC's	0.4	4	4	4	8	8	7	20
% veg. cover		27	27	27	27	33	40	40
EK_c (urban)[a]		0.17	0.16	0.14	0.14	0.17	0.20	0.18
EK_c (vegetated)[b]		0.63	0.57	0.52	0.51	0.52	0.51	0.45
% change in ET[c]		0.00	-10	-18	-19	0	18	5

a. Effective crop coefficient of entire urban canopy, including non-transpiring areas. Defined as: $EK_{c, urban} = K_{c,g}f_{u,g} + K_{c,t}f_{u,t} + K_{c,s}f_{u,s}$; where $K_{c,g}$ is the crop coefficient for grass, $f_{u,g}$ is the fraction of urban area covered by grass, and similarly for trees and shrubs.

b. Effective crop coefficient of vegetated area only. Defined as: $EK_{c, vegetated} = K_{c,g}f_{v,g} + K_{c,t}f_{v,t} + K_{c,s}f_{v,s}$; where $K_{c,g}$ is the crop coefficient for grass, $f_{v,g}$ is the fraction of vegetated are covered by grass, and similarly for trees and shrubs.

c. Estimated change in ET calculated using Equation 7, assuming the base case as the initial distribution.

Cases 2 and 3 show the effect of increasing tree cover by 50 percent and 100 percent, respectively, while decreasing grass cover correspondingly and holding shrub cover constant. The effect is a notable decrease in ET requirement of 18 percent . Case 4 shows the effect of increasing tree and shrub cover by 50 percent and 100 percent, respectively, and holding total vegetation cover constant. ET is reduced 19 percent. Case 5 indicates that we can double tree and shrub cover, and increase total vegetation cover to 33 percent with no change in ET if lawn cover is reduced to approximately 40 percent of its base value.

Cases 6 and 7 show scenarios for a total vegetation cover of 40 percent.[14] Case 6 shows ET requirements increasing by 18 percent with tree cover tripled, shrub cover nearly doubled, and grass reduced to 23 percent of the base case. In Case 7, taken as an extreme, all grass is removed and vegetation cover is equally split between trees and shrubs. This represents an increase in total vegetation cover of almost 50 percent, with only a 5 percent increase in ET demand.

Next, landscape ET requirements are calculated assuming that low-water-use species are purposefully selected. The results are shown in Table C.5. The change in water needs are modeled by reducing the crop coefficients for trees and shrubs to 0.3 and 0.25, respectively. This appears feasible based on the estimated K_cs for trees and shrubs in Table C.3 Lawn K_c is assumed to remain the same since widespread use of water-conserving warm season grasses seems unlikely for landscaping purposes since these grasses tend to be brown and dormant in the winter time.

Table C.5. Calculated changes in plant ET requirements for different landscape scenarios based on crop coefficients for low-water-use vegetation.[a] (Estimated changes are relative to the base case shown in Table C.3.)

	K_c	C2	C3	C4	C5	C6	C7	C8	C9	C10
					% of urban area covered by vegetation type					
grass	0.8	8	3	4	5	3	0	7	13	13
trees and palms	0.3	15	20	15	20	30	20	30	10	15
shrubs and GC's	0.25	4	4	8	8	7	20	10	4	9
% veg. cover		27	27	27	33	40	40	47	27	37
K_c (urban)		0.12	0.09	0.10	0.12	0.13	0.11	0.17	0.14	0.17
K_c (vegetated)		0.44	0.35	0.36	0.36	0.33	0.28	0.36	0.53	0.46
% change in ET		-31	-45	-43	-30	-23	-36	0	-16	0
relative savings (%)[b]		21	27	24	30	5	31	—	—	—

a. All column headings as in Table C.4, except where specified otherwise.

b. Water savings in Table C.5 relative to Table C.4:
(% change in ET from Table C.4.) - (% change in ET from Table C.5.)

Cases 2 through 7 assume identical vegetation distributions in Tables C.4 and C.5. The *relative savings* (Table C.5) show how much water is saved in each case if low-water-use plants are used. These estimates indicate that water savings are large. Even Case 6, which assumes a tripling of tree cover from the base case and an almost 50 percent increase in total vegetation cover, still results in a decrease of water requirements of 23 percent, over the base case of Table C.4. The savings of low-water-use plants in this case is 41 percent. Case 8 indicates that tree coverage could be tripled, shrub coverage more than doubled, and total vegetation increased to 47 percent, while still retaining more than half of the lawn area, with no increase in ET demand. Case 9 recalculates water requirements for the base case configuration using low-water-use plants. The savings is estimated at 16 percent. Lastly, Case 10 indicates that with lawn at the base case level, ET could remain constant, while increasing trees and shrubs by 50 percent or more if low-water-use trees and shrubs are used.

A comparison of the estimated average tree Kc's in Tables C.2 and C.3 suggests that the crop coefficients used in Table C.4 might be somewhat high for western cities which have already preferentially incorporated low-water-use trees. If this is true, then the relative savings of adopting low-water-use plants could be considerably lower than those shown on the bottom line of Table C.5. That is, the crop coefficients might already be closer to those used in Table C.5 than those in Table C.4, so that the relevant changes in water use would result from changes in vegetation class distribution (trees and shrubs vs. lawn) rather than by changes in species choice within a vegetation class. Answers to these questions can be settled only at a regional level, with better information on the actual species present, their numbers and water use.

Despite these uncertainties, it is reassuring to find that the estimated water savings in Tables C.4 and C.5 are consistent with landscaper's estimates of the water conservation potential of Xeriscape design. Savings from full implementation of all of the principles of Xeriscape design are estimated at up to 70 percent (Swearengin 1987). This figure includes a savings of 10 to 20 percent from irrigation efficiency, not considered here. Savings from limited lawn areas and low-water-use plants, then, could be as high as 50 to 60 percent. A detailed study by Nelson (1987) of seven multi-family dwellings with mature landscapes and a total of 548 dwelling units, reports an average water savings of 54 percent by water conserving landscapes relative to traditional landscapes.

Because individual trees are likely to have their greatest impact on energy savings by shading single family houses, we must consider typical conditions in which we find trees next to houses. In many cases the tree canopy will overlie lawn area rather than replace it, so we ought include the water used by the shaded lawn in our areal estimate of net water use.

Endnotes

[1] Although strictly speaking plants do not evapotranspire. However, following the convention for agricultural crops, we use evapotranspiration of a plant to indicate the transpiration plus evaporation which occurs on or under the plant canopy.

[2] A more sophisticated model would include returns of water by condensation (dew) which might be important in areas with high atmospheric moisture content and large diurnal temperature swings.

[3] Interview with Gary Kah, President, AgTech Associates, Dec. 19, 1989. Agtech developed the landscape water auditing program for the California Department of Water Resource's Office of Water Conservation. For a summary of audit results, see DWR (1989).

4 This corresponds with an n of 0.6, assuming that water which is not lost to percolation or runoff is left to meet the ET demand of the crop.

5 The Principal Investigator of this study is Dennis R. Pittenger, Botany and Plant Sciences Department, UC Riverside. The project is being carried out by researchers at the University of California at Riverside and the University of California Cooperative Extension Service

6 Interview with D. R. Pittenger, Nov. 29, 1989. (See proceeding note.)

7 Interview with Janet Harten, Irrigation and Soils Specialist, Department of Soil and Environmental Sciences, University of California, Riverside, 11/27/89. Project by the University of California, Cooperative Extension Service.

8 Although this is true in general, there are trees, especially riparian species adapted to growing with their roots in groundwater, which use a lot of water. Also, in high winds, with tree crowns exposed and grass areas sheltered, the ET of the exposed trees can be driven above that of the underlying lawn, or even above that of ground-level pan evaporation.

9 Potential ET is the rate of ET of plants experiencing no water stress.

10 The leaf area index is the total leaf area divided by the horizontal projection of the tree canopy.

11 Preferential shading and sheltering of understory plants could result in the ratio of the water demand of trees to low-growing vegetation being elevated in suburban areas where trees are likely to form a windbreak, and understory vegetation receives combined shelter from both trees and buildings. When better water use data from controlled experiments on individual landscape plants become available it would be worthwhile correcting water consumption estimates of tall trees during windy conditions in suburban areas.

12 Interview with Rowan Rowntree, head of Urban Forest Research, U.S. Forest Service, Jan. 19, 1990.

13 This is supported by data from Richards *et al.* (1984) from a study in Syracuse, New York. The authors found that while parks and streetsides comprise about 9 and 7 percent of the total urban greenspace, respectively, residential greenspace alone constitutes 48 percent of the total.

14 Earlier studies indicate that this amount of vegetation is achievable in a city. Similarly, Richards et al. (1984) report total greenspace in Syracuse, New York, as 58 percent . Rowntree (1984) found potential growing space for urban trees of 55 to 66 percent in four eastern US cities.

15 The per dwelling savings of the water conserving landscapes averaged $75 per dwelling unit per year, with 38 percent of the savings from water alone. In addition, considerable savings on labor, fertilizer, fuel, and herbicides (25, 61, 44, and 22 percent , respectively) were found.

References

Brown, D.E. and A.M. Winer (1986) "Estimating Urban Vegetation Cover in Los Angeles," Photogrammetric Engineering and Remote Sensing, 52(1): 117-123.

Dorney, J.R., G.R. Guntenspergen, J.R. Keough, and R.Stearns (1984) "Composition and Structure of an Urban Woody Plant Community," *Urban Ecology*, Special Issue edited by R. Rowntree, **8**(1/2): 69-90.

DWR (1989) Annual Report-July 1988 to October 1989 Landscape Water Management Program, Office of Water Conservation, Department of Water Resources, State of California, Sacramento, CA.

Jensen, M.E. and H.R. Haise (1963) "Estimating Evapotranspiration from Solar Radiation," *Journal of the Irrigation and Drainage Division,* Proceedings of the American Society of Civil Engineers, **89**: 15-41.

Jones, H.G. (1983) *Plants and Microclimate,* Cambridge University Press, Cambridge, England.

Kittredge, J. (1948) *Forest Influences,* Dover, New York, NY.

Kramer, P.J. and T.T. Kozlowski (1960) *Physiology of Trees,* McGraw-Hill Book Co., New York, NY.

McPherson, E.G. (1989) "Vegetation to Conserve Water and Mitigate Urban Heat Islands," In: Controlling Summer Heat Islands: Proceedings of the Workshop on Saving Energy and Reducing Atmospheric Pollution by Controlling Summer Heat Islands; K. Garbesi, H. Akbari, and P. Martien (Eds.), Lawrence Berkeley Laboratory, Berkeley, CA, Report No. LBL-27872, pp. 53-69.

Meyer, J.L. and R. Strohman (1989, August) Handbook for Irrigation Evaluation and Scheduling, University of California Cooperative Extension, University of California at Riverside.

Miller, P.R. and A.M. Winer (1984) "Composition and Dominance in Los Angeles Basin Urban Vegetation," *Urban Ecology*, Special Issue edited by R. Rowntree, **8**(1/2): 29-54.

MWDOC (no date) Landscape Water Conservation Guidelines for Orange County, Prepared for the California Department of Water Resources, by the Municipal Water District of Orange County, the Department of Landscape Architecture, California Polytechnic University, Pomona, and EDAW, Inc.

Nelson, J.O. (1987) "Water Conserving Landscapes Show Impressive Savings," *Xeriscape News,* Jan./Feb. [National Xeriscape Council, Inc., 940 E. Fifty-first St., Austin, Texas 78751-2241]

Oke, T.R. (1987) *Boundary Layer Climates*, Methuen, New York.

Richards, N.A., R.R. Mallette, R.J. Simpson, and E.A. Macie (1984) "Residential Greenspace and Vegetation in a Mature City: Syracuse, New York," *Urban Ecology*, Special Issue edited by R. Rowntree, **8**(1/2): 99-125.

Rowntree, A.R. (1984d) "Forest Canopy Cove and Land Use in Four Eastern United States Cities," *Urban Ecology*, Special Issue edited by R. Rowntree, **8**(1/2): 55-67.

Swearengin, R. (1987) "Water Saving Flow with Efficient Irrigation, Good Practices," *Xeriscape News,* Nov./Dec. [National Xeriscape Council, Inc., 940 E. Fifty-first St., Austin, Texas 78751-2241]

Taha, H., H. Akbari, and A. Rosenfeld (Submitted) "Heat Island Oasis Effects of Vegetative Canopies: Micro-Meteorological Field-Measurements," Submitted to *Theoretical and Applied Climatology.*

UC Cooperative Extension (no date) "California's Water Resource," Cooperative Extension, University of California, Division of Agriculture and Natural Resources, Leaflet 21379. (Can be obtained through ANR Publications, University of California, 6701 San Pablo Ave., Oakland, CA 94608-1239. (415) 642-2431.)

UC Cooperative Extension (no date) "Determining Daily Reference Evapotranspiration (ET$_0$)," Cooperative Extension, University of California, Division of Agriculture and Natural Resources, Leaflet 21426. (Can be obtained through ANR Publications, University of California, 6701 San Pablo Ave., Oakland, CA 94608-1239. (415) 642-2431.)

Walker, R.E. and G.F. Kay (1989, January) Landscape Water Management Handbook, Version 4.1, Prepared for Office of Water Conservation, Department of Water Resources, State of California.

Appendix D

John H. Parker
Susan Panzer

Sample Ordinance

Comprehensive Model Energy Conservation Landscaping Ordinance

The intent of the Comprehensive Model Energy Conservation Landscaping Ordinance is to apply energy conservation landscaping principles to conventional landscaping ordinances. Minimum landscape standards are set forth for residential, commercial, industrial and public areas, as well as for off-street parking and other vehicular use areas.

The positive impact that landscaping can have upon space cooling requirements of buildings has been documented in recent years. Air conditioning requirements can be reduced by as much as 40 to 50 percent during the hottest parts of the cooling season by using properly designed landscaping. The use of energy conservation landscaping which yields minimum energy savings is penalized.

Preservation of desirable trees and shrubs to meet reforestation requirements is also rewarded through the credit system. The preservation of such vegetation is desirable for two reasons: 1) reduced costs for the purchase and installation of new specimens, and 2) the retention of native canopy, especially of large, often irreplaceable, trees.

Energy conservation is the intent of substantial shading requirements for off-street parking and other vehicular use areas. The cooler ambient air temperatures resulting from shading would lessen the need to air condition vehicles. Furthermore, reduced heat collection by such paved surfaces should impact positively upon air-conditioning requirements of nearby buildings.

A street tree program is outlined, reflecting the desirable consequences of shading public rights-of-way, pedestrian paths and bike paths. Such shading provides a cool microclimate, encouraging the use of these paved areas. Increased use of these areas could result in reduced use of vehicular transportation. Furthermore, reduced heat collection by these paved areas would reduce heat gain of nearby buildings.

Finally, standards designed to protect solar access are established. The use of solar insolation to heat water and to passively heat buildings can significantly reduce the use of nonrenewable sources traditionally used for these purposes. Measures must be taken to assure access to this valuable energy source.

SECTION 1. TITLE

This ordinance shall be known and referred to as the "Comprehensive Model Energy Conservation Landscape Ordinance."

SECTION 2. INTENT

The intent of this ordinance shall be to assure the preservation of and provision for vegetation associated with the development or redevelopment of structures and parking areas with _(locality).,_ in accordance with the best principles of environmental management, site planning and, most particularly, energy conservation, in order to protect, maintain, and enhance the well being of the citizens of _(locality)._ It is intended by this ordinance that landscaping shall be used wherever possible to reduce the overall level of energy consumption by structures and heat gain by parking areas through modification of microclimatic temperatures. In addition, it is the intent that this ordinance shall encourage the preservation of desirable native trees and shrubs, which the community is in danger of losing, and which are best suited to the _(local area)_ environment, thereby requiring less energy input for maintenance.

SECTION 3. FINDINGS OF FACT

The _(local agency)_ of _(locality)_ finds that:

A. The installation and maintenance of landscaping areas is not only desirable but essential to promote the health, safety, welfare and general well being of the community, and the requirement of the same constitutes a proper use of police power.

B. Vegetation, if properly utilized, offers the possibility of greatly decreasing the energy used in cooling buildings which are less than three stories in height by shading walls and windows and by reducing ambient temperatures in and around buildings via evapotranspiration. A single mature tree releases about 100 gallons of water per day into the atmosphere, providing the cooling equivalent of nine room air conditioners operating at 8000 Btus per hour for twelve hours per day.

C. Trees and other vegetation:

1. absorb large amounts of carbon dioxide and return oxygen to the air, a vital ingredient for life;
2. precipitate dust and other particulate pollutants from the air;
3. abate noise pollution;
4. add beauty to streets, roadways and developed areas;

5. provide an invaluable psychological counterpoint to man-made urban settings;

6. become a valuable property asset that can affect the value and saleability of the land;

7. provide habitats for wildlife;

8. increase the amount of unpaved surface area, allowing for more efficient aquifer recharge.

D. Native vegetation is adapted to local diseases, pests, soil and climate, thereby requiring the least amounts of pest control, fertilizer and water. Thus, native vegetation is generally the most energy and cost efficient vegetation to be used.

E. Exotic vegetation can crowd out native vegetation, increase the use of fertilizers and water and degrade water quality.

F. Uncontrolled removal of vegetation before, during and after site alteration, as well as lack of protection of vegetation during construction activities, may have an adverse impact upon the ecological balance by:

1. radically changing the microclimatic temperatures of immediate areas, resulting in increased ambient temperatures and, as a result, increased energy consumption for space cooling;

2. accelerating the natural processes of erosion, sedimentation and runoff.

G. Replacement of vegetation at site alterations stabilizes the soil, reduces erosion, and enhances the beauty, quality and viability of the environment;

H. The quality of the environment can be maintained and the level of energy consumed can be minimized if proper techniques for preservation, protection, and restoration of native and non-competing vegetation is carried out at development sites;

I. The shading of paved areas will reduce the maximum ambient temperatures of such areas by approximately 10°F. By thus reducing heating loads within paved areas such as parking lots, vegetation can minimize the need to air condition vehicles. Such vegetation can also limit solar insulation absorbed by paved surfaces, resulting in lower ambient temperatures in areas surrounding paved surfaces. Such reduction in ambient temperatures may minimize the need to air conditioning structures adjacent to said paved surfaces. The use of trees to shade public rights-of-ways also creates a more pleasant environment, encouraging the use of pedestrian paths and bikeways.

J. The utilization of energy conservation landscapes yields large reductions (up to 50 percent) in energy consumed for air conditioning buildings.

K. The climate modifying effects of vegetation is usually maximized during those periods in which energy consumption for air conditioning is also at a maximum.

L. Landscaping of structures is particularly effective during hot summer afternoons when electrical utility demand peaks, thus reducing kilowatt-hour usage, electric bills, *and* the need for new power plants.

M. During the cooling season, attempts to reduce heat gain must focus on using trees and shrubs to shade (in order of priority) 1) the west and 2) the east and south exposures.

N. Based upon potential energy conservation impact on a building, a priority listing of the areas for the provision of shade during the cooling season·are as follows (from highest to lowest):

1. Windows
2. Air conditioners
3. Insulated roofs
4. Wall areas immediately adjacent to air conditioners
5. Other walls (in order of priority);
   a. west
   b. east and south
6. Horizontal surfaces adjacent to air conditioners
7. North walls
8. Solar absorbing surfaces within twenty feet (20') of the building.
9. Ground within five feet (5') of the building
10. Other adjacent ground area.

O. Energy conservation landscaping should focus on the shading of windows since more heat is gained through windows than through any other structural component of a building.

P. The use of landscaping to shade air conditioners can increase the operating efficiency of said air conditioners by 4-10 percent during the warmest periods of the cooling season.

Q. The hours of significant direct solar heat gain are:

1. West exposure - 2:30pm to 7:30pm
2. East exposure - 7:30am to 12:00pm
3. South exposure - 9:30am to 5:30pm

R. Trees to be used for energy conservation should be planted so that within ten (10) years the canopy will be within a) five feet (5') of west or east walls or overhangs or b) three feet (3') of south walls or overhangs. Shrubs to be used for energy conservation should be planted within five feet (5') of west, east, or south walls (and to a lesser extent, north walls.) so that after a period of four (4) years, the shrub will extend within one foot (1') of the wall. If vegetation is placed at distances greater than the above, a belt of sunlight can fall on the lower part of the wall, increasing ambient air and wall temperatures.

S. Reductions in heat gain through walls and windows is maximized when trees, shrubs and ground cover are combined in the landscape plan.

SECTION 4. OBJECTIVES

In order to protect, maintain and enhance both the immediate and long term health, safety, economic stability and general welfare of the present and future citizens of _(locality)_, this ordinance has the following objectives:

A. To promote energy conservation by encouraging the use of trees and shrubs for cooling through the provision of shade and the channeling of breezes;

B. To require the landscaping of buildings, areas adjacent to buildings and parking areas in order to facilitate energy conservation due to a cooler microclimate;

C. To promote and protect property values within the community by creating a more aesthetically pleasing environment;

D. To promote the use of and protect, restore and maintain the native vegetation of the community, if deemed desirable;

E. To aid in stabilizing the ecological balance in the community by contributing to the processes of air movement, air purification, oxygen regeneration, ground water recharge, and storm runoff retardation, while at the same time aiding in the abatement of noise, glare, heat, air pollution and dust;

F. To prevent unreasonable destruction of the communities' existing tree canopy;

G. To prevent damage to and unnecessary removal of protected and/or desirable vegetation during the construction process.

SECTION 5. DEFINITIONS

A. Microclimate temperature modifications: the alteration of ambient air temperatures within a small geographical area by natural or artificial means.

B. Solar insolation: the amount of solar radiation that reaches a particular area of the earth.

C. Ambient temperature: the temperature of the air within a given area.

D. Energy Conservation Landscaping: landscaping specifically positioned to minimize energy used for a) space cooling, by providing shade, cooling via evapotranspiration or channeling of breezes during the cooling season, or b) heating, by acting as "living insulation" and channeling breezes during the heating season.

E. Solar access: the ability of a structure or area to receive the full effects of solar insolation, without interference by other structures, vegetation, or any other impediment.

F. Exotic Vegetation: any species of plant not native to _(locality)_, or that areas' particular soil type, climate, geology. However, in this ordinance, the term "exotic vegetation" shall be limited to vegetation which satisfies the above definition but which, in particular, has been or may be harmful to the native vegetation or ecological systems of _(local area)_.

G. Native Vegetation: any species of plant considered to be indigenous to _(local area)_.

H. Tree: any self-supporting woody plant which usually produces one main trunk with many branches.

I. Shrub: a self-supporting woody perennial plant of low stature characterized by persistent stems and branches springing from the base.

J   Hedge: groups of three or more shrubs whose branches intertwine and/or come in very close contact with one another so that, for all intents and purposes, the shrubs form a continuous mass.

K. Site alteration: any significant change in the use or appearance of any land including, but not limited to, the clearing, removal or destructing of vegetation, dredging, filling, draining, grading or any other disturbance of the natural topography of the land.

L. Dripline: a somewhat circular line determined by the outside end of the branches of a tree or shrub, projected vertically to the ground.

M. Landscaping: living plant and natural material purposely positioned and/or maintained for functional and/or aesthetic reasons.

N. Right-of-way: public lands set aside for public traverse.

O. Pervious area: ground which allows water to percolate down through it.

P. Energy Conservation Tree: a tree qualifies as an energy conservation tree if it complies with the following standards:

1. the tree is west, east or south of the building in question;
2. the tree dripline will extend within 1) five feet (5') of west or east walls or overhangs or 2) three feet (3') of south walls or overhangs within 10 (10) years of the issuance of occupancy or use permits.

Q. Energy Conservation Shrub: a shrub qualifies as an energy conservation shrub if it complies with the following standards:

1. the shrub is placed within approximately five feet (5') of west, east or south walls (as first priority) or north walls (as a second priority) so that the outer edge of said shrub shall reach within approximately one foot (1') of said wall within four (4) years of the issuance of occupancy or use permits.
2. the shrub shall be of a species which can be projected to reach a minimum height of four feet (4') within four years of the issuance of occupancy or use permits.

R. Cooling Season: in Florida, between June 1 and September 30.

SECTION 6. ENFORCEMENT

This ordinance shall constitute a minimum standard and shall apply to _(local area)_ pursuant to Section 8. The _(local area)_ shall be the administrating agency and representatives of said agency shall inspect the landscaping of all development and redevelopment and no Certificate of Occupancy or Use or similar authorization will be issued unless the landscaping meets the requirements herein stipulated; the (local agency) shall re-inspect said landscaping at the intervals stipulated below to assure compliance with the intent of this ordinance.

a. Parking lots: One (1) year and three (3) years after the issuance of Certificate of Use.

b.   Other Vehicular use areas: One (1) year after the issuance of Certificate of Use.

c.   Building: One (1) year after the issuance of Certificate of Occupancy or Use.

If said landscaping is not in compliance with the requirements stipulated in this ordinance, the owner shall be given a period of time, not to exceed thirty (30) days, within which to comply with appropriate requirements. After a period of not more than thirty (30) days the site shall be re-inspected. If the landscaping still fails to meet the applicable requirements, fines shall be leveed against the owner(s) of said property in the amount of $___ per day of non-compliance.

If any tree for which credit was given pursuant to Section 18 of this ordinance is not alive and healthy one year after occupancy and use permits have been issued, it shall be removed and replaced with the tree or trees which originally would have been required.

SECTION 7. LANDSCAPING PLAN

A.   It is the responsibility of an applicant to include in the Landscape Plan sufficient information for the _(local agency)_ to evaluate the environmental characteristics of the affected areas. The Landscape Plan shall contain maps, charts, graphs, tables, photographs, narrative descriptions and explanations, and citation to supporting references, as may be appropriate to communicate the information required by this section.

B.   The proposed Landscape Plan shall be submitted to _(local agency)_ for approval, and shall include at a minimum:

1.   The name and address of the owner of the land for which the development or site alteration is planned;

2.   A description of how vegetation to be preserved will be protected during and after construction;

3.   A map showing:

a.   any buildings or other structures

b.   the trees and other vegetation to be preserved, indicating size, species and location;

c.   the proposal for landscaping and revegetation;

d.   the shadow pattern the vegetation would be expected to cast on the structure between 9 am and 5pm on August 6 within five (5) years of the issuance of the building permit or the shadow pattern the vegetation would be expected to cast at 3pm on August 6 within vehicular use areas after ten (10) years of the issuance of the use permit;

e.   the areas that will be covered by impervious surface;

f.   proposed rights-of-ways and utility easements;

g.   a legend of orientation

4.   A maintenance guide which shall be supplied to owners;

5.   Any other information which the developer or the _(local agency)_ believes is reasonably necessary for an evaluation of the development.

C. All landscaping shall be installed according to the plans and specifications as submitted and approved by *(local agency)* before a Certificate of Occupancy or Use will be issued.

SECTION 8. APPLICABILITY OF LANDSCAPING PLAN REQUIREMENT

A. Unless exempted pursuant to subsection B, a Landscape Plan must be submitted and approved:

1. at the same time a site development plan is submitted;
2. at the same time a site development plan is altered;
3. before the transfer of title when existing development is resold;
4. before a building permit is issued for the reconstruction or enlargement of existing buildings;
5. once three (3) years have passed after the implementation of this ordinance and existing parking and other vehicular use areas have not conformed with the requirements herein stated.

B. Exemptions: The following development activities are exempt from Landscape Plan requirements:

1. Minor landscaping maintenance, such as trimming of trees, shrubs, yard mowing and gardening;
2. Routine maintenance or improvement within an established highway, railroad or utility right-of-way;
3. The operation of nurseries operating in their ordinary course of business;
4. The use of any agriculturally zoned land for the purpose of growing plants, crops, trees, and other agricultural or forestry products, raising livestock, or for other bona-fide agricultural purposes;
5. Parking areas for single-family residences.

C. Variances: The *(local agency)* may grant a written variance from any requirement of this ordinance using the following criteria:

1. The implementation of the requirements herein stated would constitute an unconscionable economic burden; or
2. There are special circumstances applicable to the subject property or its intended uses; and
3. The granting of the variance will not otherwise significantly impair attainment of the objectives of this ordinance.

SECTION 9. LANDSCAPING QUALITY

Plant materials used in conformance with the provisions of this ordinance shall conform to the Standards for Florida No. 1 or better as given in "Grades & Standards for Nursery Plants," Part I and Part II (latest edition), State of Florida, Department of Agriculture, Tallahassee, or equal thereto. Grass sod shall be clean and reasonably free of weeds and noxious pets or diseases. Living shade trees of a leaf or flowering variety and/or shrubs shall be provided in accordance with the landscape quality standards hereinafter stated:

A. Tree Standards:

1. The required trees shall be at least eight (8') feet [five (5') feet for residential sites] in overall height upon planting and shall be graded Florida No. 1 or better, according to "Grades & Standards for Nursery Plants," Part I and Part II, (latest edition), State of Florida, Department of Agriculture, Tallahassee. Furthermore, trees shall be species having an average mature spread of crown of greater than ten (10') feet [fifteen (15') for vehicular use areas] in this geographical region and having trunk(s) which can be maintained in a clean condition over five (5') feet (not applicable for residential sites) of clear wood.

2. Palm trees may be utilized in place of the required shade trees in parking areas only if an individual specimen exhibits a mature crown of at least fifteen feet (15') in diameter. Palm trees of smaller mature canopies may not be grouped to meet the above canopy requirement.

3. Species should be those with moderate to dense canopies.

4. Trees must be long-lived and known to do well in urban environments.

5. Native species are to be emphasized.

6. The following trees shall not be utilized.

   a. members of the Ficus family with extensive root systems.

   b. malaleuca (Malaleuca leucodendra)

   c. Brazilian pepper-tree (Schinus terebinthifolius)

   d. toog (Bischofia javanica)

   e. Australian pine (Casuarina equisetifolia)

   f. poison wood (Metopium toxiferum)

   g. schefflera (Brassaia actinophylla)

   h. castor bean (Ricinus communis)

B. Shrub Standards:

1. Shrubs shall be at least twenty-four inches (24") in height immediately upon planting.

2. Native and non-competing species are to be emphasized.

C. Vines: Vines shall be a minimum of thirty inches (30") in length at planting time and may be used in conjunction with fences, screens, or walls to meet physical barrier requirements as specified.

D. Ground Cover: Ground covers used in lieu of grass in whole or in part shall be planted in such a manner as to present a finished appearance and reasonably complete coverage within one year after planting.

E. Lawn Grass: Grass areas shall be planted in species normally grown as permanent lawns in this geographical area. Grass areas shall be at least twenty-five percent (25%) sodded or seeded. Solid sod shall be used in swales or other areas subject to erosion.

F. Mulches: Mulches shall be applied at a depth of two inches (2") within the dripline of trees and shrubs at installation, unless said dripline is covered by lawn grass.

SECTION 10. TREE REMOVAL PERMIT REQUIREMENTS

No person shall cut down or cause to be cut down, destroyed, removed, relocated or destructively damaged any tree without first obtaining a permit from _(local government)_ as herein provided.

A. Required fees and application content.

1. Permission for removal, relocation or replacement of trees shall be requested by written application to the _(local government)_ in the form provided by the _(local government)_ and accompanied by the required fee as set forth in subsection B(2).

2. Tree removal fees:

    a. Non-agricultural land $_____per tree.

    b. Agricultural land: $_____per tree.

    Recognizing that the production of food is essential for the existence and health of the population, and that, where agricultural use of land is continuous, it can provide employment and income for the population indefinitely, and also taking note of the large number of tree removals which agricultural use, by its nature, necessitates, the fee to be charged applicants who seek to destroy trees in conjunction with an agricultural purpose shall be charged a reduced fee. This reduced fee, however, is to be charged only upon the applicant's submitting to the _(local government)_ a covenant running with the land for a term not less than five (5) years, indicating that the land noted therein shall not be utilized by the owner for any purpose other than an agricultural purpose. Said covenant shall be promptly filed with the appropriate officer for recording in the same manner as any other instrument affecting the title to real property and may only be released prior to its termination by written instrument of the _(local agency)_ releasing the owner from the terms agreed to. The release shall only be made to the owner, however, upon payment to the _(local agency)_ of the permit fees that would have been charged for a non-agricultural tree removal permit at current charges, less the amounts actually paid for the permit at the time of application.

3. Application for said permit may also be required to contain a legible plot or site plan, in as many copies as required by _(local agency)_ for review and processing, drawn to the largest practical scale showing the following:

    a. Location of all existing or proposed buildings, structures, improvements and site uses, properly dimensioned and referenced as to property lines, yard setback areas and spatial relationships.

    b. Location of existing or proposed utility services.

    c. Location of all existing trees, designating those to be removed, relocated, or replaced. Groups of trees in close proximity may be designated as "clusters" with the estimated total number noted. The name, common or botanical, height and caliper size of those trees to be removed, relocated, or replaced shall be shown on the site plan.

    d.   Information required in (c) above for trees proposed to be removed, relocated or replaced shall be summarized in tabular form on the plan, and shall include a statement of reasons for such removal, relocation or replacement.

    4.   Application for permit shall be reviewed by the _(local government)_ which may include visual inspection of the subject plot or site and referral of the application to such departments or other agencies having interest to determine the effect upon the public welfare, adjacent properties, or public services and facilities.

B. Conditions for permit.

    1.   Removal. No permit shall be issued for tree removal unless one of the following conditions, as determined by the _(local government)_ exists:

        a.   A site plan submitted by the applicant shows that a proposed structure, permissible under all applicable laws and regulations, can be situated on the subject parcel only if specific trees are removed or relocated.

        b.   The tree is located in such proximity to existing or proposed structures that the utility or structural integrity of such structures is materially impaired.

        c.   The tree materially interferes with the location, servicing or functioning of public utility lines or service.

        d.   The tree obstructs views of oncoming traffic or otherwise creates a substantial traffic hazard.

        e.   Any law or regulation requires such removal.

    2.   Relocation or replacement.

        a.   As a condition to granting a permit, the _(local government)_ shall have the option to require the applicant to relocate or replace a tree being removed at his expense, either within the site or with the concurrence of the _(local government)_ on public or private land within reasonable proximity to the site, including the relocation to any public land in the city retaining for future use, or donating to any citizen or group of citizens, for any purpose in the public interest and welfare, as approved by the _(local government)_.

        b.   A replacement tree shall be of a type and species having shade potential and other value, at least equal to that of the tree being removed, and shall meet the landscaping standards established in Section 9. The replacement tree shall not be of the type specified in Section 9, subsection A (5).

C. Exemptions to Permit and Fee Requirements:

    1.   The types of trees specified in Section 9, subsection A (5).

    2.   Owner-occupied properties developed for detached single-family usage, provided that where a tree is to be removed from said property without being relocated, the _(local government)_ shall be notified and given the option of relocating the tree elsewhere at no cost to the property owner.

    3.   Utilities franchised by the _(local government)_ may remove without permit or fee, after prior written notice to and approval by the _(local government)_,

trees which endanger public safety and welfare by interfering with utility service, provided such utilities cooperate with the city to preserve such trees by relocation or replacement in the same vicinity or as determined by the city for the best public benefit; except that where such trees are on owner-occupied properties developed for detached single-family usage, disposition of such trees shall be at the option of the property owner, subject to the provisions of subsection D(2).

4. During emergency conditions caused by a hurricane or other disaster, the provisions of this section may be suspended by *(local government)* until the end of said emergency period.

5. All licensed nurseries, botanical gardens, and commercial grove operations shall be exempt from the provisions of this sections, but only in relation to those trees which are planted and growing for the sale to the general public in the ordinary course of said licensee's business.

6. Public land.

SECTION 11. PROTECTION OF PRESERVED TREES

A. To receive credit for the preservation of an existing tree, the following requirements must be met:

1. The entire area within the dripline of the tree shall be naturally preserved or provided with pervious landscape material and shall be maintained at its original grade with no trenching or cutting of roots in this area. Within this area, there shall be no storage of fill or compaction of the soil, as from heavy construction equipment, or any evidence of concrete, paint, chemicals, or other foreign substances in the soil.

2. Unless otherwise authorized by the tree removal permit, no soil is to be removed from within the dripline of any tree that is to remain at its original location.

3. The tree shall not be damaged from skinning, barking, bumping and the like.

4. There shall be no evidence of active insect infestation.

5. There shall be no impervious surface or grade change within five feet (5') of the trunk.

6. Cutting and ditching for underground utility lines shall be done in such a way as to preserve and protect the root systems of trees.

B. Trees destroyed or receiving major damage must be replaced by trees of equivalent environmental value as specified by the enforcement agency before occupancy or use, unless approval for their removal has been granted under permit.

SECTION 12. LANDSCAPE STANDARDS FOR OFF-STREET PARKING AND OTHER VEHICULAR USE AREAS

All areas used for the parking or display of any and all types of vehicles, boats or heavy construction equipment, whether such vehicles boats or equipment are self-propelled or not, all land upon which vehicles traverse the property as a function of the primary use, hereinafter referred to as "other vehicular uses", shall conform to the minimum landscaping requirements hereinafter provided, save and except for those areas used for parking or other vehicular use areas under, on, or within buildings.

A. Landscaping requirements for Off-Street Parking Areas.

    1. Interior Landscaping

        a. At least ten percent (10%) of the gross lot area of all parking areas shall consist of interior landscaping.

        b. Enough shade trees shall be planted so that fifty percent (50%) of the gross lot area shall be covered by canopy within ten (10) years.

        c. The required number of trees shall consist of the number required to meet the above standard, as long as there is at least one tree for every 75 square feet of interior landscaping.

        d. Interior landscaping should consist of a mix of vegetation, including, but not limited to, trees, shrubs, and ground cover.

    2. Perimeter Landscaping

        a. All paved ground surface areas other than public right-of-way, designed to be used for parking an movement of vehicular traffic, except on property used only for single-family residential lots, shall be separated by a strip of landscape development from any boundary of the property on which the paved ground surface is located. Such strip of landscape development shall be developed in accordance with the following requirements:

            i. The strip of landscape development shall contain a wall, fence, hedge, or dense vegetation to a height of three feet (3'), except where the adjoining property is zoned for single- or multi-family residential use, in which case the required height is six feet (6').

            a) If a hedge or other dense vegetation is used, the hedge or vegetation shall be installed with plants of sufficient size and spacing as to attain a height of three feet (3') and an opacity of seventy-five percent (75%) within three (3) years of planting [four years (4) if a six foot (6') hedge is required]. If the hedge or vegetation is not in compliance with the above height and opacity requirements within three (3) years after planting [four years (4) if a six foot (6') hedge is required], the hedge or vegetation shall be completed with mature plants or replaced with a wall or fence in compliance with this sub-section.

            b) If a wall or fence is used, it shall be at least seventy-five percent (75%) opaque, with any open spaces or non-opaque areas evenly spaced and not concentrated so as to produce gaps or large holes. A wall or fence must be made of brick, stone, concrete block, pressure-treated wood, or similar materials, in accordance with prevailing building industry standards for appearance, soundness, safety, and resistance to disease and weather.

B. Other Vehicular Use Areas.

1. At least ten percent (10%) of the gross lost area shall consist of landscaping.

2. Enough shade trees shall be planted so that thirty percent (30%) of the gross lot area will be covered by canopy within ten (10) years.

3. The required number of trees shall consist of the number of trees shall consist of the number required to meet the above standard, provided there is at least one tree for every seventy-five square feet (75') of required landscaping.

C. Existing Parking Areas.

1. Where an off-street parking area, or other vehicular use area existed as of the effective date of this ordinance and such off-street parking area or other vehicular use area is enlarged in area, volume, capacity of space occupied, landscaping requirements, as herein specified, shall be met for the total (old and new) area, volume, capacity, or space so created or used.

2. Within three (3) years of the effective date of this ordinance, all existing off-street parking and other vehicular use areas shall conform to the requirements herein stated.

D. Right-of-Way Visibility

1. When an access way to parking areas and other vehicular use areas intersects a public right-of-way or when the subject property abuts the intersection of two (2) or more right-of-ways all landscaping within the triangular areas described below shall provide unobstructed cross-visibility at a level between thirty inches (30") and six feet (6'), provided, however, trees having limbs and foliage trimmed in such a manner that they do not extend into the cross-visibility area shall be allowed, provided they are located so as not to create a traffic hazard. Landscaping except required grass or ground cover shall not be located closer than three feet (3') from the edge of any access way pavement. The triangular areas above referred to are:

   a. The areas of property on both sides of an access way formed by the intersection of each side of the access way and the public right-of-way line with two (2) sides of each triangle being ten feet (10') in length from the point of intersection and the third side being a line connecting the ends of the other two (2) sides.

   b. The area of property located at a corner formed by the intersection of two (2) sides of the triangular area being thirty feet (30') in length along the abutting public right-of-way lines, measured from their point of intersection, and the third side being a line connecting the ends of the other two (2) lines.

SECTION 13. STREET TREE PROGRAM

A. Subdivision Street Tree Requirements.

1. Developers of subdivisions shall be required to provide shade trees within five feet (5') of the right-of-way of each street, pedestrian path and bikeway constructed with the subdivision. The trees shall be planted at such distances

whereby a complete canopy will shade the width of the entire street, pedestrian path or bikeway within ten (10) years. Tress shall conform with Landscaping Quality Standards established in Section 9.

or

2. Subdividers shall be required to deposit a sum equal to the cost of the purchasing, planting and required maintenance for the first two (2) years of the above required street trees with the *(local agency)*. These monies shall be used by the municipality to comply with the requirements established in subsection A (1).

B. Municipal Street Requirements.

1. Street Right-of-Ways.

   a. Medians in divided right-of-ways shall be planted with shade trees, where possible, spaced so that a canopy covering fifty percent (50%) of the divided right-of-ways will exist within ten (10) years.

   b. City and county right-of-ways within the municipality shall be rated according to the following priorities for the establishment of street trees:

      i. First Priority: Streets, pedestrian paths and bikeways which are used frequently or have the potential for frequent use. For example, those streets, pedestrian paths or bikeways which lead to stores, schools and recreation areas, as well as other popular destinations.

      ii. Second Priority: Streets, pedestrian paths and bikeways which lead to first priority streets, pedestrian paths and bikeways.

      iii. Third Priority: Other municipal right-of-ways, pedestrian paths and bikeways, including residential streets.

C. Street Tree Committee Formation.

1. A Street Tree Committee shall be established by the municipal government and shall be charged with categorizing streets according to and within the above priorities (for example, among first priority streets, pedestrian paths and bikeways, some are more frequently used than others). The committee shall then work with the *(local agency)* to develop a reasonable schedule for the establishment of street trees based upon (a) the priorities stated in subsection B and (b) cost factors.

D. Residential Street Tree Program.

1. The municipality should make every effort to encourage property owners to participate in a residential street tree program.

2. The majority of the property owners of an area abutting any street may request the establishment of street trees.

3. The property owners should be responsible for (a) the full cost of purchasing said street trees, or (b) a percentage of the purchase price, with the balance subsidized by the municipality. In both instances, however, the *(local agency)* would be responsible for installation of the trees, initial maintenance, and education of the homeowner about the necessary care of said tree.

4. Shade trees shall conform with the Landscaping Quality Standards established in Section 9.

5. Shade trees shall be planted within five feet (5') of right-of-ways, pedestrian paths or bikepaths.

SECTION 14. LANDSCAPING INCOMPATIBLE LAND USES.

A. As a condition of obtaining any development permit for any of the following incompatible land uses, there shall be provided a landscape buffer strip where indicated, according to the standards hereinafter provided.

1. Residential use other than detached, single-family homes: Along an common boundary with property in actual conforming use or zoned as single-family residential;

2. Office or commercial use: Along any common boundary with property in actual conforming use or zoned as residential, including mobile home parks and mobile home subdivisions.

3. Mobile home parks and mobile home subdivisions: Along a common boundary with property in actual conforming use or zoned as any other residential type.

4. Industrial use: Along any common boundary with property which is neither in actual conforming use or zoned for industrial use.

B. The required buffer shall be a strip of landscape development at least five feet (5') in width, which shall be developed in accordance with the following requirements:

1. Said buffer shall contain a wall, fence, hedge or dense vegetation to a height of six feet (6') within four (4) years, and said vegetation shall be at least twenty-four inches in height upon planting.

    a. When the buffer is between property used for an office, commercial or industrial use and property in actual use or zoned for single-family residential, a solid masonry wall shall be required;

    b. When the buffer is between office use and single-family residential, the _(local agency)_ may permit, as a special exception, the substitution of a hedge or dense vegetation for the masonry wall if a hedge will provide equivalent protection to the single-family residential use. The following shall be considered before such exception is granted:

        i. The scale of the office use and the adjoining uses;

        ii. The traffic generated by the office use;

        iii. The location of structures on the office site;

        iv. The existing natural features and vegetation of the site;

        v. The proposed exterior lighting and hours of operation of the proposed office use;

    c. Whenever a wall or fence is used, and is not required to be solid, it shall be at least seventy-five percent (75%) opaque and any open spaces or non-opaque areas shall be evenly spaced and not concentrated so as to produce gaps or large holes. The wall or fence must be made of brick, stone, concrete block pressure treated wood, or similar materials, in accordance with prevailing building industry standards for appearance, soundness, safely and resistance to disease and weather.

2. Within the buffer strip required by this section there shall be planted shade trees spaced so that no more than thirty-five lineal feet (35') separate their trunks. None of these trees shall be planted at a distance greater than five feet (5') from any adjoining paved ground surface. The shade trees used shall be from an approved List of Shade Trees maintained and kept by _(local agency)_.

SECTION 15. MINIMUM ENERGY CONSERVATION LANDSCAPING DESIGN STANDARDS FOR THE SHADING OF BUILDINGS

A. Unless otherwise shaded by vertical or horizontal projections, 1) all west windows shall be shaded by vegetation between approximately 2:30pm and 7:30pm during the cooling season; 2) all east windows shall be shaded by vegetation between 7:30am and 12:00pm during the cooling season; 3) all south windows shall be shaded by vegetation between 9:30am and 5:30pm during the cooling season. These requirements shall be met within five (5) years of the issuance of occupancy permits.

B. Unless otherwise shaded, air conditioners, and horizontal surfaces within eight feet (8') of them shall be extensively shaded by vegetation between 8:00am and 6:00pm on August 6. This requirement shall be met within three (3) years of the issuance of occupancy or use permits.

C. Trees to be used for energy conservation should be placed so that within ten (10) years the canopy will be within 1) five feet (5') of north walls (as a second priority) so that the outer edge of said shrubs should reach within one foot (1') of said walls within four (4) years.

D. Tall shrubs should be placed within five feet (5') of west, east or south walls (as a second priority) so that the outer edge of said shrubs should reach within four (4) years.

E. Wherever possible, trees and other forms of landscaping shall be used to shade the entrances and pedestrian paths of commercial, office and public buildings so as to reduce ambient temperatures and heat load.

F. Where possible, trees and other forms of landscaping should be used to direct winds and breezes so as to naturally ventilate those structures which have appropriately positioned windows, thereby providing a more comfortable microclimate.

G. In all cases, consideration shall be given so as to provide for the optimum placement of landscape materials in order to reduce energy used for space cooling of buildings.

SECTION 16. PREVIOUS AREA REQUIREMENTS.

A. In addition to landscaping requirements for vehicular use areas and the separation of incompatible land uses, the following figures represent the percent of gross lot area that shall remain pervious:

1. Single-family and duplex residential 30%
2. Multi-family residential 40%
3. Commercial and office 20%
4. Public land use 30%
5. Industrial 20%

SECTION 17. LANDSCAPING REQUIREMENTS FOR BUILDINGS.

At least 80 percent of the required pervious area shall be covered by tree and shrub canopy, with at least percent of the requirement consisting of shrubs. Section 18 establishes a landscaping credit system, based upon tree and shrub area, to be used for complying with this requirement.

SECTION 18. LANDSCAPING CREDIT SYSTEM.

A. Tree Credit System.

1. To calculate credit for a given tree (whether planted or preserved), multiply the estimated canopy area by the appropriate credit factor. The credit factor is determined by (a) whether or not the tree is an energy conservation tree as specified in Section 5, and (b) tree location relative to building walls.

Table D-1. *Tree credit.*

Estimated canopy within 10 years of planting or building permit issuance		non-energy conserving trees	CREDIT FACTORS energy conserving trees	
Diameter	Area		E, SE, S	W, SW, NW
15'	176 sq. ft.	.8	1.	1.2
20'	314 " "	.8	1.	1.2
30'	710 " "	.8	1.	1.2
40' or greater	1250 " "	.6	.8	1.0

2. Additional Credit.

a. If a tree shades a paved, heat-collecting surface, additional credit for said tree shall be given. To qualify for additional credit for shading heat-collecting surfaces, a tree's dripline must be within three feet (3') of said surface within five (5) years if the tree is west, southwest, east or southeast W, SW, E, SE) of said surface. If the tree is south of said surface, the tree dripline must reach the heat-collecting surface. The heat-collecting surface must be within twenty feet (20') of the building it is associated with. If a tree meets the above requirements, the following credit shall be given:

Table D-2. *Additional Credit.*

Location relative to heat-collecting surface	Additional credit
W, SW, SE, E	10%*
South	5%*

*percent of the area of said tree

Thus, if a tree meets the above requirements and is W, SW, SE, or E of a heat-collecting surface, additional credit equal to ten percent (10%) of the area of said tree shall be added to the credit calculated in Section 18 (A).

3. If a tree shades an air conditioner, additional credit for said tree shall be given. To qualify for additional credit, the tree canopy must shade both the air conditioner and the ground within eight feet (8') of the air conditioner. Furthermore, the air conditioner must be shaded between the hours specified below. If a tree meets the above requirements, the following credit shall be added to the credit calculated in Section 18 (A).

Table D-3. *Credit for hours air conditioner is shaded.*

Hours Air Conditioner Is Shaded	Tree Location To Air Conditioner	Relative Additional Credit
2:30pm-7:30pm	W, SW	20%
7:30am-12:00pm	E, SE	10%
9:30am-5:30pm	S	10%

B. Shrub Credit System

1. To calculate credit for a given shrub, multiply the estimated shrub area by the appropriate credit factor (see table below). The credit factor is determined by whether or not the shrub is an energy conservation shrub as specified in Section 5.

Table D-4. *Shrub credit.*

Estimated diameter within 4 years of planting*	Estimated area within 4 years of planting*	CREDIT FACTORS	
		non-energy conservation	energy conservation
2'	3' sq. ft.	.6	1.
3'	7' sq. ft.	.6	1.
4'	12' sq. ft.	.6	1.
5' or greater	20' sq. ft.	.6	1.

*rounded to nearest whole number

2. Additional Credit.

    a. If a shrub also shades an air conditioning unit four or more hours during a summer day, additional credit equal to ten percent (10%) of the area of said shrub shall be added to the credit calculated in Section 18 (D).

SECTION 19. PROTECTION OF SOLAR ACCESS.

A. The proposed landscape plan by its approval shall not result in the shading of a solar collector or south facing windows of a neighbor's property between 9:00am and 3:00pm on January 21.

B. In choosing the species of trees and shrubs, and the placement of such vegetation, the effect on existing or future solar access of neighborhood properties shall be considered.

SECTION 20. MAINTENANCE OF LANDSCAPE MATERIALS.

A. All landscaping, landscaped areas, landscape development, buffer areas and trees required by this ordinance shall be maintained and used in the following manner:

1. Plant material. All required plant material shall be maintained in a healthy, vigorous, disease and pest-free condition, through proper and efficient watering, fertilizing, pest and disease management, pruning, or be replaced.

2. Irrigation. All landscaped areas shall be provided with an irrigation system or a readily available water supply located within one hundred feet (100'). Where practical, and where cost is not prohibitive, drip irrigation systems should be installed.

3. Where practical, and where cost is not prohibitive, "natural methods of pest and disease control should be employed.

SECTION 21. SEVERABILITY.

Each separate section, subsection, clause or provision of this ordinance is deemed independent of all other sections, subsections, clauses or provisions herein, so that if any of the same be declared invalid, all other sections, subsections, clauses or provisions thereof remain valid and enforceable.

SAMPLE CALCULATION OF LANDSCAPING REQUIREMENTS
UTILIZING CREDIT SYSTEM

Example based upon an 8000 sq. ft. residential lot

Example 1: Pervious area requirement = 30% of 8000 or 24,000 sq. ft

Tree requirement = 75% of 2400 or 1800 sq. ft.

Shrub requirement = 5% of 2400 or 120 sq. ft.

Table D-5. *Example calculations of landscaping requirements utilizing credit system.*

All examples based upon an 8,000 sq. ft. residential lot

Example #1: Pervious area requirement - 30% of 8000 or 24,000 sq. ft
            Tree requirement - 75% of 2400 or 1800 sq. ft.
            Shrub requirement - 5% of 2400 or 120 sq. ft.

		Credit	Actual Area
Tree requirement:	two e.c.* 20' trees west of bldg.	754	628
	one e.c. 30' tree east of bldg.	710	710
	also shades air conditioner	71	
	one n.e.c.** tree	251	
	also south of driveway	15	
	TOTAL sq. ft.	1801	1652

Shrub requirement:	six e.c. 2' shrubs north of bldg.	13.5	
	thirteen e.c. 3' shrubs west, east		
	and south of the bldg	91	
	three n.e.c. 4' shrubs	18	
	22 shrubs Shrub credit:	122.5sq.ft.	

Example #2

		Credit	Actual Area
Tree requirement:	two e.c. 30' trees west of bldg.	850	710
	also shades air conditioner	142	
	one e.c. 20' tree east of bldg.	314	314
	one e.c. 20' tree west of bldg.	377	314
	one n.e.c. 15' tree	140	176
	TOTAL sq. ft	1823	1514

Example #3

		Credit	Actual Area
Tree requirement:	two e.c. 40' trees west of bldg.	1250	1250
	also shades driveway	62	
	one e.c. 20' tree west of bldg.	370	314
	one n.e.c. 15' tree	140	
	TOTAL sq. ft	1822	1564

* e.c. = energy conserving
** n.e.c. = non-energy conserving

Appendix E

Gary Moll[1]

The Best Way to Plant Trees

We at the American Forestry Association propose that the new decade inaugurated this year be called the Decade of the Tree.

During the 1990s major changes are needed in public policy and personal lifestyle to improve the ecological health of the planet. Tree planting is one of the simplest ways to start the decade on the right foot.

Perhaps no other action is more direct: Plant a tree and cool the globe. This call to action by the American Forestry Association offers each of us an opportunity to change the direction of our personal lifestyle.

Planting trees around our own homes is a logical place to start. It's a personal action that boosts our property value and does something for the environment at the same time. In addition to providing benefits ranging from aesthetics to erosion control, trees help reduce the energy needed for heating and cooling and thus the fossil fuels burned by power plants. One result is the production of less carbon dioxide, a major greenhouse gas.

When selecting a tree for planting, remember: "Buyer beware."

---

[1]The Best Way to Plant Trees," adapted from *American Forests*, American Forestry Association, March/April 1990.

Here at AFA we take the job of tree planting very seriously. We believe that major changes are needed in the way people think about trees and plant them. The American Forestry Association has drawn up new guidelines for how to plant a tree, and unless you've been reading a lot of research information lately, you will find many surprises such as don't dig a planting pit and don't add soil amendments to the planting hole.

We'll admit up front that tree planting is a more involved process than we once thought. The new information we've developed requires more than just digging a hole that fits the root ball. It requires more labor, but the result is also very rewarding. We estimate young trees will grow twice as fast when planted correctly and will live at least twice as long as trees improperly set out.

Planting a tree is a positive action that is made even more positive when the species and individual specimen are carefully selected, the tree is strategically located on the lot, and—what concerns us most in this article—the sapling is properly planted.

Studying the health and survival of community trees, plus working with city foresters around the world, has led us to make new recommendations on how to go about planting. The old standards suggested digging a hole six inches wider and deeper than the root ball. Up until a couple of years ago, the experts also suggested that community tree planters mix peat moss and other soil amendments with the soil backfill. None of this is recommended today.

Over the last few years we have been searching for clues to the declining health of community trees, and we are coming to believe that planting methods are a major culprit. Some old-timers wrinkle their foreheads and look skeptical when the old methods are challenged. They can take you out and show you tree after tree that survived and is doing fine, thank you.

So why do we feel so confident that planting techniques need updating? The main reason is that home construction has changed greatly since the good old days. Bigger earth-moving equipment and less hand labor are used in creating today's housing developments. Because of the heavier construction equipment, the soil in the average yard is less fertile and more compacted.

Digging a hole in dense, compacted soil and filling the hole with peat moss and other soil amendments is like creating a pot for the tree. The roots grow outward in the soil amendments, and the tree does fine until the roots reach the original soil and the outward growth stops. Instead of spreading into the yard, the roots encircle the planting pit. The "pot" soon fills with roots, and the health of the tree declines.

The crown continues to grow, but the roots do not. Once the tree becomes root bound, its ability to maintain itself during a drought or survive a flood is limited—leading to decline that is often terminal.

So what do we propose? Plant so that roots have a chance to grow into the surrounding soil and produce healthy, vigorous branches, foliage, and roots. Instead of a planting hole, what's needed is a large planting area that is wide but not deep, where the soil is loose and suited for root growth. The larger the area, the better.

Planting Tips

After selecting a suitable location, mark out a planting area that is five times the diameter of the planting ball. Use a rototiller or shovels to loosen and mix the soil in this entire area to a depth of about 12 inches. Organic matter can be added to the loosened soil so long as the new material is used uniformly throughout the area.

In the center of the prepared area, dig a shallow hole to set the tree, root ball and all. The hole should allow the root ball to sit on solid ground rather than loose soil. Once the ball is set in the hole, its upper surface should be level with the existing soil.

After the tree is properly situated, cut and remove the rope or wires holding the burlap in place and securing any part of the tree. Position the tree so that is perpendicular to the ground, so the main stem will grow straight up.

Backfill around the root area and gently step the soil to prevent major air pockets, but it is a mistake to pack soil too hard. Water can be used instead of your foot to help the soil settle and prevent overpacking. Rake the soil even over the entire area and lay mulch on the area using two to four inches of bark, wood chips, old sawdust, pine needles, leaf mold, or the like. Some mulches decompose quickly and will have to be replenished once or twice a year. Maintaining the mulch layer carefully will improve tree growth substantially.

Some planting recommendations suggest mounding the soil at the outer edge of the planting ring to form a water-holding berm, close to the tree. The berm will help hold water, but it may also encourage the root growth to remain within the berm, close to the tree. So berms are not recommended here; mulch should hold the water adequately.

If needed, support the tree with a flexible stake so that the trunk can sway in the wind. The movement is necessary for building the trunk's strength. Remove the stake and rope after one year, since leaving rope around the tree can kill it.

We hope to have spurred your interest in planting—especially in doing it right. Our focus here is planting, but we don't want to leave you without a few words on selecting a suitable planting location, which is the first step in the whole process.

Paramount in this consideration is energy conservation. Research by Dr. Hashem Akbari of the Lawrence Berkeley Building Laboratory in Berkeley, California, shows that energy savings can run as high as 50 percent when vegetation is properly located.

Researchers Gordon Heisler in Pennsylvania and Jack Parker in Florida have helped identify specific optimum locations. The basic model calls for shade trees on the south-facing side of a house, with the southeastern and southwestern sides being the most important locations in terms of summer cooling. The detrimental effects of winter winds are addressed by planting evergreens (pine, spruce, fir, or hemlock) on the northeastern section of your lot.

Deciduous trees are the best choice for summer shading since the foliage adds cooling benefits during the hot months, while the leaf drop in fall allows the sun to reach the windows of the house and contribute solar heat gain during the winter.

A minimum of three trees are recommended. They should be sited so they can grow vigorously; allow space for both roots and branches to develop.

Species selection should be geared toward producing medium to large trees for these strategic spots so that both the roof and the sides of the building receive shade. As the trees mature, the low winter sun will be able to reach the house from underneath the branches.

Evergreen windbreaks work best as group plantings containing at least four trees, but the more the better. Spacing between the trees should be six to 10 feet, which gives the trees some room to grow but allows branches to meet and form a windbreak as the trees mature.

As your knowledge of the landscape increases, you will be able to make many other energy-saving plantings around the home. Trees that shade air conditioners are most effective at improving the efficiency of the cooling units. Trees and shrubs can also be located to direct summer breezes through open windows, shade walls, or create air movement where ventilation is needed.

Although strategic location is the most important consideration, the impact of the vegetation is also directly related to its overall size and abundance. The effectiveness of the landscaping at moderating the climate will be increased by filling available space with small, medium, and large plants. Each plant has its niche, so it is the job of the landscaper to review site conditions and select plants that fit the local needs.

When it comes to actual selection, don't assume that the cheapest tree is the best tree. It is usually the worst. One planting recommendation that has remained unchanged over the years is that a quality tree is the best investment.

First, you need to decide which species is the right one for your spot. Be sure to get some help here if you don't know. Some trees grow well on wet sites, and others do better on dry sites. Know the conditions and find out what trees do best in your area. Matching a tree to a site is a problem that must be addressed locally.

To find answers, ask for information at your state forestry office or Cooperative Extension Service, or go to a local arboretum, garden center, or nursery.

Nurseries offer a tremendous range in quality of trees. Not all the trees are good ones. Two things must be considered by the buyer. First, is this the right tree for my site, and second, is it in good condition and ready for transplanting into the cold, cruel world?

Scientists are working with nurserymen to develop genetically superior trees, and with each passing year, better specimens will become available. As a buyer, you need to be assured that the improved genetic line has been passed along to the young plants. Selecting trees by named varieties or cultivated variety will address some of these problems.

To determine the health and condition of a tree, eyeball the trunk, branches, and root ball for signs of damage, and use the guidelines supplied by the American Association of Nurserymen (see below) to determine if the nursery has handled the tree properly. Nursery growers will refer to their management techniques as *cultural practices*.

Trimming will give the crown a strong structure and raise the branching up the trunk. Pruning the branches on the main stem needs to be done carefully. The branches help the tree put on caliper (diameter) growth, but if they are left on too long, the wounds from pruning can cause considerable damage to the tree. Roots require pruning that produces a fibrous and compact system.

By the time a tree leaves the nursery, its shape, size, and direction of growth have been modified by the nursery's cultural practices to help it survive transplanting and remain healthy.

If a tree isn't properly root-pruned, for example, most of the roots needed for survival will be lost during transplanting. The tree may survive, but it will grow slowly and require a great deal of care. There is a long list of things that need to be done by the nursery to prepare a tree for street planting. The buyer can learn a lot about the quality of a tree by asking one question: Is this tree grown to nursery standards? If no one at the nursery knows what you're talking about, the trees may not be a good choice.

The following is what you should look for when buying a tree. These recommendations are an abbreviated review of the standards published by the American Association of Nurserymen (1250 I St., NW, Washington, D.C. 20005).

The standard measure for balled-and-burlapped trees is *caliper*, or the diameter measured six inches above the ground (for trees larger than one half inch and smaller than four inches in diameter).

A proper relationship of height to caliper assures that the tree's size is in proportion to the strength of its trunk. The average height of a two-inch-caliper tree is 12 to 14 feet, and the maximum height is 16 feet.

The amount of roots left on the tree is critical to survival. For bare-root trees, a two-inch-caliper tree should have a minimum root spread of 32 inches. If the tree has a root ball, the ball must be of a diameter and depth to encompass enough fibrous roots for full recovery of the plant. The ball diameter for a two-inch tree is 24 inches, and its depth is about 16 inches.

If all these directions are followed—nursery standards, careful selection of species, proper location on your lot, and our new planting recommendations—then you'll have a solid chance of nurturing a healthy tree. Of course, you must water it when necessary, stand guard against errant vehicles, and—just to cover all bets—talk to it occasionally. A kind word never hurt anyone.

Appendix F

Southern California Edison [1]

Trees and Shrubs

Planting Trees and Shrubs, Step by Step

Trees and shrubs must be planted, watered and cared for properly to ensure they have a long, healthy life. Plant in fall (preferred) or spring in mild-winter climates; in spring in cold-winter areas. Follow these important steps.

1. Be sure site is safe for planting, as discussed on page 202. Dig planting hole twice the width and the same depth as the plant's rootball. If your soil is very sandy or heavy clay, blend one-third original volume of soil amendment, such as ground bark or other composted organic material with original soil for backfill. If your soil is good loam, use as is.

2. Fill planting hole with water to check drainage. After water drains, fill again. Water should drain in 12 hours or less. If not, select another site.

3. Gently remove plant from container. Free roots from bottom and sides. If rootbound (a tight mass of roots), use a knife to slice partway up through the rootball, and spread apart.

4. Place plant in hole, positioning it at original soil level. Fill in around rootball, firming lightly to remove air pockets. If planting a bareroot plant, follow the same procedure, but dig hole large enough to accommodate roots. Build cone of soil at bottom of hole and lay roots over cone. Then add backfill as explained above.

5. Use soil to build a watering basin around the perimeter of the rootball. Water slowly to saturate rootball area. Cover area with 2-inch layer of organic mulch to reduce moisture loss through evaporation.

6. Keep rootball soil moist (not soggy) for the first few weeks. Continue to water regularly. Gradually reduce irrigation frequency and increase amount of water applied each irrigation to encourage deep rooting. After a few months, extend basin outward several inches to allow for spread of roots.

The excerpts in Appendix F are taken from a brochure distributed by the Southern California Edison (SCE) utility company, titled "Trees: Saving Energy Naturally," 1991. The information pertains to planting trees in Southern California. It is provided here mainly as an example of the kind of information useful to a tree-planting program.

Staking

Drive two sturdy stakes, tall enough to support the trunk, about two feet deep into soil outside of rootball. Place on opposite sides of trunk. Tie trunk loosely to stakes —enough for support but not so tight that the tree cannot move on its own to gain strength. Prune only lightly, removing broken, crossing branches.

Ways to Save Water

With roughly half of residential water use going to home landscapes, it pays to select low-water-use plants. Choose plants that are naturally adapted to grow with minimum water. For example, water consumption for a mulberry *(Morus alba)*, a popular shade tree, requires almost three times more water than the similar African sumac *(Rhus lancea)*.

Figure F-1.
Proper support: Trees need to have stakes for support before their root systems gain strength.

Most of the trees and shrubs described in this booklet are low water-use plants. Some additional ways to save water include:

- Water in early morning hours when it's cool and the winds are calm to reduce evaporation loss.

- Water slowly and for long periods to encourage deep rooting. Plants will have greater reservoirs of soil area for drawing moisture and anchoring themselves.

- Learn your soil type—sandy, clay or loam—and adjust watering practices to apply just enough water for plant growth. Sandy soil drains fast, clay drains slow. Loam is somewhere between.

- Add amendments to soil so moisture is retained in the root zone longer. This is not always practical with trees and shrubs, but works well for flower and vegetable gardens.

- Water plants at the drip line—an imaginary line where rain-water would fall from leaves to the ground. This is the area where feeder roots are most concentrated.

- Use a moisture-conserving mulch such as ground bark or other composted organic material over the root area to cover soil and reduce evaporation.

- Install a drip irrigation system to water plants slowly and efficiently.

Plant Care and Your Safety

Always stay far away from power lines. Be sure to remember this when pruning trees or shrubs. And, never use an aluminum ladder. Also, be careful with tree-trimming and fruit-harvesting equipment around power lines. If you are holding a metal pole of any kind and it contact a power line, you could be killed. Also be aware that water is a good conductor of electricity. Never use electric tools such as hedge trimmers or electric lawnmowers if your hands or feet are wet, or if you're standing in water or on damp ground. Keep electric tools and cords away from damp grass and shrubs, and never use electric tools near a swimming pool.

Climate Zones

C = Coastal, IV = Inland Valleys, LD = Low Deserts, HD = High Deserts, M = Mountains. All climate zones are general, and can vary considerably. Use the recommendations in the following diagrams (Figure F-2) only as a guide. For best results, check locally to see if plants are adapted to your area.

Figure F-2.

Acacia
Acacia species

Acacia represents hundreds of species of evergreen trees and shrubs. Leaves are delicate and lacy. *A. abyssinica*, Abyssinian acacia, grows up to 30 feet high with a wide-spreading canopy. *A. farnesiana, (A. smallii)*, sweet acacia, grows to 20 feet. Leaves are green, fern-like. **Low water use.** C, IV, LD.

African sumac
Rhus lancea

Evergreen grows 20 to 25 feet high, spreading even wider. Trees gradually take on a broad, dome shape. Leaves are narrow, glossy, medium green. Creates dense shade. **Low water use.** C, IV, LD.

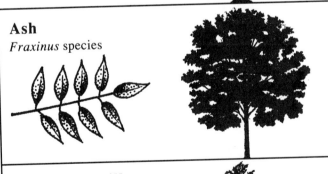

Ash
Fraxinus species

F. oxycarpa 'Raywood,' deciduous to 35 feet. Fast growth. *F. uhdei*, Shamel ash, evergreen to deciduous to 60 feet. Do not plant near power lines. 'Majestic Beauty' is an improved variety. Narrow, upright form spreads with age. Leaves are dark green in leaflets. *F. velutina* 'Rio Grande' (fantex ash) is drought and heat tolerant. **Low water use.** C, IV, LD, HD.

Australian willow
Geijera parviflora

Evergreen, grows to 30 feet; 20-foot canopy. Upright form. Graceful, willowy presence. Leaves are medium green, 3 to 6 inches long. **Low water use.** C, IV, LD, HD.

Bottle tree
Brachychiton populneus

Evergreen, fast growing to. 50 feet, 30-foot canopy. Pyramidal shape. Leaves are shiny dark green. Excellent in hot areas. Often used as a windbreak. **Low water use.** C, IV, LD.

California pepper
Brazilian pepper
Schinus species

S. molle, California pepper, evergreen grows fast to 40 feet high, with wide canopy. Branches droop willow-like, covered with bright green leaves. *S. terebinthifolius,* Brazilian pepper, evergreen, grows to 30 feet. Growth is more rounded. Leaves are glossy dark green. **Low water use.** C, IV, LD.

Carrot wood
Cupaniopsis anacardiopsis

Evergreen to 40 feet high, spreading 20 to 30 feet. Attractive, dark green, leathery leaves. Even but not dense shade. Fruit occasionally messy. C, IV.

Chinese pistache
Pistacia chinensis

Deciduous, grows up to 50 feet high and spreads as wide. Long, bright green leaflets allow filtered shade. Leaves are pinkish when new; brilliant yellow, orange and red in fall. **Low water use.** IV, LD, HD.

Cottonwood, Poplar
Populus species

Trees for fast shade. *P. alba,* white poplar, deciduous to 60 feet high. Leaves are medium green, light green underneath. 'Bolleana' (also 'Pyramidalis') is more upright. *P. fremontii,* Fremont cottonwood, deciduous grows to 90 feet. Glossy green leaves turn yellow in fall. Caution: Usually needs more water and has invasive roots. IV, HD, M.

Crape myrtle
Lagerstroemia indica

Deciduous shrub or small tree, vase-shaped to 30 feet. Often with multiple trunks. Profuse flowers in summer. 'Indian Tribe' group is disease resistant. **Low water use.** IV, LD, HD.

Desert willow
Chilopsis linearis

Deciduous, to 25 feet, spreading to 25 feet. Leaves are green and willow-like on twisted branches. Orchid-like flowers are snowy white to lavender and bloom in spring and summer. **Low water use.** IV, LD, HD.

Eucalyptus
Eucalyptus species

Large group of evergreen trees and shrubs. Fast-growing and accepting of difficult conditions. Some get quite large; can be messy. Do not plant near power lines. *E. citriodora,* lemon-scented gum, grows to 75 feet, spreading to 25 feet. *E. polyanthemos,* silver dollar eucalyptus, to 30 to 60 feet. Leaves are silvery gray-green, round like silver dollars, becoming lance-shaped with age. **Low water use.** C, IV, LD.

Floss silk tree
Chorisia speciosa

Deciduous, but for a short time. Grows to 60 feet; pyramidal form. Produces profuse amounts of pink flowers in fall. Trunks are studded with spines. C, IV.

Flowering plum
Flowering cherry
Prunus species

P. carolinana, cherry laurel, evergreen large shrub or small tree 20 to 40 feet high. Pyramidal form. Shiny, dark green leaves. White flowers in clusters in spring, blue berries in fall. Many varieties of *P. cerasifera,* cherry plum, are available. 'Atropurpurea,' purple-leaf plum, is one of the most common. Deciduous to 30 feet high. Highly ornamental dark purple leaves and white flowers. Cherry laurel: **Low water use.** C, IV, LD, HD. Cherry plum: IV, LD, HD.

Golden-rain tree
Koelreuteria paniculata

Deciduous to 20 to 35 feet. Open branching growth habit. Leaves are soft, medium green. Flowers are striking yellow and bloom in late spring. Fast-growing. Can be invasive when it reseeds. *K. bipinnata*, Chinese flame tree, is deciduous to 40 feet. **Low water use.** C, IV, LD, HD.

Hackberry
Celtis occidentalis

Deciduous to 50 feet and almost as wide. Oval leaves are 2 to 5 inches long. Tough tree. All areas where cold-hardy. **Low water use.**

Honey locust
Gleditsia triacanthos inermis

Deciduous to 30 to 55; wide canopy. Leaves are green to dark green, delicate and lacy. Excellent lawn tree. Likes heat. Many improved varieties with colorful leaves. IV, LD, HD.

Jacaranda
Jacaranda mimosifolia

Deciduous to semi-evergreen, to 40 feet, spreading 30-foot canopy. Oval irregular form. Leaves are fern-like. Lavender-blue blossoms in late spring to early summer. C, IV, LD.

Locust
Robinia species

R. ambigua 'Idahoensis' ('Idaho'), deciduous, grows to 40 feet high, upright habit. Leaves in leaflets are medium green, up to 12 inches long. Clusters of deep pink flowers in late spring. *R. pseudoacacia*, black locust, deciduous and fast-growing to 40 to 75 feet high. All areas where cold-hardy. **Low water use.**

Mesquite
Prosopis species

Deciduous to evergreen, ranging in size from small native shrubs to wide-crowned trees to 40 feet high and as wide. *P. alba*, Argentine mesquite, has blue-green leaves. *P. chilensis*, Chilean mesquite, has fern-like foliage and dark trunk. Also look for hybrid mesquites. **Low water use.** IV, LD, HD.

Oak
Quercus species

Quality trees for the West. Some of the best include: *Q. agrifolia*, coast live oak, evergreen, grows to 30 to 60 feet high. Crown becomes dome-shaped with age. Leaves are shiny green and holly-like. *Q. lobata*, valley oak, deciduous, grows to 60 to 75 feet high, spreading 50 to 80 feet wide. **Low water use.** Generally adapted. Check locally.

Olive
Olea europaea

Evergreen 20 to 30 feet high, often with multiple trunks. Wide-spreading canopy. Leaves are leathery, silvery gray-green. Dark blue-black fruit in fall can be a messy problem. Look for "fruitless" varieties; planting restrictions in some communities. **Low water use.** C, IV, LD, HD.

Ornamental pear
Pyrus species

P. calleryana, callery pear, deciduous, grows to 25 to 40 feet. 'Aristocrat' is pyramidal in form. Bright green leaves produce spectacular fall color. *P. kawakamii*, evergreen pear, grows to 30 feet. Leaves are shiny, light green with wavy edges. Flowers are white and profuse in early spring. IV, LD, HD.

Palo verde
Cercidium species

C. floridum, blue palo verde, deciduous up to 30 feet and about as wide; dense, low-spreading branches. Spring flowers are golden yellow. Leaves, bark and trunk are green. Also consider the similar *Parkinsonia* species, Mexican palo verde. **Low water use.** IV, LD, HD.

Pine
Pinus species

Large group of evergreens. Look for *P. brutia eldarica,* Eldarica pine, very fast growth to 50 feet high. *P. halepensis,* Alleppo pine, is similar to eldarica. Not quite as fast growth, not as symmetrical. *P. pinea,* Italian stone pine, grows 40 to 80 feet. *P. thunbergiana,* Japanese black pine, fast growth to 30 feet, sometimes higher. Adaptation depends on species and cold temperatures in your area. Check locally.

Silk tree
Albizia julibrissin

Deciduous, grows slowly to 30 feet or higher, with a broad canopy. Leaves have fern-like texture; pink, pin-cushion flowers in summer. All areas where cold-hardy.

Sycamore
Platanus species

P.x acerifolia, London plane tree, deciduous and fast-growing to 60 feet high with 50-foot canopy. Large, coarse bright green lobed leaves. *P. racemosa,* California sycamore, grows fast to 50 to 100 feet, spreading wide. Leaves are dark green, bark is attractive mottled tan. Tolerates heat and wind. All areas where cold-hardy.

Bottlebrush
Callistemon species

C. citrinus, lemon bottlebrush, evergreen shrub or small tree 20 to 25 feet. Narrow, round-headed form. Cylindrical, 'bottlebrush' flowers are bright red. *C. viminalis,* weeping bottlebrush, is slightly taller with drooping branches. **Low water use.** C, IV, LD.

Hopbush
Dodonaea viscosa

Evergreen, grows to 10 feet high and about 5 feet wide. Leaves are green and cover plants densely. Fast rugged growth. 'Purpurea', with purplish leaves, is more refined. **Low water use.** C, IV, LD.

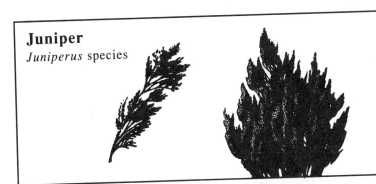

Juniper
Juniperus species

Onc of the most dependable and adaptable group needled evergreens for the West. Hundreds of cultivated varieties to choose from. *J. chinesis* and *J. scopulorum* are common upright forms. Check individual species for mature size. All areas where cold-hardy. **Low water use.**

Oleander
Nerium oleander

Popular evergreen shrubs reaching to 12 feet (or higher), and almost as wide. Long, narrow, dark green leaves on upright stems. Flowers in white, red and pink and are profuse in spring scattered through summer. Plant parts are poisonous. **Low water use.** IV, LD, HD.

Photinia
Photinia species

P.x fraseri, red tip photinia, evergreen, grows to 12 feet high. Lush, bronze-red new growth in spring turns a rich, shiny green. White flowers in flat clusters in spring. *P. serrulata,* Chinese photinia, is similar, slightly smaller and more open growth. IV, LD, HD.

Privet
Ligustrum species

L. japonicum, Japanese privet, evergreen, grows to 15 feet or higher to make an outstanding screen. Glossy, dark green leaves with whitish undersides. Berries can be messy. *L. lucidum,* Chinese privet, evergreen shrub or small tree to 30 feet. All areas where cold-hardy. **Low water use.**

Xylosma
Xylosma congestum

Evergreen shrub or small tree grows slowly to 15 feet, spreading almost as wide. Leaves are glossy, yellow-green—giving the plant a lush appearance. Excellent as a spreading shrub or clipped hedge. **Low water use.** C, IV, LD, HD.

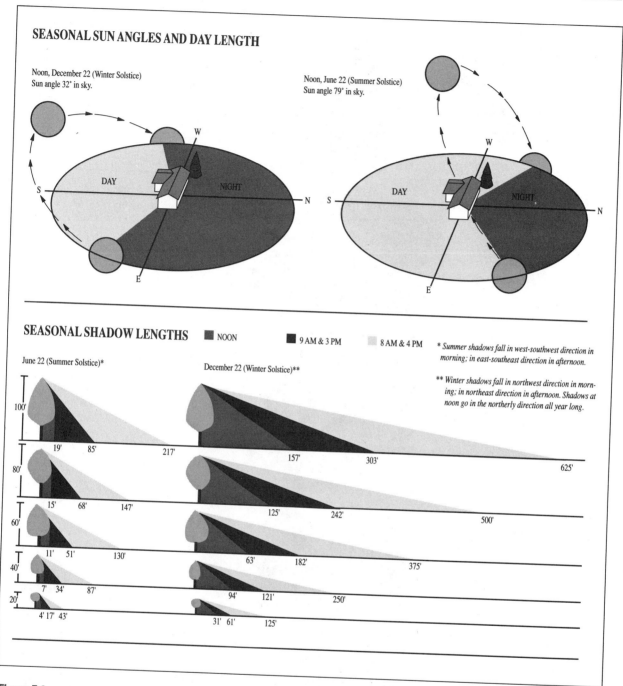

SEASONAL SUN ANGLES AND DAY LENGTH

Noon, December 22 (Winter Solstice)
Sun angle 32° in sky.

Noon, June 22 (Summer Solstice)
Sun angle 79° in sky.

SEASONAL SHADOW LENGTHS   ■ NOON   ■ 9 AM & 3 PM   □ 8 AM & 4 PM

June 22 (Summer Solstice)*

December 22 (Winter Solstice)**

* Summer shadows fall in west-southwest direction in morning; in east-southeast direction in afternoon.

** Winter shadows fall in northwest direction in morning; in northeast direction in afternoon. Shadows at noon go in the northerly direction all year long.

Figure F-3.

Sun angles and shadow lengths: These diagrams show the paths of the sun during winter and summer, and the resulting tree shadows for various times of the day. Note: These diagrams all pertain to Southern California conditions.

Appendix G

Pasadena Water and Power Department[1]

Sample Tree Planting Incentive Program

Planting trees is an effective way to save energy and improve the environment. A tree planted on the west and/or south side of your home cools your home naturally, thus decreasing the necessity for air conditioning. Energy saved from planting trees also helps to diminish peak power demand, thereby reducing the need for expensive new power plants. Additionally, trees help to improve our local air quality by filtering dirt and pollutants from the air and lessening the global greenhouse effect. You will receive, for each tree planted, either a $10 cash rebate (check) or an energy-saving compact fluorescent light bulb with a retail value of $15. Customers can receive rebates for up to three trees. Program is subject to availability of funds.

Tree Selection

There are many beautiful deciduous and evergreen trees to choose from. **Deciduous** trees drop their leaves each winter allowing sun to penetrate through to warm your house. **Evergreen** trees keep their leaves year-round. Evergreens should not be located on the southwest, south or east exposures of your home if you want to take advantage of the winter sun to warm your home. The trees on this chart (See Figure G-1) are only a few examples of the types that are suitable for the Pasadena area. For a more complete list of low water use trees and planting and maintenance guidelines, contact your local nursery or call (818) 792-POWER.

The main objective of shading your home with trees is to shield the roof and walls from hot summer sun. The more area you shade, the cooler your home will be. Larger trees which shade a sizeable area with less dense coverage are preferable to smaller compact trees which shade a modest area with dense coverage. Consult your local nurseryman or landscape professional with specific questions about the characteristics

---

[1]The information and table in Appendix G are taken from a brochure distributed by the Pasadena Water and Power Department, titled "Tree Planting Incentive Program," 1990.

and special needs of the trees you wish to plant. The Sunset Western Garden Book (1987) is one of the many publications which can provide you with additional information about the tree you select.

Tree Selection Chart

Figure G-1.

Botanic Name	Common Name	HGT/WTH	Type	Comments
Acacia bailyana	fernleaf wattle	20'/20'	deciduous	grey foliage
Albizia julibrissin	mimosa tree	30'/35'	deciduous	pink flowers
Arbutus unedo	strawberry tree	25'/25'	evergreen	red berries
Brachychiton populneus	bottle tree	40'/25'	evergreen	white flowers
Cretis occidentalis	western redbud	20'/20'	deciduous	Calif. native
Ginkgo biloba (males)	maidenhair tree	50'/25'	deciduous	fan shape leaves
Koelreuteria bipinnata	Chinese flame tree	50'/35'	deciduous	orange seed pods
Lagerstroemia indica	crape myrtle	25'/25'	deciduous	showy flowers
Platanus acerfolia	London plane tree	50'/30'	deciduous	fall color
Ouercus agrifolia	coast live oak	40'/40'	evergreen	Calif. native

Appendix H

American Forestry Association[1]

Planting New Life in the City Down the Street

Trees are as much a part of our street environment as are fire hydrants, light poles, and sidewalks. They help to define rights-of-way, as well as the age and spirit of a community. Trees are the first thing we see as we enter a neighborhood—they form our first and lasting impression of a place. They also provide significant ecological and economic benefits that far outweigh the cost of planting and caring for them.

Planting trees along a street can be a difficult task. Streets are cluttered and compacted environments for a growing tree. In addition, there are legal, political, technical, and economic issues to be considered when planting on public property.

Tree selection and planting methods essentially determine how long a tree will live. A species that grows very tall and conflicts with utility lines will suffer from heavy pruning to keep the lines unobstructed. Matching the right species and variety of tree to the site will extend its ability to survive.

Perhaps an even bigger concern is underground. Trees like the American sycamore are too big and muscular for sidewalk pits or small planting strips. Final decisions on tree selection should be based on the expected mature size of the tree. The more confined the planting area, the more knowledgeable the planter must be.

Our first street-side planting recommendation is for planting in the street lawn (or treelawn), between the sidewalk and curb. Our planting model is a five-foot-wide grass strip that extends along the full length of the street. The first step in this kind of planting is to loosen soil with a rototiller or shovel over an area including the width of the treelawn and eight feet in length, just as you would if you were planting around your home.

[1]Excerpted from *Urban Forests*, April/May 1991, vol. 11, no. 2

Preparing a treelawn for planting is like yard planting, but slightly more restricted. The prepared planting area will be a rectangle instead of a circle, and it will not be quite as large. Mark out a five-foot by eight-foot rectangle, and loosen the soil to the depth of the rootball. The ideal planting area looks like the bottom of a bowl (unless drainage is a problem—see discussion below) with the center the same depth as the ball and the outer edges only a few inches deep. Now simply follow the last five points in the section on planting trees in yards (See Appendix E).

Unfortunately, many urban streets do not have a treelawn. Instead, they have a wide sidewalk and a small pit of soil every 20 or 30 feet. Because of space restrictions, a sidewalk pit presents probably the greatest treeplanting challenge. Though there is wide agreement that new, radical approaches to planting trees in the city are needed, the sad reality is that in many cities over-restrictive sidewalk pits, or "concrete coffins," are the only street spaces available for tree planting.

As the trees in these existing sidewalk pits die, cities don't have the resources to rebuild street infrastructures to provide adequate root space. There are, however, a few things we can do to increase the life spans of trees planted in these places.

First, attempt to determine why a tree died before planting a new one. Poor drainage is a common cause, so determine if the pit will drain. Here's a simple test: Dig a small hole (10 inches in diameter and 12 inches deep) in the pit and fill it with water. After it drains, fill it again and see how long it takes for the water to soak into the ground. One inch per hour is the minimum drainage needed to support tree growth.

Next, measure the size of the pit. It should be at least 30 square feet, with four feet being the minimum width. If the pit is not six feet by five feet or eight feet by four feet, find out if there is an opportunity to expand the root space under the sidewalk. Stormdrain inlets, gardens, or adjacent lawn space within 10 feet of the pit may enhance a tree's available root space. Broken pavement is often an indication of a tree's success in reaching more space.

Another possible remedy is to enlarge the pit (the larger the site, the larger the tree will grow). After the appropriate permission has been obtained, use a cement cutter to cut the pavement and remove the surface and sub-base. Excavate all of the soil in the resulting tree pit to a depth of 24 to 30 inches. In soil of moderate to poor drainage, install an aeration ring and a drain sump.

To keep the rootball from sinking into the fresh backfill (a major cause of decline in newly planted trees), construct a compacted mound under the rootball and set the rootball in the pit so that its top is three inches above the adjacent sidewalk. Fill in the pit with the same soil that was taken out (do not add soil amendments except in very sandy soils). Finally, cover the pit with two to four inches of bark mulch.

In areas with high pedestrian traffic, brick or stone sand-set pavers can be added to the surface of the pit. Set the rootball and the soil volume lower as required. Adding these pavers, however, will have a negative impact on a tree's potential growth.

Roots and Sidewalks

If large trees are to mature successfully in an urban environment, they will inevitably have to establish roots outside the original planting hole. Root expansion is restricted by the sidewalk on one side and the curb and street on the other. The most likely root expansion is parallel to the street, and the next most likely is under the sidewalk. Though root growth under streets is unusual, root expansion under sidewalks is both a common problem for public-works departments and opportunity to improve tree health in the future.

When tree roots hit the compacted soil under pavement, they tend to grow in a thin, shallow soil zone along the underside of the pavement where there is more oxygen and moisture. Once they grow beyond the sidewalk and into more soil, a new system of fine roots takes advantage of available water and nutrients. This new growth changes the function of the roots under the sidewalk from absorption to transport. As the flow of water and nutrients increases, the diameter of the transport roots also increases, and as the roots enlarge, they can lift and damage the pavement.

Attempting to stop sidewalk damage by cutting tree roots and replacing sidewalks is expensive and can be fatal to the tree. Sidewalk and root conflicts can be solved only when urban foresters and city engineers work together to address the needs of both the trees and the pavement. Discussion should take place when sidewalks are being installed or repaired, and when new trees are plated. The best solutions are found when new trees and new pavement are installed at the same time. Select a tree for the largest available planting space, and provide adequate space for root growth such as aerated rooting channels under the pavement.

Preventing a conflict where trees and sidewalks already exist is the most difficult conflict to resolve. Creating more space around the tree is the best answer. This can involve cutting away part of the sidewalk or diverting the walk to allow more space for tree growth. Even when more space is created, a tree expert should be consulted to prevent serious damage to roots.

When new trees are planted where sidewalks already exist, various methods can be employed to reduce conflicts. Various types of root barriers can be installed to physically deflect roots. Though the barriers deter root damage to sidewalks, they also limit tree growth. Barriers that encircle the tree's roots are the most restrictive to root development. This kind of barrier is being used with some success in parts of the country where soils are well aerated and not wet. Any use of these devices east of the Mississippi River is questionable because soil density and moisture levels are higher there.

The most promising root barrier is one that deflects the roots only where sidewalk and street protection is needed. Barriers can be placed next to the edge of the pavement, for eight feet on either side of the tree, for example, and provide protection for the sidewalk while allowing more root space than encircling root collars will.

Even more creative elements are now being added to root-deflector systems. One new product acts as a barrier and a conductor, not only deflecting roots but also providing a pathway for them to follow. The pathway attempts to provide improved soil moisture and aeration for root development.

Open Spaces

Open spaces, greenways, and parks offer some of the best opportunities for tree planting because newly planted trees will have adequate space to grow. In addition, many trees per acre can be planted in parks, with less need to ensure the survival of each tree. Open-space planting offers a good opportunity to plant smaller trees, and more of them.

Small-tree planting may prove to be the salvation of our inner-city greenways, riparian corridors, highways, and boulevard medians. Planting bare-root seedlings, whips, and saplings is a citizen-sized effort that encourages volunteer participation. But keeping these young trees alive requires forethought—careful species selection and handling, and impeccable timing for the planting event. The most important factor is the drive of the citizens who plant them. Concerned citizens must be willing to follow through by watering and weeding during the first three years.

Whether the purpose of a planting event is soil conservation, beautification, or windbreaks, the precautions are the same. The gathering of trees and people should occur on the same day. The planting site should be cleared of debris—trash and underbrush removed, and the grass cut. Individual planting holes should be clearly marked for the volunteers.

Perhaps the biggest problem with planting small trees in open areas is damage from people. Small trees often go unnoticed by groundskeepers and become victims of lawn mowers, or are damaged by visitors or vandals. A relatively new product that is helping to establish small trees is called a tree shelter. It is a biodegradable polypropylene tube fits around the tree, supplying both protection and improved growing conditions.

To plant with a shelter, clear an area two feet in diameter—removing all grass—and cultivate the soil to the depth of the root mass (equivalent to the rootball on a larger tree). Plant the tree in the center of the area with the roots level or slightly higher than the surrounding soil. Install the tree shelter, and water the new tree slowly and thoroughly.

Many of the available planting areas in a city strain a tree's ability to adapt and survive. The average tree planted in a downtown sidewalk of a big city, for example, lives only seven to 10 years. Finding a space will allow a tree to live a long time is one of urban forestry's great challenges.

If your community is going to plant trees this year, scout out the best locations. They are generally the largest areas of soil (the most important factor) with the fewest above-ground restrictions. The soil in the larger planting areas can be worked to dramatically improve the life of the tree.

During your search for planting locations, you will undoubtedly find some that are unsuitable because of their soil content. Therefore, work with planners, engineers, and community foresters (if available) between planting seasons to improve quality of these sites so that you can plant in them next year without undue strain on the tree.

One of the environmental goals for the 1990s should be to plant more trees and to take responsibility for their survival. You can take an important step toward ensuring a tree's survival by planting it the new AFA way—this is the best information we have to date. Please use it and pass it on to your friends, neighbors, and community leaders.

They say it is difficult to get experts to agree on anything. But in writing this article, our experts found many areas of agreement In fact, on this final point there was absolute agreement: Planting a tree is a simple act, but it takes three long years to establish a tree. Planting it right is the first step!

A Little Tree Glossary

Backfill: To return soil to a planting area from which it was originally taken.

Bare-root seedling: A tree ready for transplanting that has had the soil around its roots removed.

Brick or stone sand-set paver: Brick or stone set in sand and placed around a tree to allow water infiltration and give protection from pedestrians.

Drain sump: A pipe that helps to drain excess water from a planting hole.

Greenway: A linear open space that stretches into or around cities, usually containing trees, shrubs, and grassy areas.

Riparian Corridor: The green area along a waterway such as a river, stream, or lake.

Rootball: The clump of soil containing the roots of a tree.

Rototiller: A power-driven machine that uses metal teeth to chop up and mix soil.

Sapling: A young tree that measures two to four inches in diameter.

Sidewalk pit: The small patches of soil found amid the sidewalks of the most urbanized sections of a city. The pits are designed as a sort of "street planter" for trees or other greenery.

Treelawn: The grassy area between street and sidewalk.

Well-aerated soil: Soil that has been loosened, breaking up compaction and adding air space.

Well-developed soil: Undisturbed soil with a many-layered profile, rich in organic matter at the top and minerals near the bottom.

Whip: A young tree; often a bud graft on an established root system that has developed a main stem but very few branches.

Abstract

Summer temperatures in urban areas are now typically 2 to 8°F higher than in their rural surroundings, due to a phenomenon known as the "heat island effect." Research shows that increases in electricity demand, smog levels, and human discomfort are probably linked to this phenomenon. *Cooling Our Communities: A Guidebook on Tree Planting and Light-Colored Surfacing*, produced by the U.S. Environmental Protection Agency, is the first action-oriented guide that addresses the causes, magnitude, and impacts of increased urban warming, suggests strategies which can be taken to combat the problem, and estimates the level of possible benefits that may be achieved.

Two of the most cost-effective methods of reducing heat islands are strategic landscaping and light-colored surfacing. Strategic landscaping refers to planting trees and shrubs around buildings and throughout communities to provide maximum shade and wind benefits. Light-colored surfacing means changing dark-colored surfaces to ones which effectively reflect—rather than absorb—solar energy. The guidebook shows that well-placed vegetation around residences and small commercial buildings can reduce energy consumption, typically by 15 to 35 percent. Savings from lightening surface colors may be as high or greater, but are still being measured. If widespread planting and lightening occurs, it could also help lower summer temperatures and reduce the production of smog.

Cooling Our Communities is a compilation of the most current scientific research that is underway to understand the effects of urban heat islands. It provides citizens with practical recommendations for implementing mitigation strategies in their communities, and contains lessons learned from successful tree planting programs. The publication has been developed for the benefit of lay readers, but also includes several technical appendices to assist those seeking more specific information.

To order a copy of *Cooling Our Communities: A Guidebook on Tree Planting and Light-Colored Sur-facing*, indicate stock number 055-000-00371-8 and send $13 for each copy in a check made out to the Superintendent of Documents or provide your VISA or MasterCard number and expiration date, and send it to New Orders, Superintendent of Documents, P.O. Box 371954, Pittsburgh, PA 15220-7954. Or FAX your credit card order using 202-512-2250.

Order Processing Code:
* 6172

Superintendent of Documents **Publications** Order Form

☐ **YES,** please send me ____ copies of **COOLING OUR COMMUNITIES: A GUIDEBOOK TO TREE PLANTING AND LIGHT-COLORED SURFACING,** S/N 055-000-00371-8 at $13.00 ea.

The total cost of my order is $_____. International customers please add 25%. Price includes regular domestic postage and handling and is subject to change.

May we make your name/address available to other mailers? ☐ YES ☐ NO

Please Choose Method of Payment:
☐ Check Payable to the Superintendent of Documents
☐ VISA or MasterCard Account

Customer's Name and Address

(Credit card expiration date)

Zip

(Authorizing Signature)

1/92

Mail To: Superintendent of Documents, P.O. Box 371954, Pittsburgh, PA 15250–7954

Summer temperatures in urban areas are now typically 2 to 8°F higher than in their rural surroundings, due to a phenomenon known as the "heat island effect." *Cooling our Communities: A Guidebook on Tree Planting and Light-Colored Surfacing,* produced by the U.S. Environmental Protection Agency, is the first action-oriented guide that addresses the causes, magnitude, and impacts of increases in urban warming, suggests strategies which can be taken to combat the problem, and estimates the level of possible environmental and economic benefits.

Two of the most cost-effective methods of reducing heat islands are strategic landscaping and light-colored surfacing. Strategic landscaping refers to planting trees and shrubs around buildings and throughout communities to provide maximum shade and wind effects. Light-colored surfacing means changing dark-colored surfaces to ones which effectively reflect—rather than absorb—solar energy. *Cooling Our Communities* provides citizens with practical recommendations for implementing these mitigation strategies in their communities. The guidebook was developed for the benefit of lay readers, but also includes several technical appendices to assist those seeking more specific information.

To order your copy, simply fill out the front of this card and mail it to the Government Printing Office with your payment.

Summer temperatures in urban areas are now typically 2 to 8°F higher than in their rural surroundings, due to a phenomenon known as the "heat island effect." *Cooling our Communities: A Guidebook on Tree Planting and Light-Colored Surfacing,* produced by the U.S. Environmental Protection Agency, is the first action-oriented guide that addresses the causes, magnitude, and impacts of increases in urban warming, suggests strategies which can be taken to combat the problem, and estimates the level of possible environmental and economic benefits.

Two of the most cost-effective methods of reducing heat islands are strategic landscaping and light-colored surfacing. Strategic landscaping refers to planting trees and shrubs around buildings and throughout communities to provide maximum shade and wind effects. Light-colored surfacing means changing dark-colored surfaces to ones which effectively reflect—rather than absorb—solar energy. *Cooling Our Communities* provides citizens with practical recommendations for implementing these mitigation strategies in their communities. The guidebook was developed for the benefit of lay readers, but also includes several technical appendices to assist those seeking more specific information.

To order your copy, simply fill out the front of this card and mail it to the Government Printing Office with your payment.

Summer temperatures in urban areas are now typically 2 to 8°F higher than in their rural surroundings, due to a phenomenon known as the "heat island effect." *Cooling our Communities: A Guidebook on Tree Planting and Light-Colored Surfacing,* produced by the U.S. Environmental Protection Agency, is the first action-oriented guide that addresses the causes, magnitude, and impacts of increases in urban warming, suggests strategies which can be taken to combat the problem, and estimates the level of possible environmental and economic benefits.

Two of the most cost-effective methods of reducing heat islands are strategic landscaping and light-colored surfacing. Strategic landscaping refers to planting trees and shrubs around buildings and throughout communities to provide maximum shade and wind effects. Light-colored surfacing means changing dark-colored surfaces to ones which effectively reflect—rather than absorb—solar energy. *Cooling Our Communities* provides citizens with practical recommendations for implementing these mitigation strategies in their communities. The guidebook was developed for the benefit of lay readers, but also includes several technical appendices to assist those seeking more specific information.

To order your copy, simply fill out the front of this card and mail it to the Government Printing Office with your payment.